REGIONAL DEVELOPMENT AND PLANNING IN INDIA

By the Same Author

— Development: A Saga of Two World
— Urbanization, Urban Development and Metropolitan Cities in India *edited by Prof. S.K. Aggrawal*

About the Author

Dr. Vishwambhar Nath was one of the leading development economists of India. After getting a Master's degree in Geography from Government College, Lahore in 1946, he received his Ph.D. in Geography from the University of Marryland in 1949.

Returning to India, Dr. Nath Joined the Planning Commission of India and was tasked to lead the Project Evaluation Organization (PEO).

In 1957, Dr. Nath joined the Indian Administrative Service (IAS) and served as a District Collector in the Sawai Madhopur and Pali districts in Rajasthan. In Sawai Madhopur, Dr. Nath helped with the creation of country's best known Tiger reserve—the Ranthambor Sanctuary.

In 1963, he re-joined the Planning Commission as the head of its Natural Resources and Urban Planning Division. He was deeply involved with many projects, including the plan for the Calcutta Metropolitan Region.

In 1966, Dr. Nath was deputized to the united Nations Development Programme and began his UN service as a Professor of Economic and Social Development at a newly formed Development institute in Kuwait. Later assignments included Development Planning positions in Sierŕa Leone and Gambia.

Dr. Nath spent a year as a Visiting Professor of Geography at the University of Kentucky, and after retiring from the UNDP, he spent two years as a Visiting Scholar at Boston University.

Returning to India in 1986, Dr. Nath was attached to the Centre for Policy Research in Delhi and continued his writing and scholarly work until his passing on September 10, 2002.

About the Editor

S.K. Aggarwal is at present Professor of Geography at Delhi University. He has studied Geography at the universities of Punjab (India), Akron and Kent State (USA). He has taught geography in the US and India and delivered lectures and conducting research on wide ranging topics on Urban Management, Environmental Health and Mega Cities. He was co-editor of the widely received book on Asian City: Processes of Development, Characteristics and Planning published by Kluwer. He has been a Visiting Professor at the University of Bonn, and a Fulbright Scholar at the University of Akron, Ohio. Among several research and teaching assignments within India and abroad, Professor Aggarwal has been honored to be a Full Member of the International Geographical Union (IGU), Commission on Health and Environment and IGU Task Force on Mega Cities. Professor Aggarwal is on Board of Asian Urban Research Association (AURA) located at the University of Akron, USA. He has been associated with WHO-SEARO and Asian Development Bank for conducting research related to Healthy Cities and Resettlement issues and policies in South-East Asia respectively. More recently, Ministry of Education and Research (BMBF), Germany has honoured him to be on their panel of experts on selection and evaluation of Research Projects on Emerging Mega Cities in the developing countries.

Regional Development and Planning in India

Dr. V. Nath

Edited by
S.K. Aggarwal

CONCEPT PUBLISHING COMPANY, NEW DELHI-110059

Cataloging in Publication Data—DK
Courtesy: D.K. Agencies (P) Ltd. <docinfo@dkagencies.com>

Nath, Viswambhar, 1923-2002.
Regional development and planning in India / V. Nath ; edited by S.K. Aggarwal.
p. cm.
Includes bibliographical references.
Includes index.

ISBN 13: 9789351252672 (P.B.)

1. Regional planning—India. 2. Rural development—India. 3. India—Economic policy. I. Aggarwal, Surinder K., 1943- II. Title.

DDC 338.954 22

ISBN-13: 978-93-5125-267-2 (P.B.)

First Published 2009

Published and Printed by
Ashok Kumar Mittal
Concept Publishing Company
A/15-16, Commercial Block, Mohan Garden
New Delhi-110059 (INDIA)

Phones : 25351460, 25351794
Fax : 091-11-25357103
Email : publishing@conceptpub.com

Acknowledgements

As mentioned in Volume I we are making an effort to publish Dr. Nath's writings on Economic Development in five volumes. Each volume focuses on specific area of development and planning in India. The volumes are not being published sequentially but by subject matter, with the generous assistance of experts on the subjects.

During his lifetime, Dr. Vishwambhar Nath had the privilege of working in many important areas of economic development. He was the Chief of the Urban Planning Division of the Planning Commission and played a significant role in preparation of the Plans for Calcutta Metropolitan region. Urban Development and Planning of Metropolitan Cities is the focus of the first volume in the series.

In a short assignment with the Population Census Commission in the early 1950s, he worked on the idea of demarcation of agro-climatic regions in India and worked with sustained interest on the subject of Regional Development and Planning in India, the focus of this volume.

Dr. Nath's involvement in the Programme Evaluation Organization of the Community Development Programme as its Director during the 1950s led to his strong interest in the organization of social structures in village India and rural society's response to economic development interventions in post Independent India. Dr. Nath conducted intensive socio-economic surveys in three villages in Eastern Rajasthan, where he was posted as Collector. In Punjab he studied the effect of the Green Revolution on social structure in rural Punjab to gauge how far the development in the villages is self-sustainable. The Rajasthan study forms part of a separate volume while the Punjab study will form part of the volume on Planning and Development in India.

As an administrator (District Collector) and Chief District Development Officer, Dr. Nath observed the problems of administration and implementation of economic development plans in situations created by decentralized planning and local self-government under the Panchayati Raj institutions. His writings on the subject will form part of the volume on Administration and Planning in India.

I had the privilege to see how Dr. Nath's interest in these areas of development evolved, and how he could knit them together.

While he worked on various issues of development, it is my privilege to bring them together in Volumes so that all his thoughts are available to researchers and planners. The author passed away in September 2002 and was involved in academic writing until the last day of his life.

The essays included in this book reflect the fine people who worked with and for Dr. Nath in the institutions named above. A great many people are responsible for the growth and development of India since 1950, and this book and the country owes a debt of gratitude to them.

I have received encouragement and assistance in this task from Dr. Surender Agarwal, Head, Department of Geography, Delhi University. Dr. Agarwal, in spite of his very busy schedule, took on the task of editing this volume and the volume on Urbanization, Urban Development and Metropolitan Cities in India. Dr. Agarwal has made significant contributions by giving a meaningful structure to this collection of essays. Dr. Agarwal has also written a detailed introduction to the volume on Urbanization. I am grateful to Dr. Aggarwal, without his support my task would have been so much harder.

I am also grateful to Mr. Ashok Kumar Mittal of Concept Publishing Company for publishing both volumes and persisting with the task, in spite of delays which would creep in from many and unexpected corners.

Last, but not the least I am thankful to my three children, Virendra, Arvind and Jyoti in supporting and encouraging me to undertake the task, in spite of the fact that I am not a student of development planning and it would be a difficult task for me!

December 2007 **Kamla Nath**

Contents

Introduction

Prof. S.K. Aggarwal

A major problem in planning for every large country is that of development of its different regions. It raises questions of regional allocation of resources, location of major projects, and rates of growth of production, income and employment in different regions, and allied questions of inter-regional movements of goods and people. Planners in every country are concerned with these questions. The plans must contain clearly articulated policies in respect of them and appropriate programmes to implement the policies. In case of large countries, such as India, the national plan must be accompanied by regional plans for States and smaller areas.

However, regional planning problems had not until recently, received adequate attention from planners in many countries. The national plans continued to be concerned primarily with overall growth of the economy and with sector-wise and project-wise allocations of investment and other resources. Regional allocations of investment, rates of growth of different regions or special measures needed to accelerate growth in the depressed or retarded regions received only secondary attention. One reason for inadequate interest in regional problems is that the issue of spatial location of economic activity has not received enough attention in economic analysis. Some economists have given attention to it from time to time; but it has not been in the mainstream of economic thought. This is due mainly to the fact that space and distance introduce a complicating factor in economic analysis. Most economists have chosen to ignore them and have been content to record that decisions relating to location of enterprises are made by entrepreneurs on consideration of such factors as location of natural resources and markets. The influence of other factors, such as—availability of capital, entrepreneurial skill and skilled labour in attracting industries to particular location has been recognized and it is also admitted that some locations can only be explained on the basis of historical accident. The agglomerative tendency of industries is recognized in Marshall's concept of external economies. A German Economist, Alfred Weber, made an attempt to develop a systematic theory of location of economic activities; but his work had not received much attention until recently. A considerable advance has been made in this field in recent years, especially as a result of the work of Losch and Walter Isard; even so, the theory of location remains one of the less developed branches of economic thought.

The issue of development of regions began to engage the serious attention of planners, administrators and economists during the depression years of the 1930s, when there was acute economic distress in some regions. This distress, it was found, was not a temporary phenomenon but a semi-permanent state, caused either by chronic depression in the industries on which the regions had depended or by the fact that the regions had been by-passed in the economic development process.

In recent years the issues of location of economic activities and regional development have been brought to the attention of planners and economists from another direction – the phenomenal growth of metropolitan regions. The agglomerative tendency of economic activities has been seen in a particularly pronounced form in the post-war period of rapid economic growth: it has resulted in metropolitan cities and other major industrial regions of every country growing more rapidly than other areas. This trend, coupled with the trend towards dispersal of settlement from the central areas of cities to the suburbs, has created gigantic conurbations.

The issues of location of economic activities and development of regions have considerable importance in developing countries, such as India. The disparities in levels of development within these countries, *e.g.*, between the metropolitan cities and the hinterland areas are as great (if not greater than) as in the developed countries. Moreover, the tendency towards further concentration of modern economic activities in the metropolitan centres is very strong. The strength of this tendency is borne out in India, by the experience of industrial location during the period of the Plans. In this period, in spite of the preference of Government for dispersal of industries and of various measures taken by it to achieve this objective, about 70 per cent of all new factories or substantial additions to old factories have been located in the cities; 40

per cent in and around the 1 million cities alone. Such concentration of modern activities in the metropolitan cities creates a growing cultural hiatus between them and the rest of the country. It creates what Lewis calls a drift towards a "polarized dual society" (Lewis, 1963, p. 178).[1] Secondly, rapid growth of the cities, resulting from such concentration, has created difficult problems of housing, water supply, transport and other urban services. These problems have reached crisis proportions in the largest cities, such as Kolkata, Mumbai and Delhi; their solution requires large investments and major administrative and technological innovations.

The issues of location and regional development are important in India for another reason also. In a country of India's size and diversity of economic and social conditions, it is essential that people of different regions have a feeling of benefiting adequately from the development process. They must see that projects are located in their regions and that production, employment, income and levels of living go up. But concentration of economic activities in metropolitan cities or in a few other favoured regions can only create a feeling among people of the rest of the country that they are being asked to bear the burdens of economic development without benefiting adequately from it. This will lead, in a federal democracy, to increasing political pressures on locational decisions, of which we have seen some evidence in recent years. Therefore, in order that locational decisions do not become the subject of political pressures, but are guided by techno-economic considerations, it is important that the principles of spatial distribution of economic activities and the policies relating to development of regions are clearly defined. This requires, as a corollary, that regional science—the theories of location and of growth of regions, and the techniques of regional analysis—is developed rapidly in India.

REFERENCE

1. Lewis, John P. (1963), *Quiet Crisis in India*, Asia Publishing House, Mumbai.

1

Regions for Planning[1]

INTRODUCTION

The region is a conceptual tool for understanding the diversity in space and for organizing space for particular purposes. Every science has its regional scheme based on distribution of the phenomena in which it is interested. Thus in medical science there are regions showing distribution of cholera, malaria and other diseases. Frequently, regions are based on distribution of a group of related phenomena. Climatic regions are an example. The concept of regions based on multiple related phenomena is found to be particularly useful in sciences such as geography, economics and sociology. Geographers distinguish regions based on distribution of the physical phenomena—geological structure, topography, climate, hydrology, soils and natural vegetation—or regions based on distribution of these phenomena and human phenomena such as agricultural land-use, population density and the settlement pattern. Sociologists and cultural anthropologists distinguish cultural regions based on distribution of various cultural phenomena. All such regions are demarcated on the basis of internal homogeneity and external contrast; the areas included within them have certain common characteristics which set them off from areas outside. The economists also distinguish regions on the basis of homogeneity in economic characteristics. Industrial regions are an example. But the concept of economic regions based on the principle of inter-relationship is also used in economics. An economic area has been defined by Losch as the market area of a commodity, and an economic region as a system of such market areas (Losch, 1964 p. 115). Such an economic region may include areas with widely divergent economic characteristics. Typically, it will include an industrial producing centre and a consumption area which may be largely rural. The two are considered as forming part of an economic region because of their economic relationship.

Both these principles, homogeneity and inter-relationship, have their utility in demarcating regions for planning.

Planning Regions

Planning regions have to serve as the spatial units for formulation and implementation of development plans. They must, therefore, be demarcated, keeping in view the objectives of planned development and the nature of the principal development programmes. Secondly, since institutional and administrative arrangements for plan formulation and execution will have to be made with these regions as the units, they must be related to the existing politico-administrative structure of the country and its territorial divisions. Since most planning is done by government (or by agencies established by government), it is most convenient to adopt the territorial divisions or administrative regions as the planning regions. Planning and development agencies can be established for these regions simply by expanding the existing departments or adding new ones. Secondly, arrangements for association of the people's representatives with the planning process can also be made most conveniently with them as units, because legislatures, local bodies and other democratic institutions are already established for them. Other planning regions have undoubtedly to be adopted for particular purposes. But the need for them must be clearly established, because their acceptance involves supplementing or replacing the administrative regions.

Planning in India is the concurrent responsibility of the Central and the State Governments. It is being done with the States (and Union Territories) as the primary units. Below the State level the principal units of administration and planning are the district, the block and the village. Administrative and institutional arrangements exist at these units for formulation and execution of plans, and for association of popular leaders with planning. These administrative regions are in fact the principal planning regions of the country. However, they are not adequate for all planning purposes and have to be supplemented by other regions for some purposes of planning, and may even have to be replaced for other purposes. Thus, for development of water resources it is convenient to adopt a river valley or a river system as the region; in metropolitan planning it is necessary to plan with the metropolitan area of the city as the unit. Similarly, for planning of transport or development of power resources, regions may have to be specially delineated keeping in view the particular requirements of the planning task. Secondly, even when administrative units are adopted as the planning regions, it is useful for the planners to be aware of similarities, contrasts or economic relationships between areas situated in different administrative units. Thus, the Himalayan areas of U.P., Punjab, Himachal Pradesh and Jammu and Kashmir have certain common physical features of topography, climate and soils and common patterns of resource use and economic activity. In all these hilly areas arable land is limited, specialized forms of agriculture (*e.g.*, horticulture), and grazing and exploitation of forest resources are important economic activities. Population is sparse, water supply and communications are difficult problems, and there is urgent need for programmes of conservation of soil and water. These common features, problems and needs have to be kept in view and arrangements for co-operation in plan formulation or implementation have to be devised between the States and Union Territories concerned. A regional scheme which expresses the common links between these areas is, therefore, useful for planners.

The planning tasks in India can be divided into the following four categories:

- (i) Agricultural and related development programmes—land reclamation, soil conservation, irrigation, animal husbandry, forestry and fisheries;
- (ii) Development of industries, power, transport and communications;
- (iii) Development of social services—education, medical care, social welfare etc.; and
- (iv) Urban development.

The classification follows broadly the sectoral classification in the Five Year Plans. Urban development has been added. It is not a separate sector of development but it has been listed here because urbanization affects the economy in such a variety of ways and urban development is a task of such importance that it was felt that it should be listed separately in order to focus attention on it.

In agricultural and related development programmes, primary emphasis is on scientific and more intensive exploitation of the resources of land and water. This has to be done by changing present production techniques and by undertaking various resource development programmes. Since regional variations in the methods of resource use and the resource development economy—patterns of agricultural land use and cropping, development of livestock husbandry, forestry or fishing—are related primarily to the physical factors, regional schemes based on analysis of the physical factors and associated human factors of agricultural land use and rural settlement, furnish the basic mosaic for planning the development programmes. Such schemes bring out the contrasts within the country and within individual States which are most significant for planning purposes. Further, they bring out for each region (and its smaller divisions) the basic physical and human factors, and the potential and limitations of the physical environment. The scheme of "Regions for Resource Planning" developed by the Regional Planning Unit of the Indian Statistical Institute (unpublished) and the scheme of Resource Development Regions and Divisions recently published by the Planning Commission (Government of India, 1964) are both schemes of this type. The latter is described below.

Such schemes are useful also for planning of social service programmes, especially in the rural areas, because planning of these programmes has to be related primarily to the rural settlement pattern. They are useful to a limited extent for planning of industrial, power, transport and associated development programmes. They furnish the basic facts on location of mineral and power resources, and agricultural raw materials, and of distribution of population which have to be taken into account in planning of these programmes. Thus, the scheme of Resource Development Regions and Divisions published by the Planning Commission distinguishes the Eastern Plateaux and Hills Region. This region, consisting of the plateau areas of Bihar, Orissa, West Bengal, Eastern Madhya Pradesh and two districts of Maharashtra, has been demarcated primarily on the basis of geological and topographic factors. But by distinguishing it with the highly mineralized areas which contain most of the coal, iron ore, manganese and other mineral resources of the country, have been separated from the adjoining areas of the Gangetic Plain or of the Deccan which are poor in minerals. Visualizing this mineral-rich area as one region is very useful in planning of industrial, power and transport programmes. However, it appears that regional schemes based on the principle of homogeneity are not adequate for planning of such programmes and that schemes based on the principle of inter-relationship have to be used. The latter are useful because they indicate how regions are related with one another and with the national economy and the potential or limitations for development which these relationships hold. Thus for any region the scheme of Resource Development Regions and Divisions would indicate only its agricultural, mineral, forest and other resources, but it would not indicate the potential or limitations for development which its location with reference to other regions creates. Consider the South Bihar Plain area (consisting of the districts of Shahabad, Patna, Gaya, Monghyr and Bhagalpur) as an example. It has a very large population in relation to its agricultural land, has few mineral resources and would appear to have a limited potential for industrial and urban development. But its location next to the coal and steel centres of Bihar and West Bengal and athwart the principal transport routes of Northern India hold for it enormous possibilities of industrial and urban growth.

As an illustration of schemes based on the principle of inter-relationship, a scheme of metropolitan regions has been described below. The scheme distinguishes four metropolitan regions, which are the hinterlands respectively of the metropolitan cities of Kolkata, Chennai, Mumbai and Delhi. The scheme is based on the concept of central places[2] each me tropolitan city is regarded as an apex central place, which is linked through a system of secondary and lower order central places to every part of its hinterland.

Accordingly, we consider four sets of regions:

(i) Administrative Regions,
(ii) Resource Development Regions/Agro-climatic Regions,
(iii) Metropolitan Regions, Transition Zones or Corridors, and
(iv) Rurban Corridor.

ADMINISTRATIVE REGIONS

States (and Union Territories), districts, blocks, and villages constitute the different units in the structure of administrative regions. The planning process in India provides for formulation of plans with them as units and inter-relation of plans of different units. The plan of each State is drawn up within the framework of the goals, investment magnitudes and physical achievement targets of the national plan: but it reflects in its details—the financial and physical magnitudes of different sectors and the particular projects included in it, the development potential of the State and the needs and aspirations of its people. The plans of districts are related similarly to the plan of the State, and of smaller units to the plan of the district. Such inter-relationship between plans of different units is an essential aspect of the national planning process. It enables plans to reflect national goals and objectives on the one hand and local needs and aspirations on the other. Institutional arrangements have been established at various area levels for participation of the people's representatives in the planning process. The national and State legislators frame the policies for planning; the local leaders participate in detailed planning and implementation of programmes for their areas. The responsibilities of the local leaders in planning have increased, and much greater attention has begun to be given to local planning after the establishment of the Panchayati Raj institutions. The district plan particularly is being given increasing attention, because it is felt that the area of the district is sufficiently large for formulation of an integrated development plan and officials and non-officials of sufficient calibre and experience are available for preparation of the plan. If the present trends continue the district will in time emerge as a distinct unit of planning in addition to the nation and the State.

The administrative regions have some characteristics which enhance their claims of being accepted as planning regions. Most States of the Indian Union are quite large in size so that adequate planning organizations can be built up for them. Secondly, the areas of most States are co-terminus with the linguistic regions of the country and their people have a certain sense of linguistic-cultural unity. The importance of linguistic regions as basic planning regions can scarcely be over-emphasized in a large, multilingual country. The districts similarly are of sufficient size to be adopted as primary units of local planning. The population of most districts ranges between one and two million and their area ranges between two and five thousand square miles. Secondly, since the boundaries of most districts follow natural features such as rivers or hill ranges and have remained unchanged for long periods, and the district headquarters town is the principal administrative, commercial and educational centre of the area, there is among their people a well-developed feeling of "belonging to the district". There are of course districts which are quite unsuitable for local planning because they are too large or too small or contain areas of sharply contrasted physical and economic characteristics[3]. But the number of such districts is small.

Among the administrative units below the district level, the community development block is the most important for purposes of planning because the institutional and administrative structure of planning and development—the Panchayat Samiti and the community development organization—have been built up round it. A typicai block consists of about 100 villages with a population of 50,000 to 100,000 but there are variations in different areas. Below the block level, the traditional unit of rural community life, the village, has also a certain importance in planning. The aspirations and needs of the rural people are articulated first through the village Panchayat and agricultural and rural development programmes must be formulated in the first instance with the village as the unit.

Supplement to Administrative Regions

(i) *Special Areas* : This structure of administrative regions is used mainly for planning of agricultural and related development programmes, social service programmes and others which are the responsibility of the State Governments. It is useful for planning of these programmes because it enables planners to relate programmes for successively smaller areas to local conditions and the needs and aspirations of the local people. But it has to be supplemented in various ways in order to meet planning needs for which it is found to be inadequate. One set of supplements consists of areas of special problems or promise for which special development programmes have to be undertaken and special administrative or institutional arrangements have to be established. Metropolitan areas of cities, industrial complexes, areas of river valley projects or other resource development projects, and backward areas are the most important among such special areas. In each case the boundaries have to be demarcated keeping in view the particular objects of planning and development. They have to be defined precisely in some cases but not in others. The boundaries of "metropolitan areas" have to be defined with precision because they have to be given the force of law. Control over urban land use which is an essential element in metropolitan planning cannot be enforced without legal sanctions. The boundaries of areas of irrigation and other resource development projects may also have to be defined precisely, because the areas which will receive irrigation or other benefits and those which will not receive such benefits have to be clearly distinguished. On the other hand, boundaries of backward areas need not be defined so precisely. The boundaries of special areas may change relatively quickly. The metropolitan area of a city may have to be enlarged from time to time as the city expands. The areas of irrigation projects may also be enlarged as the scope of the projects is enlarged. On the other hand, backward areas may be reduced progressively in size as backwardness is liquidated.

(ii) *Zones, Macro-regions and Commissioners' Divisions*: Another set of supplements to administrative regions consists of groups of States and districts and are useful for planning at inter-State and inter-district levels. Inter-State action is required for water resource development, power generation and distribution, and various other development programmes. There is considerable experience of inter-State co-operation for water resource development in India; the river valley projects undertaken during the last 15 years are outstanding recent examples of such co-operation. But as each case requires agreement among the States concerned, adequate institutional arrangements are essential for securing inter-State co-operation. The need for inter-State action in power generation and distribution has also begun to be recognized increasingly. The power systems of most adjoining States are already inter-linked. Formation of regional power grids has been under consideration for some time: the grids are visualized as the first step in the establishment (eventually) of a national power grid.

Since the re-organization of the States in 1956, an institutional arrangement for inter-State action has existed in the Zonal Councils. These Councils have been constituted for the five Zones—Northern, Central, Eastern, Southern and Western—into which the country is divided. Each Zone consists of two or more States and adjoining Union

Territories. The agency of the Zonal Councils could be used for planning and co-ordinated execution of programmes of development of inter-State interest more effectively than has been done so far.

Zones also provide a useful conceptual framework for macro-regional divisions of the country: most macro-regional divisions are variations on the Zonal scheme[4]. Macro-regions are useful for planning of various activities of the Central Government and for regional economic and social analysis. They can be very useful in planning flows of basic commodities—coal, iron and steel, cement, petroleum products, chemical fertilizers, foodgrains and agricultural raw materials—and deciding locations of industrial units keeping the flow patterns in view. This concept has been best developed in U.S.S.R., which has been divided into a number of "major economic regions" each based on one or more major industrial complexes. However, the related Soviet concept of self-sufficiency at major economic region level, very attractive in a country with long distances, sparse population and relatively under-developed transport, has distinct limitations in India. As the bulk of the coal and iron ore deposits of India are located in Eastern India, this region must remain the premier iron and steel producing region of the country and large flows of coal, steel and heavy engineering goods from the region to other parts of the country must remain an essential feature of the Indian economy. Ignoring these facts and attempting to achieve self-sufficiency at macro-regional level could lead to a distorted and wasteful pattern of resource development. Macro-regional schemes are useful for regional economic and social analysis because they make possible presentation of data on regional differences within a large country in terms of a limited number of units. In U.S.A., the Census Divisions are used extensively for this purpose, and the practice of using macro-regions is growing in India. The National Sample Survey, the Energy Survey and various studies of the National Council of Applied Economic Research present data on regional differences within India primarily by macro-regions.

In most of the larger States of India there has existed for a long time an intermediate unit between the State and the districts—the Commissioner's Division. These Divisions, consisting of 5 or 6 districts were formed for co-ordination of work in the districts; but many of them express also the most significant differences in physical and economic conditions within a State. In any case, these Divisions furnish, as the Zones do at the macro-regional level, the starting point for dividing large States into a limited number of relatively homogeneous units. Distinguishing such units is useful in planning for a large State because it provides to the State and the local planners a frame of reference for comprehending the diversity within the State and for modifying the development programmes accordingly. Such modification is particularly necessary in agricultural and related programmes which have to be adapted to the physical conditions and agricultural and settlement patterns of each area.

With these two sets of supplements, the structure of administrative regions consists of: nation, macro-region or Zone, State, division, district, block and village, and the special areas. The latter cannot be integrated into the administrative structure, because their boundaries would frequently cut across the boundaries of States and districts. But since planning arrangements for them can be made without serious disturbance to the administrative structure, they can also be considered along with the administrative regions.

RESOURCE DEVELOPMENT REGIONS/AGRO-CLIMATIC REGIONS

The second regions that are important for economic development are agro-climatic regions. They are regions which have similar conditions of topography, soils, climate, vegetation, etc. The ministry of agriculture regularly issues forecasts of crop production based on the incidence and amount of rainfall during the monsoon and post-monsoon seasons and reports sent by the various states on areas sown with different crops, areas which may have been damaged because of floods or unseasonal rains or those in which crop production would be low because of deficient rainfall. These forecasts based on data obtained from the Indian Meteorological Department about the amount and distribution of rainfall in the monsoon and post-monsoon seasons in Tamil Nadu and Kerala and winter rains in Punjab, Haryana and western U.P. have become increasingly accurate because of improvements in reports sent by different states. The Indian Meteorological Department has divided the country into 35 divisions for each of which it publishes data on the amount of rainfall and its incidence within the monsoon and post-monsoon seasons in different parts of the country. These forecasts which are of vital importance for farmers as well as for residents of urban areas for irrigation and generation of power and providing drinking water to the cities and villages have also become increasingly accurate because of improvement in the methods of forecasting.

The scheme of Resource Development Regions and Divisions of India published by the Planning Commission is based on analysis of data of topography, geological formations, soils, rainfall, and agricultural land use, cropping pattern, population density and occurrence of mineral resources. The data have been analyzed for each district of the country.

The scheme recognizes five primary or major natural regions of the country: the Himalayas, the Northern Plain, the Peninsular Plateaux and Hills, the East Coast Plain, and the West Coast Plain. Each of these is divided into one or more regions to make a total of 14 regions on the mainland of India. The fifteenth region is formed by the Islands in the Bay of Bengal and the Arabian Sea. The regions are divided further into sub-regions, divisions and sub-divisions. The scheme distinguishes 61 divisions, each of which is located entirely within the territory of a State. The divisions are formed by intersection of boundaries of the regions and the States or by further division of the area of a region located within a State. Each division is a unit, homogeneous in physical and socio-economic characteristics, and located entirely within the territory of one State which can be adopted as a planning unit by the State Government. The objects of the scheme are:

1. To provide a framework for understanding the variety of physical conditions and resource development potentials in different parts of the country.
2. To furnish to those concerned with planning at the State level, a scheme of division of their States into internally homogeneous units (Government of India, 1964).

Since the resource development division consists of a group of districts, it can be easily integrated into the structure of State planning. Its principal usefulness is in relating development programmes more closely to the different physical and socio-economic conditions of different parts of a State. The scheme also enables planners to keep in view the similarities between areas located in adjacent States.

The agro-climatic regions are regions which have similar conditions of topography, soil and climate which are different from those of other regions. *The concept of agro-climatic regions was developed by the Census Commission of 1951*[5]. It was refined and made more scientific by the Census Commission of 1961. Such regions are used by the Ministry of Agriculture for its season and crop reports which forecasts the total output of crops in both the monsoon and post-monsoon seasons. The forecasts are remarkably accurate.

In large states such as U.P. and Bihar there are more than one agro-climatic region. U.P. has 5 and Bihar has 3. But in small states such as Punjab, Haryana, Kerala and Assam there is only one agro-climatic regions. Micro-regional variations could not be ignored. Thus in H.P. there are areas in the lower Himalayas which are the centres of agriculture, horticulture and population and others. In the great Himalayas, which are thinly populated and snow-bound for most of the year, there is hardly any agricultural output. Thus there is considerable intra-regional variations in various large states, but not in small states. For example, U.P. and western U.P. are relatively developed and eastern U.P. and peninsular U.P. is poor and backward.

METROPOLITAN REGIONS

In this scheme the country is divided into four metropolitan regions—the hinterlands respectively of the metropolitan cities of Kolkata, Mumbai, Chennai and Delhi. Each hinterland is a macro-region consisting of two or more States together with Union Territories or parts of States. It can be divided further into sub-regions, divisions and smaller units going down to the service area of the small town (or large village) with population between 5,000 and 10,000, which performs various commercial and other service functions for a group of villages. Towns of different sizes located in a metropolitan region are considered to be central places of different orders; the metropolitan city is considered to be the apex central place of the region.

The areas included within a metropolitan region are dissimilar in physical features, land use and cropping pattern, population density and various other characteristics. The metropolitan region of Delhi includes the Himalayan areas of Jammu and Kashmir and Himachal Pradesh, the Punjab plain as well as the desert of Western Rajasthan. The region of Kolkata includes areas as dissimilar as Northeast and North Bihar. But all parts of a metropolitan region are bound together by the bonds of functional relations with the metropolitan city. The relations are primarily commercial—distribution of goods is the principal element in them—but they are also cultural and administrative. Three of the metropolitan cities are ports but the fourth, Delhi, is an inland city. The external trade functions which the port cities perform for their metropolitan regions are shared in case of the Delhi region between Kolkata and Mumbai. But the concept of the metropolitan region does not involve as a necessary condition that the metropolitan city be a port or that it be the only port in the region. It only involves that the metropolitan city be so important as a commercial, administrative and social service centre that it can be recognized as the apex centre of the region. Each of the four cities has this position in its metropolitan region. The cities are connected with every part of the hinterland through a succession of smaller towns—sub-regional centres, district towns, mandi centres, etc. These are central places of different orders, each of which is connected upwards with higher order central places and downwards with lower order places; it is also connected with its own particular hinterland (service area) for the specific services that it performs for it. In this way, a whole system of functional relationships—economic, socio-cultural, administrative—focuses eventually on the sub-regional and the metropolitan cities, and the influences emanating from these cities travel to every part of the hinterland.

Formulating such a scheme of metropolitan regions has many limitations at present. First, because of virtual lack of data on economic relationships between the metropolitan cities and their hinterlands, the regions cannot be demarcated precisely. Studies on demarcation of the hinterland have been carried out most extensively for Kolkata[6] and the boundaries of the Kolkata region can be drawn somewhat more precisely than those of the other regions. The regional transport surveys conducted under the auspices of the Planning Commission make available considerable data which will make possible more precise demarcation of the other three hinterlands. Similarly, studies on the economic relationships between cities and towns of different sizes within a metropolitan region and between them and their service areas, needed for dividing the metropolitan regions into sub-regions, divisions and smaller units, are virtually lacking. In Appendix I, central places of six classes have been listed, which implies that it should be possible to have a size hierarchy of six units, going down from the metropolitan region to the service area of the very small town or large village which functions as rural service centre. But this classification is only illustrative and will need to be verified by studies in the different metropolitan regions. It is most likely that central places of all the six categories are not fully developed in every region. However, the hierarchical order provides the framework for seeing the cities and towns of different sizes as linked parts of a spatial system.

As important as the paucity of data is the fact that the city-region relationship is not as well developed in India as it is in industrially advanced countries. Since, the bulk of the population is rural, depends upon subsistence agriculture and has limited extra-village economic relationships, the influence of the metropolitan city, or of any urban area for that matter, is quite weak. But this influence is increasing as means of communication improve and modern social services and consumer goods are used by the rural people to an increasing extent. One visible result of this increase is use by large commercial firms of the four metropolitan cities as focal points for distribution of products within the regions. Various agencies of government and such institutions as the Life Insurance Corporation are also using these cities as regional headquarters for their activities. The smaller cities are similarly beginning to be used increasingly as focal points for distribution of products or radiation of various activities, within their respective influence areas.

The metropolitan regions may be roughly indicated as follows:

1. The Kolkata Metropolitan Region—Assam, Nagaland and the Union Territories in North East India; West Bengal, Bihar, Eastern U.P., and Eastern Madhya Pradesh, except the extreme Southern portion.
2. The Chennai Metropolitan Region—Chennai, Kerala, most of Mysore and most of Andhra Pradesh.
3. The Mumbai Metropolitan Region—Maharashtra, Gujarat, Southern Madhya Pradesh.
4. The Delhi Metropolitan Region—Punjab, Jammu and Kashmir, Himachal Pradesh, most of Rajasthan, Western U.P., and Northern Madhya Pradesh.

Transition Zones or Corridors

It is useful to distinguish transition zones or corridors between the metropolitan regions. These are areas in which the influence of two metropolitan cities overlaps, *i.e.* the advantages of obtaining services from the two cities are nearly competitive and the local people have a choice of obtaining services from one or the other city. The choices are exercised in favour of different cities at different times or for different commodities. Central U.P. is such a transitional zone between the metropolitan regions of Delhi and Kolkata. The transition zones are roughly indicated below, they can also be indicated more precisely when more detailed data become available:

1. Between the Kolkata and the Chennai Regions—extreme South Eastern Madhya Pradesh and North Eastern Andhra Pradesh (the hinterland of Visakhapatnam).
2. Between the Chennai and the Mumbai Regions—the Northern fringe of Mysore.
3. Between the Mumbai and the Delhi Region—Southern Rajasthan, and Central Madhya Pradesh.
4. Between the Delhi and the Kolkata Regions—Central U.P.

The transition zones will be seen on an all-India map as arc—shaped belts of varying widths. Their northern apex is in Central U.P. in the vicinity of Allahabad. From this point they go southwards dividing in Central Madhya Pradesh into three arcs going North-West, South-West and South-East respectively.

The metropolitan regions are units of the same size order as the macro-regions. In some cases they are very close to the zones or other commonly used macro-regions. The Chennai Metropolitan Region is co-terminus with the South India Region of many macro-regional schemes. The Mumbai Metropolitan Region differs only slightly from the Western India Region of macro-regional schemes—it includes Southern Madhya Pradesh. The metropolitan regions based as they are on the economic fact of exchange of goods and services are even more useful than the macro-regions for planning, production and distribution of basic commodities. They are useful also for planning of power, transport and similar programmes. In fact they appear to be the most useful macro-units for working out the regional implications of the long-term perspective of development. The national projections of population, its distribution between urban and rural areas and among various economic activities, of supply and demand of basic commodities and of requirements of power and transport can most conveniently be broken down in terms of the metropolitan regions. Programmes for attaining the targets of development can then be formulated with each metropolitan region as the unit. It appears also that inter-State relationships for purposes of resource development are also visualized most fruitfully in terms of metropolitan regions.

But the metropolitan regions have their greatest utility in urban planning which will have to move in the not distant future from planning for cities to planning of entire hinterlands as units. The need for adopting in case of the large cities, a sufficiently large "metropolitan area" as the unit of detailed land use planning, and a still larger "peripheral region" as the unit of less detailed, directional planning has, already been recognized. The "metropolitan area" concept, first used in the Delhi Plan, is now being used in the plans of all major cities of India. The Delhi Plan also visualized planning for its peripheral region which is now being called the National Capital Region. This is an area of about 400 square miles located in U.P. and Punjab. In case of Kolkata, the CMPO has demarcated outside the Kolkata metropolitan district a Southern Plain Region, as the unit for less detailed, directional planning. The Maharashtra planners are already thinking in terms of planning with the Mumbai-Poona Region as the Unit. In Gujarat, the entire strip between Ahmedabad and Surat, which is experiencing rapid urban-industrial growth, may be adopted as a planning unit. The process has to be carried further and entire hinterlands of metropolitan cities have to be viewed as planning regions. For each such region, the likely growth of the urban population can be forecast within the national perspective of economic development. This total can then be distributed in towns of different sizes located in different parts of the region. The location and size of some towns will, no doubt, be determined by such factors as distribution of natural resources and topographic conditions. Thus, the steel and heavy engineering centres of the Kolkata metropolitan region will be located mainly near the coal fields or iron ore deposits. But location and size of most of the towns in a metropolitan region can be planned in accordance with accepted policies of dispersal of economic activity and balanced regional development. Growth of local, district and multi-district centres can be planned in the perspective of the expected growth in the economy of their service areas. In fact, each such town can be built up as a focal point of modernization of agriculture and of the rural economy, which provides a constellation of services, ranging from distribution of supplies required for modern agriculture (chemical fertilizers, steel, petroleum products, power-driven implements) to facilities of modern education, medical care and recreation. The relations between these towns and their service areas can be improved through improvement of means of transport and communications. The more suitable among them can be developed as local growth points by establishment of various agro-industries and other industries. Some towns can be planned deliberately as growth points to stimulate the economy of stagnant regions or to serve as counter-magnets which will relieve the pressure on large cities. As one city or area approaches saturation point, growth can be transferred to other cities or areas within the metropolitan region.

Urban planning of this kind, with metropolitan hinterlands as units, is an essential counterpart of perspective economic planning. The metropolitan regions furnish the most useful conceptual framework for such planning, because the different cities and towns within each region can be viewed as inter-linked and mutually interacting parts of a spatial system.

RURBAN CORRIDORS

These are areas in which there is a succession of cities and towns with intervening villages becoming rapidly urbanised. There are at present three well developed Rurban corridors:

(i) Central Punjab, parts of Haryana, Delhi and its extension from Delhi to north east Saharanpur with several sugar mills towns in between in U.P. The corridor has a number of cities and agricultural towns and there is large productivity. In U.P. there are several cities such as Ghaziabad, NOIDA, Meerut, Moradabad and sugar mill towns extending north to Saharanpur. Traffic along the road is heavy so that construction of an expressway from Meerut to Delhi is suggested but no progress has been made on it. The metropolitan area extends along the highways north to Panipat in Punjab and south or southwest to Faridabad and Gurgaon in Haryana. Traffic between Panipat and Delhi and Delhi and Faridabad is heavy and construction of the expressway from Meerut to Faridabad and from Panipat is suggested. The expressway will have to bypass Gurgaon also because traffic along the road between Gurgaon and Delhi which connects Delhi and Jaipur is rapidly increasing and remains congested despite the fact that most of the industrial units are located off the roads near Gurgaon. The 2-lane highway is being widened to six lanes to accommodate the traffic.

(ii) The second highly developed corridor includes coastal Gujarat from Ahmedabad to Mumbai and from there south west to metropolitan Pune. There are a large number of cities and towns in this area and the villages in the area are being rapidly urbanised. The 170 kilometres rail-cum-road strip between Mumbai and Pune are also being rapidly urbanised despite the obstacles of heavy rains and the Western Ghats. Traffic along the road is very heavy except in the monsoon season. The Pune metropolitan area has expanded also because rainfall in it is not very heavy. An extension of this corridor includes sugar mill towns in western Maharashtra.

(iii) The third well-developed corridor is from Dhanbad in Bihar through Durgapur-Asansol and Vardhaman to Howrah and Kolkata. As mentioned earlier the jute mill towns located along the Hooghly river are part of it. The corridor extends southwest towards Kharagpur in West Bengal but that city is not part of it. 45 jute mill towns located along the Hooghly river and towns and villages south of Kolkata that supply milk fruit and vegetables to the city are part of it. The corridor is expanding north to the residential township of Kalyani, 60 kilometres north of Kolkata. A southeastern extension is to Midnapur. Traffic along the roads and railway lines is heavy despite recurrent flooding during the monsoon. A second bridge on the river Hooghly and 15 kilometres of an underground railway from Dum Dum airport to the city centre have been completed to ease the flow of traffic. However, despite these, parts of Kolkata and Howrah and the roads and railway lines from Kolkata west to Delhi and southwest to Chennai get flooded for brief periods during heavy downpour in the monsoon.

The state governments of Maharashtra and Gujarat are doing their best to build bypasses and widen and improve the roads in coastal Gujarat between Mumbai and Pune and in the two cities. However, they are constrained by paucity of funds. The Tatas are steadily expanding electric and water supplies to Mumbai so that there is no interruption of these in the highly congested city. All efforts to decongest Mumbai have failed for various reasons.

(iv) A mini-corridor is developing between Bangalore to Mysore city and it includes several small towns on the road between Bangalore and Chennai and Bangalore and Mumbai. Steady expansion of the corridor is inevitable.

The road between Mysore city and Bangalore never gets flooded during the rains because the cities are located on a 3500 ft. high plateau. The road passes from Mysore city to Vrindavan gardens a most beautiful garden patterned after the gardens of Shalimar in Kashmir. The area grows high yielding rice and there are a number of rice and sugar mill towns. Farmers and labourers have full time work in the highly productive agriculture and in the rice and sugar mills. Their women folk are busy raising cocoons of silk worms on mulberry leaves found on the bushes; the climate is suitable for raising such worm. Thousands of weavers are busy making silk sarees and producing silk for other garments. Besides, the government owns a silk mill in Mysore city.

Bangalore has become the largest centre of the information technology industry due to the presence in the city of two institutes of science and consequent produce of large number of graduates in basic sciences. The information technology industry is the fastest expanding industry at present and such expansion is expected to continue for another decade or two. The government of Karnataka is making every effort possible to ensure that it remains concentrated in and around Bangalore. There is uninterrupted water and power supply and state-of-the-art information technology parks. Roads are being resurfaced and widened to reduce congestion on them.

Bangalore has become a multiple industry city after Second World War. Hindustan Aircrafts which was established in its environs for repair of aircraft has now diversified to manufacture small trainer aircrafts. Hindustan Machine Tools which makes basic light machine tools, watches and the Indian Telephone Industries established in the 1950s to manufacture telephone receivers and other telecommunication equipments has steadily expanded its output to meet increasing demand. A number of private enterprises are also manufacturing telephone receivers and telecommunication equipment.

The corridor is expanding towards Chennai upto Hossur for a distance along the road to Mumbai. The attraction of Bangalore and its environs is so great that a number of industries including manufacture of motor vehicles are being located in its environs. The long-term prospects for the mini-corridor is infilling and linear expansion along the roads to Chennai and Mumbai.

The central Punjab-Haryana-Delhi-western U.P. corridor is also experiencing infilling and expansion in new direction to include Chandigarh the capital of Punjab and Haryana and its environ particularly the small towns of Mohali and Pinjore in Punjab. The biggest company manufacturing pharmaceutical drugs is planning to establish a large factory for manufacturing drugs in Mohali located about 13 kilometres south of Chandigarh. There is already the city of Gurgaon and large industrial estates of Bhiwani is also getting filled up with medium sized and large industries owned by entrepreneurs based in Delhi or Jaipur. Rajasthan government is planning to locate other industrial estates in this area. The road between Delhi and Jaipur which has a heavy flow of tourist traffic and goods traffic is being widened and improved. Establishment of industries in it would mean expansion of the corridor.

Chandigarh could itself become the centre of information technology because the large number of Punjabi non-resident Indians who have become multi-millionaires would like to invest in establishing of the industry in the capital of their own state. It has a first rate teaching hospital and a university so that there is a large pool of graduates in science and technology and pharmacology.

Metropolitan cities and their environs and urban corridors are likely to remain the principal centres of factory industries and modern services. The prospect for the immediate future is for expansion and infilling of the corridors because of their many advantages for industrial development.

Urban Development

The chapters on Regional Development in Indian Planning (Ch. 6) and The Growth of Indian Agriculture: A Regional Analysis (Ch. 12) relate to regional development in the Five Year Plans and the experience with them, especially in relation to state level of economic development and rates of economic growth. It was found that inspite of policy for reduction of disparities in development the urban population of India is increasing progressively. It has increased from 17 per cent of the total population in 1951 to 28 per cent by 1991 and could exceed 30 per cent by 2001.

There is a pronounced tendency for the urban population to concentrate in the cities and in the large metropolitan cities with a population of 1 million or more. In 1991, over 60 per cent of the urban population lived in the cities; more than half of it was in the metropolitan cities. The number of such cities has increased progressively from 5 in 1951 to 23 in 1991 and is expected to rise to between 36-40 in 2001.

The metropolitan cities are the political, commercial, industrial and cultural capitals of the regions in which they are located. The capitals of 10 of the 16 large states of India are metropolitan cities. These cities are the principal distribution centres for a wide range of products—from textiles to consumer durables in the region in which they are located. Furthermore, most of them are important industrial centres. The craftsman and traditional handicrafts of the region are concentrated in them. The industrial units located within them or in their environs produce a large variety of goods—textiles, readymade garments, shoes, furnishings, furniture, processed foods and a variety of other goods to meet the demands of the city and the regions. The largest metropolitan cities—Mumbai, Kolkata, Chennai, Delhi, and Bangalore, are major industrial centres. The industries located in them include everything from pharmaceutical drugs, processed foods and garments to passenger cars and in some cases high and light trucks.

This concentration of industries and modern services in metropolitan areas is primarily due to availability within them of large pools of capital, technical and managerial personnel and of skilled and unskilled workers. Unskilled and skilled workers are attracted to them because of availability of jobs in industries and those of the rickshaw pullers and domestic servants to skilled employees in manufacturing plants. Furthermore, some of them are distribution centres of various goods within their hinterlands.

In the Mumbai metropolitan area in which the skilled workers are primarily from adjoining districts of Maharashtra, others may come from Punjab or distant parts of Maharashtra. White-collar workers come from Maharashtra as well as from Karnataka, Tamil Nadu and Kerala. There is a very large number of workers from eastern Uttar Pradesh and Bihar who do the unskilled jobs such as of rickshaw pullers, watchmen with banks and other companies, porters on railway stations, etc. In Delhi, similarly, construction labourers are from Rajasthan but white-collar workers come from Bengal, Maharashtra, Tamil Nadu, Karnataka and Kerala.

Most of the metropolitan areas experience rapid growth of population because of large in-migration. Many development plans aimed at dispersal of population and economic activities from them to towns and cities located on their periphery in order to reduce pressure on their essential services, such as electricity, water supply, facilities for waste disposal have not succeeded for various reasons.

The principal reasons for this are concentration within them of entrepreneurs, skilled labourers and the professionals needed for starting and work in the units. Furthermore, large market of the cities is itself a major attraction for manufacturers of a wide range of products choosing to locate their units within them or in the environs. Some of the large cities are also financial centres, with a stock exchange, head offices or large branches of banks or the Life Insurance and General Insurance Corporations and offices of institutions such as the Industrial Development Bank of India created by the Government of India to give loans to new or existing industrial units.

Some of the large cities are cultural capitals of the states or regions in which they are located. Located within them are the writers and poets that enrich the regional language and the painters and sculptures that enrich its culture. The changes in lifestyle introduced by the residents of these cities are adopted in time by the people of the region.

Urban Development Programmes: In contrast to rural development, no country-wide programme of urban development has been undertaken. In case of a number of cities long-term development plans for expansion of electricity, water supply, the sewerage system and facilities for disposal of solid waste and finally, housing to meet the needs of the growing population had been drawn up in the 1960s and 1970s. The plans also indicate the land use in and around the cities—thus indicating the areas for locating new housing colonies, markets, offices of companies and location of industrial units. However, no long-term plans were drawn up for most of the cities, and no follow up plans have been made after expiry of the first long term plans. The principal reasons for this are discussed later.

The principal problems of the metropolitan cities are to expand the physical and social infrastructures in conformity with growth of population and economic activities. The physical infrastructures include supply sources of electricity and water, intra-urban road, and public transport system and finally, improvement or relocation of slums in which the poor population of the cities lives. As long as concentration of capital finance and entrepreneurial talent remain in the metropolitan cities, people will be attracted to them like bees to a honeycomb.

APPENDIX-I

Hierarchy of Central Places in a Metropolitan Region

1. Metropolitan City.
2. Sub-regional centre—the principal town and service centre of the sub-region.
3. Multi-district centre-principal town and service centre of a group of districts. Some of these towns are also headquarters of Commissioners' Divisions.
4. District centre—the principal town and service centre for the whole or a major part of the district. Most of these towns are also district headquarters.
5. Mandi centre-town with an established permanent market (not weekly *hat*) serving an area approximating a community development block or a taluk. It may also be the headquarters of the block or taluk.
6. Rural service centre—small town or large village functioning as a service centre for a group of villages.

NOTES

1. "Regions for Planning", *Indian Journal of Public Administration,* New Delhi, Vol. XII, No.1, pp. 1-17 (1966).
2. For discussion of the hierarchial order of Central places, see Isard W., 1960.
3. Some districts of Bihar and Madras with population of three to four million are recognized as being too large for efficient local planning. The Madras districts have been bifurcated for purposes of planning, and a similar bifurcation of the Bihar districts will be useful. On the other hand many of the districts of Rajasthan, Madhya Pradesh and Himachal Pradesh are very small.
4. One such scheme is that used by the Energy Survey Committee which divides the country into the following six energy regions:

   (i) Northern: Punjab, Himachal Pradesh, Delhi, Rajasthan and Jammu and Kashmir.
   (ii) Central: U.P. and Madhya Pradesh.
   (iii) Eastern: Bihar, West Bengal and Orissa.
   (iv) Assam: Assam, Tripura and Manipur.
   (v) Southern: Andhra Pradesh, Mysore, Madras and Kerala.
   (vi) Western: Maharashtra and Gujarat.

   The only unsatisfactory feature of the scheme is inclusion of U.P. and Madhya Pradesh in one region. There are marked physical and socio-economic differences between the two States which are marked by their inclusion in one region. Each State is large enough to constitute a region by itself.
5. Make reference to the booklet of the Census Commission of India by V. Nath and Gopalaswamy.
6. See for instance, Lastie Grean: *The Economic Hinterland of Calcuta*, published by Asian Publishing House, Mumbai.

REFERENCES

Government of India, *Regional Planning Unit*: Mimeographed.

Government of India (1964): *Resource Development Regions and Divisions of India*, Planning Commission, India.

Government of India (1965): *Report of the Energy Survey of India Committee*, New Delhi.

Green Lastie, *The Economic Hinterland of Calcutta,* Asia Publishing House, Mumbai.

Isard, W. (1960): Methods of Regional Analysis, M.I.T. Press, Cambridge Mass.

Losch, A. (1964): The Nature of Economic Regions in Friedmann, J. and Alonso W., *Regional Development and Planning: A Reader*, Cambridge, The M.I.T. Press, Mass.

2

Regional Development Policies[1]

INTRODUCTION

India has reached a stage in its planning when formulation of comprehensive policies on the spatial location of economic activities and the spatial pattern of development has become essential. The need for such policy formulation is underscored by the growing regional development pressures which, if not satisfied, could seek expression in counter-productive activities; by the possibilities of large costs to the economy from wrong decisions on locations of large projects, taken under regional pressures; and by the lack of adequate policies in the neglected areas of industrial location and urban growth.

The observed increase in inter-state differences in levels of economic development conforms to the theory that intra-national regional disparities increase in the early stages of economic development and begin to be reduced only in later stages (Friedman and Alonso, 1965 pp. 3-7). Increase in regional disparities generates pressures for regional development, which can create serious strains on the political systems of the developing countries.

REGIONAL DEVELOPMENT PRESSURES

Regional development pressures are an important part of the political process in India. They find expression in various ways, notably:

(i) Demands of backward regions on State and Central governments for special programmes for relief of backwardness;

(ii) Demands of the State governments on the Central government for larger financial allocations for their plans and for location of large, centrally financed projects. Similar demands for location of projects come from backward regions; and

(iii) Competing claims of States for larger allocations of inter-State natural resources such as waters of inter-State rivers.

There is considerable evidence of intensification of the pressures in the last few years. Demands for additional resource allocations and special measures for relief of backwardness have come from an increasing number of 'backward regions,' and there is a growing trend towards linking regional economic and political aspirations, and using "neglect by the State government" as an argument to support demands for constituting backward regions into separate States. The most notable instance of the latter was in the 1969 agitation for the creation of the separate State of Telengana (*Economic and Political Weekly*, 1969. pp. 278-280). But the argument has been used in other separate State demands—Haryana, Vidarbha, the hill areas of Assam and others. The competing claims of States for location of centrally financed industrial and other projects have become so strong that locational decisions have been delayed, sometimes for long periods, in order to satisfy (or at least not to offend) the various claimants.

The history of location of the public sector steel plants provides a good illustration of intensification of competing claims and their effects on decision-making. The decisions relating to the location of the first four plants – at Rourkela, Bhilai, Durgapur and Bokaro – were taken quickly and without controversy in the 1950s and early 1960s. But the decision on location of the fifth plant became the subject of prolonged controversy as a result of the pressures exerted by the rival claimants – Andhra Pradesh, Mysore, Tamil Nadu and Goa[2]. The controversy inspired among other things, public demonstrations and riots in Andhra Pradesh in 1966. The decision to locate plants in three States—Andhra Pradesh, Mysore and Tamil Nadu—finally, announced in 1970, while it satisfied these States, was promptly hailed also as having been dictated by political expediency (*Economic and Political Weekly*, August 1970, pp. 1326). It was followed by a demand, accompanied by a *bandh*, for location of a second steel plant in Orissa (*ibid*).

The controversies over development of water resources of inter-state rivers have become so intractable, because of internal pressures on the State governments 'not to surrender their interests' that the process of negotiation to reach agreement is becoming an exercise in futility. The Krishna and Narmada river dispute had to be referred to judicial tribunals after negotiations, among the States concerned, extending over several years, had failed to produce agreements and the Kaveri river dispute appears to be destined to a similar fate (*Hindustan Times*, 1970, p. 1).

STRAIN ON POLITICAL SYSTEM

Regional development pressures are found in other federal countries, such as USA and Yugoslavia, as well as in countries like UK, Italy and France which have unitary government: they are part of the complex of political processes through which different interest groups in a country seek to obtain more favourable resource allocations for themselves. Growth of such pressures is an inevitable result of the process of political development—increasing political awareness and participation. An important factor contributing to growth of group pressures in India is the fact that Central and State governments have such a dominant role in allocation of investment: public sector investment is directly decided by them and private sector investment is greatly influenced by their policies and programmes, enforced through systems of incentives and sanctions. With increasing political awareness and participation, the awareness of this role of the governments is increasing and leaders of various groups including regions seek to influence investment decisions in favour of their constituents. The political developments following the general elections of 1967, particularly the formation in several States, in the absence of a clear majority of any political party in the legislature, of weak and unstable coalition governments dependent upon support of diverse interest groups, and coming to power of regional parties such as the DMK in Tamil Nadu, may also have contributed to growth of regional development pressures. A detailed study would be interesting.

Although regional development pressures impose a strain on the Indian political system, to regard them as mere manifestations of fissiparous regionalist tendencies is to disregard the dynamics of political development in a large country having great physical and social diversity. It is essential for the success of planning in India that the people of every State and region feel that they are being fairly treated in allocation of development resources and that the Plans aim to meet their needs and develop the potential of their region as well as of any other. In regional development policies it will be necessary to arrive at acceptable compromises between the demands of maximizing national economic growth, and promotion of regional welfare and satisfaction of regional aspirations. The two objectives need not be entirely or even necessarily in conflict. In situations such as India's, in which there are large unemployed or underemployed resources (particularly manpower), regional-welfare-oriented policies could contribute to national economic growth by eliciting significant additional resources for development programmes.

There are three areas of regional development in which formulation of new policies, modification of existing policies or more effective implementation of policies is most needed. The areas are:

(i) Development of backward regions;
(ii) Industrial location; and
(iii) Urban growth.

DEVELOPMENT OF BACKWARD REGIONS

The pressure for development of backward regions is the strongest and most persistent among regional development pressures and, as mentioned above, it can be harnessed in support of the political objective of creation of separate States. Under the strategy for development of backward regions, outlined in the first three Five-Year Plans, the prime role was given to development of infrastructure and social services; it was expected that the handicaps of the regions would be mitigated through such developments and that industries and other economic activities would be attracted to them (Planning Commission, 1961, p. 147). But development of the regions had to be financed from within the allocations for the State plans; the Five-Year Plans did not provide significant additional funds for it. In backward regions, having large tribal populations, those with problems such as famine, or those in which national priority programmes such as border communication were implemented additional funds were available under appropriate welfare or development programmes. In backward regions, endowed with mineral resources such as those of the Coal-Steel Belt of Bihar, Orissa and Madhya Pradesh, large investments were made, mainly by the Central government, in mineral and industrial projects.

But many backward regions did not come under any of these categories and did not receive additional funds. The most notable among them are the backward regions of the Uttar Pradesh (UP) and Bihar plains, which have moreover such large populations. According to Levels of Regional Development in India 59 per cent of the total population of UP and 78 per cent of that of Bihar, a total of 80 million people, were in districts classified as being at the bottom or next level of development (Registrar General, India, 1964, p. 19). These backward districts of the two States contained also 45 per cent of the total (all-India) population of such districts (*ibid.*, p. 26). These two States and adjoining Madhya Pradesh and Orissa, is the largest contiguous area of backwardness – the backward heart of the country. Relief of backwardness of such large populations is beyond the resources of individual State government; backwardness and poverty of large sections of the population themselves reduce the revenue raising capacity of the State governments and the development expenditures in the States. Thus, UP and Bihar had the lowest per capita State plan expenditure under the first three plans (Nath, V. Jan. 1970, Table 8.1 Col. 10). In the case of the Fourth Plan also, projected per capita State plan outlay in the two States remains below that in most other States[2].

First Steps

Effective action for relief of backwardness will require as first steps: (i) demarcation of backward regions on the basis of uniform, nationally accepted criteria; (ii) transfer of financial responsibility for accelerated development of the regions from the State governments to the Central government and provision of adequate funds for it in the Central plan; and (iii) formulation of development programmes, separately for each regions as per needs for progress, after surveys of their resources, physical and socio-economic blocks. Demarcation of backward regions using uniform criteria is essential for objective assessment of the magnitude of the problem of backwardness and to remove complaints of differential treatment. The need for transfer of financial responsibility arises from the above-mentioned inability of the State with the largest populations in backward regions to take effective action for relief of backwardness. The financial provisions for development of the regions will have to be large enough to accelerate economic growth in them significantly so that the regions can overcome their handicaps within a measurable period and can participate adequately thereafter in national economic growth. Otherwise, as a result of the processes which increase regional disparities in development, the regions will be condemned to long-term stagnation and poverty.

Specific regional programming may not appear important because a large proportion of the development expenditure in all backward regions will have to be on infrastructure, social service and resource development programmes. The need for it arises from the need to relate such expenditures more closely to the resource potentials and problems of individual regions. The need may be illustrated by reference to three groups of backward regions:

(i) In the regions of the Coal-Steel Belt of Bihar, Orissa and Madhya Pradesh, in which a number of mineral or industrial projects have been located during the period of the Plans (and more will be located in future), special programmes are needed to prepare the tribal and other rural populations for the *opportunities* and *perils* of urban industrial development. The new projects have brought to these populations new employment opportunities in industries and services as well as opportunities of increasing incomes through production to meet the new demands for agricultural products, particularly high-value perishables such as milk, vegetables and poultry products. At the same time, aggressive immigrants such as contractors, moneylenders and traders have exposed the populations to exploitation. The Third Five-Year Plan had envisaged area development programmes, including education and skill formation for the local populations, in the vicinity of the steel plants and other projects located in these regions (Planning Commission, 1961, p. 149). Little information is available on actual formulation and implementation of the programmes. But judging from frequent inter-group conflicts and alienation of the tribal people around Ranchi and some other project areas, it would appear that the protective programmes at any rate have been inadequate or ineffective.

(ii) In the backward regions of the UP and Bihar plains, where there is very high pressure of population on land—population densities exceeded 1,000 per sq. mile in many districts—but agriculture continues to be stagnant and there are hardly any mineral resources, the development programmes must extend over a broad front, with objectives ranging from achieving technological breakthroughs in agriculture and water management (including effective control over periodic floods) and improvement of communications to social and institutional reforms (Planning Commission, 1964)[3]. The problem of development is more difficult in these regions than in most others because their populations are so large and special efforts extending over a long period will be required.

(iii) Finally, in regions like famine-prone Western Rajasthan, which have severe environmental handicaps and limited development potentials, the programmes may primarily be of the 'holding operation' variety. An important objective of the programmes in such regions may also be to prepare the local people, especially the youth, for emigration to regions of better economic opportunity. Projects of development of natural resources should be scrutinized with particular care. If their benefit/cost ratios are very low, it should be examined whether regional welfare would not be promoted more effectively by undertaking more productive projects in adjoining regions, to which the people of these regions could be attracted.

Role of Large Projects

Both by stressing development of infrastructures, social services and related activities in the backward regions and by advocating location of large projects on basis of techno-economic efficiency, judged from the national perspective, the planners had sought to dissociate location of large projects from development of backward regions. But the linkage between political demands for relief of backwardness and those for location of large projects remains strong. Leaders of backward regions generally consider location of a large project to be the most important measure of regional development, and State governments frequently use backwardness as an argument to support their demands for location of large, centrally financed projects. There are several reasons for the popularity of large projects in regional development. The principal economic reason is the linkage effect, embodied in F. Perroux's growth pole concept. The Third Five-Year Plan recognized the effort by designating the steel plants and other projects located in the backward regions of the coal-steel-belt (albeit on national techno-economic efficiency criteria) as 'regional growth nuclei' to which other developments would be attracted (Planning Commission, 1961, p. 149). But the non-economic reasons are perhaps more important in India. Regional aspirations and demands can be focused far more effectively on a large project than on a variety of development programmes; the completed project serves as an excellent symbol of successful pursuance of regional demands. Another reason is the importance given to large projects in the Five-Year Plans: successive Plans have publicized the large projects included in them so much that the Plans have come to be identified with the projects by the public.

Since location of large projects is likely to remain an important issue in regional development and since costs to the national economy in departing from optimum locations, in response to regional pressures, are likely to be very large – the costs arise both from higher construction costs and loss of output from the frequently longer gestation periods in non-optimal locations – it is essential that the regional growth effects of large projects should be carefully studied. The steel plants and other projects located in the backward regions of the coal-steel-belt will furnish useful data for the study. Analysis of experience in other countries, notably France and Italy in which considerable efforts have been made in the post-War period for development of backward regions, will also be useful. Some of this experience may indicate that the regional growth effects of large projects are frequently over-estimated or that backward regions cannot take adequate advantage of the growth potential of large projects because of deficiencies of infrastructure and human resource development.

The latter is illustrated by the recent French experience with the natural-gas based industrial complex of Lacq in southwestern France which was expected to serve as a growth pole for this backward region because "the complex of Lacq responds perfectly well to the definition that F. Perroux has given of propulsive industries (asymmetric effects, rate of growth superior to the national average).... In fact, however, the effects of the Lacq complex have been quite modest, contrary to original hopes and despite the creation of some induced industries." (Hansen, 1968, pp. 176-77). "The case of Lacq well illustrates the difficulties involved in trying to induce self-sustained growth in a lagging region through EOC (economic overhead capital) even when the government is necessarily compelled to locate the EOC facility in such a region. Indeed, considerations of rational resource allocation from a national point of view have led the government to direct most of the EOC benefit stream to other regions. Moreover, one of the principal barriers to the Lacq complex becoming a development pole for its region has been the more or less traditional attitude of the indigenous population. Thus, while the advantages that EOC brings to a lagging region are undeniable, their effectiveness also depends on the degree to which SOC (Social overhead capital) has developed the region's human resources." (*Ibid.* pp. 182-83).

INDUSTRIAL LOCATION

Reference has been made to the ambivalence of the planners on the subject of industrial location in Chapter 8. It has been explained that while advocating industrial dispersal, particularly avoidance of concentration of industries in the developed industrial areas, and fostering regional patterns of development in case of consumer goods and processing industries, the planners had specifically avoided advocating use of the industrial licensing power of the government, its principal instrument for directing private sector locations, for securing industrial dispersal. The evidence reviewed in the chapter indicated that (i) while big-city locations had been avoided in case of the public sector industrial units, private sector industrial growth had concentrated in the cities, and (ii) that while some industrial development had taken place in backward States like Orissa and Madhya Pradesh, mainly as a result of location of public sector industrial units, the most rapid industrial growth had been in the relatively developed States of Maharashtra, West Bengal and Gujarat (Nath, V. Jan. 1970, Table 8.1, Col. 16).

The Fourth Five-Year Plan refers to positive measures, such as concessions and subsidies, to promote industrial development in backward regions and negative measures to prevent further concentration of industries in metropolitan region, because "the socio-economic costs of servicing such large centers are particularly heavy"

(Planning Commission, 1970, p. 311). This clear statement marks a significant advance over the earlier ambivalence, although the negative measures have not been specified and among the positive measures, the subsidy "to the extent of one-tenth of the total capital cost for projects costing up to Rs 50 lakhs both in the private and public sector" (*ibid.*, p. 310) will be available in only one or two districts of each State.

The concept of positive and negative measures to secure industrial dispersal is not new, however. Such measures have been adopted in some states, notably Maharashtra. The Maharashtra Government has sought to prevent further concentration of industries in Bombay City and to direct industrial growth to the less developed regions of the State by (i) prohibiting or actively discouraging location of industries in Bombay city; (ii) constructing industrial estates and areas (through the Maharashtra Industrial Development Corporation) in the less developed regions; and, (iii) giving financial incentives for location of industries in these regions. The technical assistance provided by the State Industrial and Investment Corporation of Maharashtra to firms wishing to locate industries in these regions constitutes a noteworthy recent addition to the positive measures. An evaluation of the experience of Maharashtra (and other States) with positive and negative measures will be useful in detailed formulation of such measures at the national level.

Need for Comprehensive Policy

While recommendations on particular aspects of industrial location, such as those contained in the Five-Year Plans are useful, they do not constitute by themselves a policy on industrial location. There is urgent need for formulation of a comprehensive policy on the subject in view of its importance to regional development and the spatial distribution of economic activity. The policy should be based on an analysis of the economics of industrial location in India and the changing patterns of industrial location in the developed countries under the impact of the techno-economic changes of recent decades in transport, communications, generation and distribution of power and industrial organization. These changes, notably extensive use of road transport for carrying both workers and goods and use in industry of power, generated in large central stations and transmitted over regional or national grids, have imparted flexibility to industrial location that did not exist earlier, in the coal-rail era. As a result, most industries have become foot-loose and regional location has acquired greater importance than site location. At the same time, locations near large cities and other existing industrial regions are preferred, in order to avail of the external economics of agglomeration and to have the advantage of proximity to markets; locations in most industries have become market-oriented (Chauncy, 1954, pp. 315-348). But the large land requirements of assembly-line production induce most industries to seek locations outside the centers of cities, in the peripheral regions (Moses and Williamson, 1967).

One result of this combination of factors has been emergence in USA, Western Europe and Japan of giant urban industrial complexes (megalopolises) which continue to grow in size in spite of increasingly difficult environmental and organizational problems created by such large concentrations of population and economic activity. In the developing countries including India, the pull of the cities on industries is even stronger because the modern infrastructures, needed by the industries, and concentrations of entrepreneurial, professional and labour skills are found in the cities. Industrial location trends in India and selected developed countries should be analyzed in detail in order to have an adequate factual basis for formulation of the policy on industrial location.

URBAN GROWTH

If the area of industrial location has been characterized by a degree of ambivalence and incompleteness in policy formulation, that of urban growth has been marked by passivity and neglect. Statements on urban development and planning appear under the chapters on Housing in the Second and the Third Five-Year Plans (Planning Commission, 1956. pp. 568-570 and 1961, pp. 689-693). They contain some useful recommendations such as those relating to control of urban land values, town planning legislation and formulation of urban plans. But the primary responsibility for urban development is placed on the municipalities. The Third Plan, while recognizing the increasing seriousness of the urban problem, because expansion of housing and urban infrastructures was not adequate for the needs of rapid urban growth, does not advocate a more active role for the Central and State governments in urban development. This passivity did not arise from lack of knowledge of urban problems: the universities and research institutes had undertaken during the 1950s, with assistance from the Planning Commission, itself, a most comprehensive set of city surveys. Besides there were studies by individual scholars and reports by expert groups including the Ford Foundation Advisory Groups appointed in connection with formulation of the master plans of Delhi and Calcutta. It may have been due to an inadequate appreciation of the relationship between urban growth and national economic development and of the role of cities and towns as essential infrastructures of economic development, and unwillingness or inability to provide adequate funds for financing urban development programmes.

The Consequences

It is not our purpose to go into the causes of this passivity; but it is necessary to mention its consequence. The most important consequence has been, failure to develop: (i) a system of urban planning, and (ii) adequate financial arrangements and organizational structures for implementation of urban development programmes. Urban plans are not formulated as part of the system of formulation of national and State plans and are not related to the latter. Formulation of urban plans remains *ad hoc* and dependent upon the initiative of the individual municipality. As a result, plans are not formulated for most cities and towns. Even the modest effort at formulating plans for a limited number of urban places, under the direction of the State Town Planning Departments but with financial assistance from the Central Government, begun towards the end of the Second Plan, has suffered a serious setback because of a drastic reduction in the financial provision for it in the Fourth Plan[4]. Financial assistance from the Central or State governments for urban development remains tied to particular schemes; a system of assistance for such programmes has not been evolved.

The thinking that urban development is the responsibility primarily of urban local bodies persists despite abundant evidence of the inability of most bodies to undertake development programmes of any size. No effort has been made to give to the municipalities an organizational structure, suitable and adequate for the need of rapid expansion of the urban plan: there is no urban counterpart of the community development and Panchayati Raj organization. There has also been a curious disregard of the relation between urban and rural development. The best indication of the disregard is given by the fact that neither the community development nor the Panchayati Raj organizations have provided for any formal interaction between the rural development organizations and the municipalities. Of late, there is some realization of the need for urban-rural interaction at the local or micro-regional level.

Following the experience in some areas, notably Punjab, of the inadequacy of marketing and storage facilities available in the *mandi* towns to handle the larger grain output resulting from the high-yielding varieties programme, there has been some discussion of developing "growth centers" (The Ford Foundation, 1969, pp. 1-7). There is greater recognition also of the fact that the market towns and similar places are the most suitable locations for the various infrastructures of modernization of agriculture and rural life—distribution centres for improved seeds, chemical fertilizers, pesticides and other supplies; facilities for sale, servicing and repair of modern agricultural implement; soil testing laboratories; facilities for marketing and processing of agricultural products and for distribution of durable consumer goods, etc. This role of market towns had been emphasized earlier by several writers, notably E.A.J. Johnson, who advocated in a report, published by the National Council of Applied Economic Research, a large programme of building 10, 000-12,000 market towns over the period of several plans as an important part of the strategy for economic development in India (National Council of Applied Economic Research, 1965). The Working Group on Incentives for Industrial Development in Backward Areas have recommended development of "growth points" in these areas (Development Commissioner, New Delhi 1969. pp. 9).

But the growth centres or growth points represent only the last (or the first, depending upon how one looks at it) element in the urban hierarchy, which extends through district and division headquarters towns, larger market towns or industrial centres and the State capitals to the national or macro-regional centres such as Bombay, Calcutta, Delhi and Madras. The towns and cities at different levels in the hierarchy are central places for their regions, performing essential services for them (Berry and Pred, 1961, pp. 1-15). The magnitude and range of these functions will increase progressively as the regional and national economies grow and as the central place role of the urban places is articulated more effectively as a result of rural modernization and closer integration of local, regional and national economies. As a result most of the towns and cities will increase in size. In cities like Bombay and Calcutta, where continued growth will create difficult problems, the pressures of growth could be reduced somewhat by preventing further concentration of industries or by diverting some growth elsewhere, as is being done by developing Haldia to relieve the pressure on the port of Calcutta. But most of the large cities, including Delhi and Madras, still have very large growth potential and it will not be desirable to curb it unduly. Indeed from the progressive increase in the number of regional offices of national firms (and of the Central Government) in these cities and from industrial growth in their peripheral regions, much of it oriented specifically to exploiting regional markets, it appears that the regional central place role of the cities is in the process of active development.

Policy for Urban Growth

A policy on urban growth should be based on recognition of (i) the certainty of rapid urban growth during the next several decades; (ii) the vital role of towns and cities as growth centres and central places for regions of different size; and (iii) the fact that as the economy develops the spatial economic relations within it will be expressed primarily through its system of urban places. Perspectives of long-term urban growth and of its distribution among urban places of different sizes and functional characteristics should be prepared. It should be recognized also that whatever the rate of growth of the urban population or the proportion of the urban population in the total, the total size of the urban population would be very large. Thus if the proportion is only 30 per cent by 2000 AD—semi-developed Yugoslavia had this proportion in 1960—the total urban population will be between 270 million and 300 million, depending upon whether the total population in that year is closer to the Planning Commission's projection of 890 million (Planning Commission, 1970, p. 31) or the United Nations' 1963 projection of nearly 1 billion[5]. The prospective sizes of the large cities as well as the probable future numbers and locations of cities and towns should be seen against the background of such totals. The largest cities need (and must) not grow to the gigantic sizes projected by Kingsley Davis (1962, pp. 25); but there can scarcely be any doubt that they will be very much larger than they are now. Further, while India must evolve its own distinctive urban patterns suited to its demographic and social conditions and, present and emerging industrial, transport, communication and power technologies, the effort to evolve the patterns must begin with a recognition of the essential role of urban places in economic development. A policy of neglect is entirely self-defeating. Even if the objective is to prevent concentration in the largest cities and to keep down urban growth, it cannot be achieved by a neglect of urban areas.

The operative parts of the policy on urban growth should relate to: (i) institution of systems of formulation of urban development plans, their inter-relation with national and State plans and their financing from national and State resource pools in the same way as rural development plans are financed at present; (ii) reorganization of municipalities to equip them adequately for rapid urban expansion; and (iii) a major effort in the area of urban design, aimed at evolving urban patterns which keep costs of expansion low and maximize its growth-inducing influences on the neighbouring rural regions. The latter objective can be achieved for instance by urban designs which encourage commuting of workers to cities and towns from neighbouring villages. The costs of expansion of housing and urban infrastructures will remain low if a significant proportion of the workers in urban industries and services are commuters; rural development will be fostered by flow to the villages of incomes from urban jobs, new ideas and knowledge of new production techniques and patterns of living.

CONCLUSION

India has reached a stage in its planning when formulation of comprehensive polices on the spatial location of economic activity and the spatial pattern of development has become essential. Growing regional development pressures which, if not satisfied, could seek expression in counterproductive activities; the possibility of large costs to the economy from wrong decisions on location of large projects, taken under regional pressures, and the need for adequate policies in the neglected areas of industrial location and urban growth emphasize the need for such policy formulation. In this context, it is necessary to urge again the need for basic data on various aspects of regional development and growth and for studies on such subjects as the regional growth influence of large projects, to which reference has been made in this and other chapters.

The most urgent need is for data on State and district incomes. State income estimates should be made using identical concepts and techniques in all States and should be extended to the 20-year period of the Plans so that the economic performance of different States in this period can be compared. District income estimates are essential for precise delineation of the spatial pattern of economic development and growth. Studies such as the 1961 Census study on Level of Regional Development are useful and we hope that the Census Commissioners will publish similar studies as part of the other Census documents. Publication of agricultural growth rates for States by the Economic and Statistical Adviser to the Ministry of Food and Agriculture has brought out regional differentials in agricultural growth. But the growth data are not being updated and data on various indicators of agricultural modernization are spotty and difficult to obtain even for States. These deficiencies should be made up and data on agricultural growth and modernization should be published also for districts. The need for district-level data has increased in recent years with markedly different impact of the high-yielding varieties and other agricultural development programmes in different parts of large states like Utter Pradesh. Data on industrial employment, value added in industry and other indicators of industrial growth should be available for districts so that trends in industrial location can be analyzed with precision and the locational preferences of industries for urban places of different sizes can be determined; the latter will be useful for policy formulation on urban growth.

As regards regional studies, the most urgent needs are for—(i) surveys and studies in selected backward regions and regions of location of large projects to which reference has been made above; and (ii) studies of city-region, inter-city and inter-regional economic relations. The studies are useful for planning of growth centres and formulating a policy on urban growth. The nature and sizes of the facilities proposed to be located at the growth centres can be determined realistically only if the nature, range and magnitude of existing economic relations between them and their complementary regions are known. These studies provide also the factual basis for policies on distribution of the projected urban growth of a period among urban places of different sizes, functional characteristics and spatial distribution. Studies of inter-regional economic relations are essential for understanding the spatial organization of the Indian economy. They have received some attention in recent years: regional transport surveys were conducted on behalf of the Planning Commission during the sixties and studies by individual scholars have also appeared (Berry 1966 and Reed 1967).

NOTES

1. *Economic and Political Weekly*, Mumbai. Vol. VI, Nos. 30-32 Special Number July 1971.
2. Location of public sector steel plants could have become a subject of controversy if the claim of all the four contending States—Orissa, Madhya Pradesh, Bihar and West Bengal – were not satisfied by location of a plant in each. But location of every major public sector project did not become the cause of controversy and an occasion to exert political pressures. The great majorities of the locational decisions were taken on techno-economic considerations, on basis of reports of expert groups, and were accepted by all concerned, although as indicated in Chapter 8 Table 8.1, Col 13, the decisions did result in large differences in Central investment in the States.
3. State-wise figures, obtained by dividing the projected State Plan outlays under the Fourth Five-Year Plan (p. 67) and by the 1971 Provisional Population Totals, Registrar General India: Paper 1 of 1971, are as follows:

States	*Projected Fourth Plan Outlay per capita (Rupees)*
Andhra Pradesh	99
Assam	177
Bihar	94
Gujarat	171
Haryana	227
Jammu and Kashmir	344
Kerala	118
Madhya Pradesh	92
Maharashtra	178
Mysore	120
Orissa	102
Punjab	218
Rajasthan	117
Tamil Nadu	126
Uttar Pradesh	109
West Bengal	73
India	121

4. A detailed survey of the development problems of Eastern Uttar Pradesh and recommendations on a development programme for it, appear in Planning Commission: Report of the Joint Survey Team, Uttar Pradesh, New Delhi, 1964.

5. The funds have been reduced from Rs. 11 million in the Third Plan to Rs. 5 million in the Fourth Plan. But the effect of the reduction is much greater than these figures indicate because the programme was getting built up during the course of the Third Plan period, when plans were started for a number of cities and towns. Continuation of planning in these places alone would have required a much larger provision than contained in the Third Plan.
6. United Nations: "World Population Prospects as Assessed in 1963" (ST/SOA/Ser A41), New York, p. 67. The median variant, with fertility declining from 1970, gave a population figure of 981 million for 2000 AD.

REFERENCES

Berry, B.J. L. (1966): "Essays in Commodity Flows and Spatial Structure of the Indian Economy", University of Chicago, Research Papers, No 111.

Christaller, W. and Losch, A. in Berry, B.J. L. and Pred, A. (1961): "*Central Place Studies: A Bibliography of Theory and Applications*", The Regional Science Institute, Philadelphia.

Davis, Kingsley (1962): "Urbanization in India: Past and Future", in Turner, R.: "*India's Urban Future*", University of California Press, Berkeley and Los Angles.

Development Commissioner (Small Scale Industries) (1969): "Fiscal and Financial Incentives for Starting Industries in Backward Area", Report of the Working Group, New Delhi.

Economic and Political Weekly (1969): "Telengana Turmoil" and "Keeping the Lid on Telengana", Vol. IV No 2, February 1.

——, (1970): "The Politics of Steel", Vol. V, No 30, August 8.

Foundation and the Council for Social Development 1 (1969): "Pilot Project for Social development: "Pilot projects for Integrated area Development", New Delhi.

Friedmann and Alonso, W. (1965): "*Regional Development and Planning –A Reader", MIT Press, Cambridge*.

Hansen, N.M. (1968): "French Regional Planning", Indiana.

Harris, Chauncy D. (1954): "The Market as a Factor in the Localization of Industry in the United States", *Annals of the Association of American Geographers*, Vol. XLIV, No 4.

Hindustan Times, July 9, 1970.

Kuznets, S. (1954): Presidential address delivered to the American Economic Association, December 29, 1954, as quoted in Williamson, J.G.: *op. cit.*

Moses, L. and Williamson, H.W. (1967): "Location of Economic Activities in Cities", *The American Economic Review*, Vol. LVIII.

Nath, V. (1970): "Agricultural Growth in the 1970's –An Analysis," *Economic and Political Weekly,* Vol. V, No 52, December 26.

——, "Regional Development in Indian Planning" *Economic and Political Weekly,* Vol. V, Nos. 3, 4 and 5, January 1970.

National Council for Applied Economic Research (1965): "Market Towns and Spatial Development in India", New Delhi.

Planning Commission (1970): *Second Five-Year Plan, 1956*; *Third Five-Year Plan,* 1961; *Fourth Five-Year Plan* 1969-74, New Delhi.

Reed, W.E. (1967): "Arial Interaction in India: Commodity Flows of the Bengal-Bihar Industrial Area", University of Chicago, Research Paper, No 110.

Registrar General, India (1964): "Levels of Regional Development in India", Census of India, 1961, Vol. I, India, Part I A-1 Text Delhi.

Williamson, J.G. (1965): "Regional Inequality and the Process of National Development—A Description of Patterns", *Economic Development and Cultural Change,* Vol. XIII, No 4, Part II.

3

Organisation for Regional Planning and Development

INTRODUCTION

Regional planning is often associated with the creation of special agencies, perhaps because of the Tennesse Valley Authority (TVA) in the United States and the Damodar Valley Corporation in India, highly publicized agencies, created for specially demarcated river valley regions. However, regional planning does not necessarily involve the creation of special development agencies. The question of organization has to be considered in the context of the existing administrative structure of the country, and the administrative structure of India provides for formulation and execution of plans with states, districts and blocks as units. The plans relate national goals, policies and objectives to local needs and aspirations. Plans for successively smaller units are drawn up within the framework of the goals and policies formulated by the larger units, but on the basis of the needs, development potential, and aspirations of the smaller units. Administrative and institutional arrangements exist at various area levels to coordinate different programmes and produce integrated plans of development. It is true that the approach is sectoral and the plans are, in essence, aggregations of sectoral plans with marginal adjustments to meet the requirements of regional inter-relations. But they could be made more truly regional with appropriate changes in emphasis and techniques.

However, in some cases, it becomes necessary to go outside the existing administrative structure, demarcate regions, and create agencies. Examples of such cases are:

1. Metropolitan regions,
2. Industrial complexes,
3. Backward or depressed regions,
4. River basins.

Each of these represents a case of concentrated, special development effort. The regional approach can make a significant contribution to orderly progress in each case, it can increase efficiency, accelerate growth, and maximize welfare.

SCALE OF PLANNING – LOCAL AND REGIONAL

Metropolitan planning, and to an extent industrial complex planning, differ from the other two in scale and in the nature of the planning tasks and in the administrative and legal measures required for formulation and implementation of plans. Planning for a small geographical area and its details of site and location are essential aspects of metropolitan planning. As a result, metropolitan planning authorities inter-act primarily with local authorities, *e.g.* municipalities and Panchayati Raj institutions. As most Indian cities are located within the area of only one state—Delhi is a conspicuous exception — metropolitan planning authorities are set up by the state governments and function under state law. Planning for industrial complexes also has some of these attributes—planning for a small geographical area, concern with site, with municipal problems of water supply, transport, and power, and interaction with local authorities. But the focus is on industrial development, and such distinctive problems as selection of industries for the complex and their specific sites assume importance. These questions have to be considered in determining the character of the industrial complex, its overall size, and the efficient utilization of basic and intermediate industrial products it produces. Selection of industries may not merely involve selection from among numerous applicants. In case of new complexes such as Bhilai and Rourkela which are located in a backward region, it will involve, in the initial stages, active encouragement of ancillary and derived products industries. Location of such industries is essential to ensure that the complex attains its growth potential and that the large investments in overhead facilities are adequately utilized.

Metropolitan planning is concerned with regional economic planning. Such regional aspects as analysis of economic growth in the hinterland are important in planning for cities like Kolkata and Mumbai. This policy involves selection of a number of growth points in the hinterland in an effort to relieve the pressure on the city. However, regional economic planning is not the primary object of metropolitan planning. It is somewhat more important in planning for industrial complexes, because analysis of the relations of an individual complex with the industrial region in which it is located, and of the flow of goods between the city and various points within the region, are important. But both metropolitan and industrial complex planning is concerned primarily with small geographical areas and physical planning.

In planning for backward regions or regional water resource development, however, the focus is regional and the principal object of planning is regional economic development. In regional water resource development, engineering construction is the starting point of the work of the regional agency. But then it may go into soil conservation, land reclamation, agricultural extension and the like. It may regard the new resources of water and power as instruments of economic and social regeneration. In planning for backward regions, attention is even more pointedly focused on regional economic growth, because this is the sole object of the work of the regional agency. The agency may take up various resources development or industrial development activities; but these are only the means to an end. Such agencies have a vital interest in programmes of agricultural improvement, rural industrialization, social welfare, and even institutional reform. They are concerned also with such matters as improvement of transport and communications, expansion of power supply, concessions in taxes, and rates of power and water, because an important objective of their activities is to attract investment to the region.

Both regional water resource development and backward region development agencies interact primarily with state governments; most of the tasks entrusted to them are the responsibility also of various functional developments of state governments. Entrusting these tasks to the regional agency means that the departments concerned lose their jurisdiction within the region. Where the region extends across several states, the departments of the entire state are affected. Therefore, when creating the regional agency, and assigning its various functions, someone must decide that the existing departments are not adequately equipped for these tasks, or that they are of such magnitude that the creation of a special agency is necessary. Where inter-state action is involved, someone must decide that the necessary coordination of plan formulation and execution is best achieved through a regional agency. This judgment has to be made for the major or primary tasks of the regional agency, as well as for secondary functions. It is particularly important in case of the latter, simply because they are secondary. If they are entrusted to the regional agency it will have to set up its own organization to carry them out. Therefore, it is necessary to be certain that the advantage of closer coordination with the engineering wing of the regional agency (which is all that transfer of the functions to the regional agency will secure) is not outweighed by the difficulties of creating a new organization. The alternative of leaving the secondary functions with the concerned department of the state government may in many cases prove to be easier and more efficient.

STATUS AND EXPERIENCE

Metropolitan Planning

The need for establishing metropolitan planning agencies has been accepted in India. Such agencies have already been established in Kolkata and Delhi and are likely to be set-up in others. The model Town and Country Planning Act recommended by the Town and Country Planning Organization envisages establishment of such agencies wherever necessary. The principal organizational issues in metropolitan planning relate, therefore, not to the need for establishment of metropolitan agencies, or to their primary purpose, but to such questions of detail as the following:

1. Inter-state action between different agencies concerned with different aspects of development in large cities. In Kolkata and Mumbai, different agencies exist or may have to be set up for land use control, water supply and sanitation, and transport. Establishment of specialized agencies is necessary for efficiency, but this raises problems of coordination between agencies.
2. Inter-state action for directing growth of cities like Delhi, whose metropolitan regions extend into more than one state.

3. Inter-state action in economic planning for the hinterland area of cities like Kolkata and Mumbai, in which an industrial dispersal policy has to be followed and economic growth in the hinterland has to be considered for formulating the policy.

Planning for Industrial Complexes

The need for integrated planning of industrial complexes is not as widely accepted as the need for metropolitan planning. The only noteworthy instance of planning for an industrial complex is the regional plan being prepared for the Asansol-Durgapur complex. But the metropolitan and industrial aspects of planning for this important complex have not yet been integrated. In the case of other industrial complexes, there is no similar planning effort.

The question of preparing a regional plan for the South East Resource Region has attracted attention in recent years. The region is the principal producer of iron and steel and is destined to be an outstanding industrial region. A number of studies have been made of various aspects of the economy of the region, with a view to obtaining data for formulating plans.[1] The Town and Country Planning Organization has initiated work on a plan for the whole region. Constitution of an inter-state Board for integrated planning and development of the region has been advocated. This recommendation is of interest, because this is a very large region; extending across the territories of six states, it has great resource potential and a number of mineral, power, water, forest and agricultural development projects are in progress. These projects raise important issues of regional development, because metropolitan areas, industrial complexes, backward regions, and regional water resource development are all represented. Inter-state and inter-agency cooperation is another essential aspect, because development has to be carried out at various levels.

Regional Water Resource Development

The only regional agency constituted so far for inter-state river development is the Damodar Valley Corporation. It was established in 1948 under an Act of the Indian Parliament with the object of developing the water resources of the Damodar river, which flows between Bihar and West Bengal. The principal activities visualized for the Corporation were flood control, power generation, irrigation, and navigation. The Corporation is headed by a Board, consisting of nominees of the Centres and the two states concerned. The establishment of the Corporation was inspired by the TVA. The region is backward, but it has a great potential for resource development. Floods were a major problem, and the Corporation had to construct a number of dams and power stations to control floods and to develop the water resource. It was conceived, as the TVA. had been conceived 15 years earlier in an atmosphere of great hope and enthusiasm, in which bold measures were considered necessary for solving economic and social problems, so there was similar enthusiasm and idealism among its staff in its initial years. The shift in emphasis in the Corporation's activities—from flood control and hydropower generation to thermal power generation—has been similar to the shift in the activities of the TVA.

But this experiment in securing water resource development through a special regional agency has been faced from the beginning with many problems, prominent among which are those of relations with the government of Bihar and West Bengal (Prasad). The Corporation has constructed a number of dams and reservoirs and operates a large power system in Eastern India. But the experience has not been encouraging enough to lead the Central or State governments to set up similar regional agencies for other inter-state river valley projects. On the contrary, an Inter-state Control Board has been adopted in preference to the regional development agency. For example, the Bhakra-Nangal project is directed by a Control Board. This multipurpose irrigation and power project on the Satluj river is the largest undertaken so far in India. The catchment area and the Bhakra dam are located in Himachal Pradesh, a Union Territory (now state); but the bulk of the irrigation and power benefits go to the Punjab, with Rajasthan the second beneficiary. Overall responsibility for planning the project, allocation of benefits and costs between different states, and coordination of execution were entrusted to an Inter-state Control Board made up of representatives of the Central government and the governments of Punjab, Rajasthan and Himachal Pradesh. Within the framework of the policies formulated by the Board, detailed plan formulation and execution of programmes were left to the state governments. Construction of the Bhakra and Nangal dams, certain engineering structures connected with power development, and the Punjab part of the canal system were directed by the Punjab Irrigation Department. The Punjab Electricity Board installed the power generation, transmission, and distribution facilities. The Rajasthan irrigation and electricity authorities similarly constructed the canals and electric transmission and distribution facilities within Rajasthan. The Bhakra Control Board ensured that work in different states was adequately coordinated and problems were promptly solved.

It might be argued that since Punjab had an overwhelming interest in the project it is not a good example of the use of a Control Board. But the same arrangement is being continued in the second phase of the project, in which benefits are more evenly shared between Punjab and Rajasthan. This phase involves construction of dams and the Satluj-Beas link channel in Himachal Pradesh and Punjab, and of the Indira Gandhi Canal in Rajasthan. The irrigation benefits will go entirely to Rajasthan and the Punjab will only get power.

The Chambal Project, an irrigation-cum-hydro-power project (Rajasthan and Madhya Pradesh are the two states concerned, and they derive almost equal benefits) is another example of overall planning and coordination by an Inter-state Control Board and execution by respective departments of state governments. This administrative arrangement has proved so satisfactory that it has now become the accepted arrangement for inter-state river development in India.

This experience demonstrates the importance of identifying carefully the different tasks involved in regional planning and development, making a clear judgment on which tasks can be accomplished through existing organizations and which tasks require new arrangements. In these cases existing state departments were quite capable of execution, and a new agency was needed only for overall policy making and coordination. The Control Boards succeeded because state irrigation and electricity departments were already well established and could be expanded to meet the challenge of new tasks. The tasks were so important that state governments had to develop the organizations to execute them with energy and speed. (These conditions may not be present in all cases requiring regional planning and development as, the case of the Dandakaranya Development Authority illustrates).

The Rihand, Rajasthan Canal and Sundarbans projects illustrate some other aspects of regional planning for development of water resources. In each of these cases the "region" is located entirely within the area of a single state and regional planning can be done by an agency set up by the state government. But each illustrates a different aspect of water resource development.

Rihand is a hydro-electric project located in southeastern Uttar Pradesh. Development of hydel power has attracted a number of industries to the area, most important among which are cement and aluminium. Preparation of a regional plan has been advocated for the area (Hosse, 1964) in order to stimulate and direct industrial and urban development. Planning in this case should have two aspects: (i) detailed planning as an industrial complex in the immediate vicinity of the project, and (ii) economic planning for the entire region to receive power from the project.

The Indira Gandhi Canal will irrigate a large area in the Rajasthan desert. Preparation of a regional plan is important, because the area is virtually uninhabited and development of irrigation must be accompanied by colonization. The plan should be focused on colonization and should locate villages, towns, roads, railways and other essential facilities. The regional plan is being formulated by the Rajasthan Canal Board: integration of construction and regional development in the same agency has obvious advantages in this difficult area.

The Sundarbans, located south of Kolkata, is an area of mangrove swamps crisscrossed by a number of estuarine and riverine channels. Reclamation by constructing a series of embankments has been recommended (NADECO, February 1964). The engineering work is highly specialized and will require a large capital outlay. It will have to be accompanied by construction of roads and other facilities and followed by programmes of colonization, development of agriculture, and creation of a fishing industry. The engineering work could be entrusted to an autonomous Board (or Corporation), an administrative device which has been found to be very useful for undertaking large and specialized programmes. Some of the associated regional development tasks could also be entrusted to the Board; but the others, such as construction of roads and various service facilities, development of agriculture and fisheries, should be done by the respective departments of the state government. The regional plan should be formulated by the Board with assistance from the concerned state departments. The Board could be an agency of the state government, or if the project is financed by the Central Government, it could have on it representatives of both the Centre and the State.

However, its efficient functioning will depend upon the state cooperation.

Development of Backward Regions

Experience with development of backward regions is limited. However, the problem of backward regions is receiving greater attention now, and in the last few years a number of backward regions have been selected for development. The "Special Areas" selected by the Ministry of Rehabilitation, the Hill Areas, the desert Area of Rajasthan and the Eastern Districts of Uttar Pradesh have been designated development targets. The principal objective in backward region development is to accelerate the regional growth process, usually by means of development programmes and administrative and institutional reforms. The regional plan must outline the strategy of development, besides indicating the various development measures needed. It should be prepared by a regional agency, either a special development agency or a coordinating body having on it representatives of the various agencies and departments concerned. Execution of various parts of the plan may be entrusted to the functional departments of state government(s).

Most backward regions are situated within the territory of a single state; agencies for their development can be set-up by the state government. But in cases where the region extends across the territories of two or more states (hill areas, desert areas) inter-state action is required. The precise nature of such action must be identified and appropriate arrangements devised. In the examples mentioned above, inter-state action should be limited to overall planning and coordination of programmes.

Developing backward regions may involve tasks for which the existing departments of the state government are not equipped. Backward regions may also be sparsely populated tribal regions which have received very little attention in the past. Both these conditions exist in the Dandakaranya Area (south eastern Madhya Pradesh and southern Orissa) in which the Dandakaranya Development Authority is working. This Authority is the only example of a central agency constituted to develop a backward region. It was established in 1959 when the Central Government was faced with the problem of resettlement of large numbers of displaced persons from East Pakistan. It was decided to settle them on forest land reclaimed with the help of large tractors. The Dandakaranya Development Authority was created because rehabilitation is a responsibility of the Centre and because the two state governments concerned were not equipped to take up the highly specialized and difficult job of reclamation. The Authority has also established production-cum-training centrrs which settle displaced persons in non-agricultural occupations. Its work will initiate a process of growth; there should be rapid development of the extensive mineral, power and water resources of the area in the coming years. But the Authority is not a regional development agency. Its purpose and the scope of its activities are more limited. It has been working in a difficult area and has been engaged in a difficult task. Its work has been criticized from time to time; but it will teach valuable lessons for development programmes in backward regions.

CONCLUSION

Regional planning is multi-dimensional and stresses attention to inter-sectoral relationships in development. Acceptance of the need for regional planning and the initiation of planned development in a region does not necessarily mean that a special regional planning and development agency must be set up. The need for such an agency is most clearly demonstrated in metropolitan and related industrial complex planning. In other cases especially regional water resource development and backward region development, where the tasks relate to regional economic development and are similar to those carried out by functional departments of state governments, the case for establishment of special regional agencies is not so strong. Experience in this field is limited. But it demonstrates the need for precise definition of the tasks envisaged in regional planning and development, so that they can be divided between existing administrative agencies (suitably strengthened for the purpose) and others for which separate administrative arrangements are required. It demonstrates also that the area of regional planning and coordination of programmes is much wider than that of regional execution of programmes. In a number of instances where regional planning and development have to be undertaken, all the advantages of integrated development can be secured if formulation of the regional plan and coordination of implementation are entrusted to a regional body.

A regional executive agency becomes necessary only in the few cases in which coordination or speed of execution cannot be achieved within the existing administrative structure.

NOTE

1. Examples are Survey of the Damodar Valley Region conducted by the Universities of Calcutta, Patna and the Kharagpur Institute of Technology; and the Regional Transport Survey, under the auspices of the Planning Commission.

REFERENCES

Hosse, H.A (1964): Report on a Plan for the Rihand Region. Submitted to the Government of India, New Delhi, (Unpublished).

NADECO (1964): Enclosures in the Western Sundarbans – A Technical feasibility Study. *The Hague*.

Prasad: *The Damodar Valley Corporation – A Brief Study*. Indian Institute of Public Administration, New Delhi (Unpublished).

4

Area Development: Planning at District and Block Levels[1]

INTRODUCTION

Area development relates to development of areas demarcated with a particular objective in view. Areas of large resource development projects—irrigation, power, industrial, areas designated as backward, and units of local administration, district and blocks, are examples of such areas. Area development is a special case of regional development, in which the spatial units of development are defined not on physical or economic considerations, but with particular developmental objectives in view. Usually, such areas are smaller than geographic or economic regions. This chapter outlines some concepts relating to area development planning at the district and block levels.

A basic concept in area development, as in all regional development, is that the plans for the area are conditioned by its physical conditions, natural resources and social and economic situation. These indicate the development potential, the needs and the problems of the area: the development plan must develop the potential, meet the needs and solve the problems. Accordingly, systematic assessment of resources, needs and problems is the first step in the planning process. The assessment is done by compilation and analysis of existing information, supplemented by fresh surveys, to the extent necessary. The needs are articulated most effectively by the representatives of the people—members of Panchayati Raj institutions, municipalities and legislatures.

AREA DEVELOPMENT AND THE NATIONAL PLAN

Area development is part of the national planning process. The plans for an area are conditioned by the general framework of the national plan, its policies and programmes, and its resource constraints. These prescribe the framework for "area planning", its overall goals as well as its limitations. The area plan is related also to the plans for larger spatial units of which the area forms part and of the smaller spatial units into which it is divided. The plan for a district has to be related on the one hand to the plans of the state and the regional division in which it is located, and on the other to plans of the blocks (and other smaller units) which are included within it. This linkage, upwards and downwards, is an essential part of planning for an area.

The development plans for districts and blocks, which came under the influence of an expanding metropolis or of large industrial or resource development projects, must reflect adequately the influence of these major developments. Providing in the local plans adequate complementary inputs, which would enable the local area to obtain full benefits from the resource development project or to withstand the disturbing influence of metropolitan development (unduly large areas in the peripheral regions of cities often get diverted to non-agricultural uses) is one method of reflecting this influence.

Approaches to Local Area Planning: "Area Development" and "Programmes"

Here it would be useful to distinguish between the "area development" approach and what may be called "programmes" approach to planning. The latter implies that certain development activities decided at the state or national level are carried out more or less uniformly throughout the area of the state or the country. The plan for a local area, built up entirely through this approach is an aggregation of such activities—primary and secondary schools, health centres, roads, water supply schemes, etc. The two approaches—"area development" and "programmes"—are not contradictory or mutually exclusive; they are, to an extent, complementary. The "area development" plan has to be formulated within the framework of the objectives and priorities of the national plan, and will have a large component of the national or state programmes mentioned above. On the other hand, even when the "programmes" approach is followed, decision-making in relation to particular programmes in an area has to be related to its local conditions and needs. Thus, the number of primary schools to be opened in an area and the specific location of the schools, can be decided only on consideration of local factors. The influence of local factors is much greater in planning of more advanced or specialized services and resource development activities. Elementary service facilities such as primary schools, can be created more or less uniformly in all areas; but the same cannot be done in case of advanced service facilities such as secondary school, college or polytechnics. Location of the latter has to be decided on careful consideration of various local factors, because faulty locational decisions will lead to inefficient service to the people and waste of resources. Resource development activities require even greater attention to local factors.

But the "area development" and the "programmes' approach are two different approaches to planning, and emphasis on one or the other leads often to different planning decisions. The "programmes" approach flows from constitution of departments at state or national level for particular development programmes—Education, Health, Agriculture. Exclusive reliance on it often results in inadequate consideration of local needs and problems, because of the inherent tendency of departments to decide the pattern of a programme at headquarters and to follow it in all areas. The result often is that attention is given to less necessary activities in preference to those needed more urgently in the local area; sometimes, unnecessary facilities are created. On the other hand, undue concern with area development would lead to inadequate attention being given to national (and state) objectives and priorities. One could generalize, perhaps, to say that the "programmes" approach is more suitable in planning of social services—especially elementary services such as primary schools, health centres and approach roads. These are needed everywhere and can be planned at the state (or even national) level on basis of criteria and patterns which can be defined with precision, *e.g.*, one primary school for 100 children of school going age; a metalled road within one or two miles of every village. The "area development" approach on the other hand has distinct advantages in planning of resource development programmes. It is also frequently more suitable than the "programmes" approach in planning of more advanced services.

Area development includes both resource development and human development. Expansion of social services, building up the infrastructure of development and institutional reform are the principal instruments of the latter. The relative emphasis on resource development and human development activities in an area, at any point of time, is indicated by its stage of development—status of exploitation of resources and the potential for further development, status of development of social services, etc. However, it is well to point out that development of social services and the infrastructure is an essential prerequisite of resource development, and until these are developed sufficiently, the progress of resource development activities will also remain slow. Thus, a large programme of resource development—mining of coal and iron ore, setting up power stations, steel plants and other industries—appears to be the obvious priority in the resource rich area called the Coal-Steel-Belt of Eastern India. But the area is backward. It is hilly and forested, has poor communications and few towns and has a large proportion of tribal people. This backwardness of the area hampers resource development activities in various ways. Development of social services and the infrastructure—improvement of communications, opening of schools, hospitals, training centres for craftsmen, modernization of the towns—will not only accelerate progress of resource development activities, but will also enable the local people to participate in these activities more actively and to benefit from them. They will be able to obtain employment in new industries and attain higher levels of income and consumption. Similarly, institutional reforms and changes in social attitudes, *e.g.*, in the attitude relating to work, are prerequisites for development of certain areas. The backwardness of area like Eastern U.P. is attributed in part to the tradition of *Zamindari* and prevalence of growth-inhibitive attitudes (*e.g.*, people of high castes should not touch the plough).

Integrated Development

Integration of different development activities undertaken within an area is a fundamental concept in area development. It has been accepted in case of rural development programmes for a long time and was reiterated and reinforced when a unified agency for rural development was created in the Community Development Organization. The structure of the Community Development Organization with a team of subject-matter specialists working under a Block Development Officer, emphasized co-ordination between developments in different fields—agriculture, animal husbandry, minor irrigation, soil conservation, co-operative social education, etc. Constitution of Block and District Development Committees and designating the Collector as the leader of the team of development officers further emphasized co-ordinated development and creation of Panchayati Raj institutions has given it a statutory institutional framework.

A primary requisite in co-ordinated development is securing appropriate relationships in magnitude, space and time between different development activities. Thus the quantum of operative credit and supplies of chemical fertilizers, improved, seeds, etc., in a Community Development (CD) Block should be related closely to the agricultural extension efforts of the block staff. In other words, if use of chemical fertilizers is being advocated by the staff and is being encouraged by making available supplies on credit given through the co-operatives, it should be ensured that the supplies and credit match the demand created by the efforts of the extension staff. Acceptance of this basic principle underlies the practice of formulating family production plans in the Package Programme districts, and regulating supplies and credit in accordance with these plans.

A second aspect of integrated development concerns the relationship between major resource development projects and local development activities. This relationship may be explained by the examples of power generation and irrigation projects. The villages located near a power project can derive benefit from it only if a programme of rural electrification accompanies the project. Power taken to the villages will, in the present stage of our rural economy, be used for irrigation, cottage and small scale industries, etc., only if adequate loans are given to farmers, artisans or small industrialists for installation of electric motors and purchase of power driven machines. Therefore, in order to carry the benefits of the power project to the villages it is necessary to secure appropriate relationships between programmes of power generation, rural electrification and financial assistance. Similarly, the waters of an irrigation project can be effectively utilized by farmers only if suitable technical assistance is given to them for changing their cropping pattern, from dry drops to irrigated crops, and financial assistance is given for measures like levelling, reclamation and preparation of land. Such assistance should be adequate in *magnitude* and should be available at the appropriate *time* and *place*.

In cases where the interrelationship between the large projects and complementary local developments has been appreciated and the latter have been provided adequately, the result has been rapid resource development and appreciable rise in economic and social levels of the people (*e.g.*, the Bhakra Canal area of the Punjab). But where this relationship has not been appreciated, and complementary inputs have either not been provided or have been provided inadequately or late, the potential created by the resource development projects has been utilized very slowly or inadequately. This experience emphasizes the need for working out in detail the complementary inputs in case of each major project and ensuring that these are provided adequately, in time and at the right place. In case of irrigation and power projects, sufficient experience has been gained in recent years for working out *norms* of investment on the projects and complementary local development inputs. These norms should be worked out for a few selected projects and should be available for guidance for new projects.

The major industrial and other resource development projects have been called "nuclei of development" in the Third Plan (Planning Commission, 1961, p. 149). This concept of the nucleus emphasizes the potential of these projects for attracting various developments to their areas, and initiating a process of area development. Appendix I lists the developmental inputs related to a major irrigation project and a steel plant. These have been divided into three major groups:

(i) associated,
(ii) complementary, and
(iii) derived.

The associated inputs are essential for the functioning of the project itself. The relation between them and the project is so direct and clear that they are generally provided as part of the project itself. But the complementary and the derived inputs, which are not so directly related, deserve more attention for area development, because it is the adequacy of these inputs and the speed with which they are created in the area, that determines the pace of its development. The complementary inputs are necessary for realization of the development potential of the project. The derived inputs have a similar role, but they have been classified separately, because they "derive" from or follow the functioning of the project.

Primary Growth Factors

The major projects could also be called primary growth factors, *i.e.*, primary development activities to which secondary and tertiary activities are attracted. The term could also be used for certain negative factors, presence of which retards development of an area. Prevalence of malaria, bad communications and low literacy are examples of negative growth factors. These too have to be regarded as "primary", because their removal needs first attention in any scheme of development of an area. The importance of removing them is often under-estimated. Thus, demands for development of backward areas usually take the form of demands for locating large projects in them. It is not sufficiently appreciated that removal of the negative factors is equally important, though less spectacular. Indeed, as mentioned above, the progress of the large projects will themselves be seriously retarded, if the negative factors are not removed.

Regional Growth

Another useful concept in area development is that of "regional growth". The economies of any area—blocks, districts or larger units—will grow with economic growth in the country. In most cases, this growth will mean change from exclusive dependence on primary industries to diversification of the economy. But in this process, the need for investment will increase progressively. The concept of progressive acceleration of the development process, and of the need for progressively larger investments is well recognized in planning at the national and state levels. The progressive increase in outlays and development activities in successive Five Year Plans is the best evidence of this. But at the level of the small area—the block and the district—the notion that a period of intensive development can be followed by one of lower investment (and development activity), because the area reaches "self-sufficiency" and is less in need of outside investment, seems to recur in Indian planning. The incompatibility of this concept with the dynamics of development was demonstrated by experience of the first community projects and blocks[1] in which an expenditure of about Rs. 22 lakhs per block for three years (or four years if the subsequent extension of time is taken into account) was followed by a post-intensive phase expenditure of about Rs. 1 lakh per year. But the idea seems to persist, as is evident from reference to it in intensive development projects of various kinds (agriculture, small industries, integrated development of districts) which are proposed from time to time. The idea has a certain attraction perhaps—it can be used as an argument to initiate intensive development in a limited number of areas. But there is a danger in adhering to it, because in any project undertaken with this idea there is bound to be a slide-back in development and frustration among the people when the period of intensive development is followed by the normal (slack) period.

It is true that after a period of intensive development, the character of inputs needed in an area changes—from elementary services to more advanced services, from service activities to resource development activities, etc. It is true also that the people's capacity to pay for development activities increase and they are able to undertake themselves many activities (*e.g.*, drinking water wells) for which they would have required outside assistance earlier. But the savings in investment resulting from this change are more than compensated by the need for larger investments, *e.g.*, in more advanced services, and resource development activities, with the result *that the total quantum of investment needed in the area is much larger.* The people may not need assistance for irrigation or drinking water wells; but they will want electric motors on wells and piped water supply schemes, which are far more expensive. Therefore, whenever any area is taken up for intensive development, it should be clearly recognized that it is being put on a road on which it will need progressively larger *total investment* as time passes.

AREA DEVELOPMENT AT DISTRICT AND BLOCK LEVELS

The need for drawing up plans with districts and other local areas as units has been appreciated from the beginning of planned development. The First Year Plan referred to district (and other) plans and the role of local institutions in the planning process. But a concerted effort to formulate plans at district and lower levels was made only at the time of formulation of the Second Five Year Plan. It was symbolized by the phrase "planning from below". As part of this effort, plans with districts and blocks as units were drawn up in a number of States. The Second Plan document defined the scope and content of the local plan (Appendix-II) and the manner of its preparation in considerable detail. Districts and blocks have since been recognized as important planning units; formulation of plans for them has been recognized as an integral part of the national planning process and an important function of Panchayati Raj institutions. Plans for districts and blocks were formulated as part of the Third Five Year Plan and similar work has been in progress in most States in connection with formulation of the Fourth Plan. It is of interest to note that the scope of the district plan as defined in the Planning Commission's Memorandum on the Fourth Plan is very similar to the definition contained in the Second Plan.

However, experience with drawing up district plans at the time of the Second Plan and in subsequent years highlights some of the difficulties and problems of such planning (and points to the needs for safeguards), which may be summarized as below:

(i) The tendency towards formulation of plans without adequate regard for resources which can be expected to become available—the tendency of plans to become catalogues of local needs and aspirations. This tendency was responsible, in part, for some of the planning effort made at the time of preparation of the Second Plan not yielding the expected results. But as a result of the Second Plan experience; an approximate indication of resources is now given in advance by the State Governments to the local institutions and officers.

(ii) The tendency to emphasize immediate need fulfilment in preference to longer term resources development, to emphasize consumption-oriented activities in preference to production-oriented activities.

(iii) Emergence of competing claimants for social service facilities, works, etc., among which the planning agency must decide. Size-inflation of plans results often from the tendency to please as many rival claimants as possible.

(iv) The need for accurate and adequate factual data—the need for conducting surveys of resources of local social and economic conditions and technical possibilities.

(v) The need for posting sufficient technical staffs, both for surveys and for plan formulation. The very real difficulty of providing such technical staff constitutes a major constraint in local planning.

Area Development and Programme Planning—Experience of Community Development Programme

The need for local planning has been realized from the beginning of the community development programme and the scope and content of local planning has also been defined fairly and clearly. But, within the area of local planning, the present practice is that priorities for different programmes and schemes, and the pattern of each scheme—content, staff, finance, institutional arrangements, etc., are worked out in great detail at the State (or even national) levels and decision-making at local levels is concerned largely with selecting locations and beneficiaries. The Panchayati Raj institutions, like their predecessor officials of the community development blocks or other development departments, often function primarily as allocating or distributing agencies, deciding where a primary school or a primary health centre should be located and who should get a *taccavi* loan, after the number of schools and health centres, to be opened in each block, the details of staff, equipment and buildings for these and the amount of *taccavi* loans to be sanctioned in a block, had been decided at the State level. The typical situation in meetings of the Panchayat Samitis is somewhat as follows: The Block Development Officer (BDO) or another Extension Officer reads out a circular from the State Government which informs all Panchayat Samitis in the State that a particular scheme is to be implemented and gives the financial pattern and other details of the scheme. The meeting thereupon proceeds to decide which particular villages, persons or groups should benefit from the scheme. There is seldom any attempt to see whether the scheme is not suitable for the area of the Panchayat Samiti, whether another scheme would be more suitable or even to attempt to modify the pattern of the scheme in any way. Nor would such attempts be very feasible under the present procedures of sanction and implementation of development programmes.

This practice of deciding patterns of development activity in detail at the State level and leaving the local institutions only the distributive functions has been the subject of considerable argument. Those opposed to the practice have argued that it does not allow plans to be formulated by local people in accordance with their needs and aspirations or the natural resources and development potential of their areas, with the result that less needed activities are often taken up in preference to those which are needed more and would have given better results—at times money is wasted on schemes which are not needed—and local people are not sufficiently enthusiastic about development programmes. This, they argue, results in development programmes not having the desired effect in terms of participation of people, and retarded economic development of the area. The protagonists of the practice have defended it on grounds of administrative efficiency, securing minimum level of development in all areas and ensuring that national and State priorities are reflected in local plans. Allocation of funds between different heads of development and on individual schemes within each development head is regarded as the chief instrument of securing development according to priorities. Working out detailed patterns of each scheme is considered essential for administrative efficiency and avoidance of waste, because it is argued that effective supervision and assessment of performance would be impossible in the absence of these.

It is also pointed out by many that so long as funds for development activities are provided by the State (or Central) Governments and the staff of Panchayati Raj institutions form part of State cadres, the tendency towards detailed planning of programme at State (and even Central) level will continue. They go on to argue that the Panchayati Raj institutions can have an effective role in planning for their areas only if they have their own staff and raise their own resources. The argument has some force. There is no doubt that when funds are given by the State Government there is a tendency for it to indicate not merely the schemes on which these may be spent but also in considerable detail the manner in which the schemes may be executed. On the side of Panchayati Raj institutions also, there is a tendency to regard the schemes as those of the State Government, and to execute them according to the instructions of the latter. The immediate history of Panchayati Raj institutions—their having been constituted in succession to the C.D. blocks and having inherited the programmes and funds of the blocks and other development departments—strengthens these tendencies. But financing by State Governments and technical staff forming part of State cadres is likely to be continued and the exercise of initiative in local planning by Panchayati Raj institutions has to be achieved within this situation. The alternative of Panchayati Raj institutions having their own staff and raising their own resources will, in the present stage of rural development and growth of these institutions, only result in greatly restricting their role in development besides reducing staff efficiency. It will reduce these institutions to the position of former district boards.

The tendency towards planning of programmes at State or Central level has been encouraged by the fact that in much of the rural development activities of the last 13 years, the object has been to provide elementary services and facilities—primary schools, primary health centres, drinking water wells and approach roads, co-operative credit societies, a basic agency for agricultural extension—which lends itself very well to planning through "programmes". The second reason for adopting the "programme" approach was that until local consciousness of development needs grew, it was necessary to provide certain leadership from above, and to take up basic activities which were clearly the most urgent needs of most areas.

This approach did create imbalances and difficulties in the community development programme. But since many of these were felt by the State Governments themselves, there was a tendency to resolve them through appropriate action between the State Governments and the Central Ministry of Community Development. Thus, when it was found by some State Governments that many of the activities included in the first community projects were not suitable for their areas, the Central Ministry allowed the States very considerable freedom in deciding the content of the programme within each major field of development activity. But the process was not carried lower, to district or block levels to any appreciable extent, and once the pattern of activity in any field had been decided at the State level, it was applied without major modification to all blocks of the State.

The Need for Shift in Emphasis

But, as a result mainly of the development that has taken place during the last 13 years, the situation is changing. Firstly, as the need for elementary facilities has been met, emphasis is shifting to providing more advanced facilities. Planning of these requires much greater attention to local conditions, and it is not possible to apply a uniform pattern to all blocks. Thus, it is not advisable to decide that each block shall have so many secondary schools, marketing societies or centres for training of craftsmen. Block-A may need more secondary schools and marketing societies than Block-B because it contains a number of small towns in which secondary schools are desired by the people and which serve as *mandi* centres for the villages in their vicinity. Block-B on the other hand may be more suitable for location of a training centre for craftsmen or a polytechnic because a large factory located within it could provide employment to the trainees. The need for attention to local factors is even greater in case of resource development activities. Even a comparatively simple activity, *e.g.*, a processing factory (cotton gin or sugar mill) has to be planned primarily on consideration of specific local factors such as availability of raw materials, nearness to market, and advantage of transport. Thirdly, experience with development activities has created among the local people much greater awareness of the need for development and of the specific development activities needed in their areas. They are more anxious to participate in the planning process and are more vocal in expression of their needs and aspirations. Finally, the programme pattern approach cannot provide adequately for intersectoral relations or for special planning needs of metropolitan, river valley project or industrial regions. The number of such projects and the areas coming under their influence is growing with economic growth in the country with the result that the need for area development is being felt in an increasing number of districts and blocks.

District as the Primary Unit of Local Planning

The emphasis on resource development activities and provision of more advanced services along with the other factors mentioned above, makes the district a more important unit of planning than the community development block. Let us take the examples of education and co-operation again. The community development block was quite a suitable unit for planning a net-work of primary schools, because the object was to provide every village, (or in case of very small villages or hamlets, a group of two or more neighboring units) with a primary school. But it is not an equally suitable unit for planning location of middle schools and may have positive disadvantages when adopted as the unit for planning of secondary schools. Similarly, while location of credit co-operatives could be planned with the block as the unit, location of marketing and processing societies has to be planned with a larger area as the unit, because of the need for attention to specific location factors mentioned above.

The need for making the district the major unit of local planning is also felt for other reasons. Effective local planning will require a considerable measure of decentralization of decision-making from the State level to local levels. Such decentralization is more feasible at the district level than at the level of the block. There are several reasons for this. First, the district has the full complement of District Level Officers who can provide the specialist assistance needed for drawing up local plans and making fruitful modifications in schemes drawn up at the State level. On the non-official side, the Zila Parishad has the top-level leadership of the district. Second, for reasons of administrative feasibility, especially maintaining effective communication between the State and local levels, the district is more suitable than the block as a unit of local planning. The State Development Departments or the State Governments find it more feasible to deal with a limited number of Zila Parishads and District Level Officers than with a large number of Panchayat Samitis and Extension Officers. Third, since intra-district variations (in physical or socio-economic conditions) are generally not very large, the need for making further modifications in programmes to suit the requirements of particular blocks is comparatively small, after the pattern has been decided at the district level.

Here, it is necessary to draw a clear distinction between the units of planning and the unit of implementation of programmes. The fact that the district is accepted as the unit of planning of a particular programme does not mean that it should necessarily be the unit for its implementation also. In some cases, the combination will be useful; but over a large field of development activity covered by the district plan, execution could just as well be done through the Panchayat Samitis. The district is a more suitable unit than the block for planning the content of the minor irrigation programme, *i.e.*, deciding the emphasis that minor irrigation should receive in the total agricultural production effort in the district, and the specific schemes which should be taken up, but implementation of a large part of the programme is best done by the Panchayat Samitis. The decision regarding the unit of planning and the unit of implementation should be taken separately for each development programme keeping in view its nature, the technical staff and other resources required for it, and the structure of Panchayati Raj institutions in the State.

Appropriate Inter-action between Town and Villages

Let us consider an average district. Its headquarters is located in a medium-sized town which performs various services for all or most of the villages and small towns located within it. Frequently, the town is also the major commercial centre of the district. The sub-divisional headquarters towns, important *mandi* towns, and other medium-sized towns have similar roles for parts of the district. Within each block, the block headquarters town has a similar role in relation to villages of the block area. In addition, there are in most blocks one or more small towns (or large villages) which perform similar functions for groups of 25-30 villages.

One effect of the developments has been that the inter-action between these towns and the villages served by them has increased, and the towns have a much more important role in the economy and social life of the villages. The village people come to the towns more frequently and obtain many more of their requirements from them than they did in the past. The very activities of Panchayat Samitis—distribution of *taccavi* loans, distribution of permits for supply of chemical fertilizers, cement or corrugated iron sheets, deciding appeals from decisions of Panchayats, and various elections—have added to the frequency of the town visits. Many village leaders and affluent cultivators visit such towns almost daily. Most of the towns have expanded considerably in recent years, on account of growth of commerce, resulting from larger agricultural production and higher incomes in the surrounding villages, and of their service functions. This expansion will continue as the role of the towns as service centres for the surrounding villages becomes more important, because as agriculture gets modernized and rural electrification and rural industrialization make progress, these towns will have an increasingly important role as centres for distribution of new materials and of servicing and repair of power driven implements and machines. This, for the simple reason that facilities for distribution of new materials and repairs and servicing of machines cannot be created at more than a few central places.

Yet, very little attention has been given so far to examining the inter-relationship between these towns and their surrounding villages and ensuring that development of the two is complementary and mutually beneficial. Indeed there are many instances of defective planning resulting from a failure to appreciate this relationship. The location of facilities like primary health centres and secondary schools has generally been decided on considerations like availability of local contribution, with the result that in many cases the facilities are located not in the place which is the natural centre of the area to be served by it, but in the place which came forward to pay the required contribution. In many blocks, the block headquarters town itself is not well located for serving the needs of the block area.

The first community projects did contain the nucleus of the idea of securing appropriate interaction between towns and villages. The programme of these projects included development of *mandi* centres, improvement of communications between them and the villages and using the centres for providing an increasing range of services and dissemination of new ideas to the villages. But the idea was gradually dropped, because other problems were considered more urgent. Moreover, the C.D. and N.E.S. Blocks which followed the first community projects had such small budgets that these more intensive development activities, could not be accommodated within them.[2] However, the time has now come when this relationship should be given adequate attention. The place of the district and block headquarters towns and of the smaller centres within each block, in the development of their service areas should be clearly recognized, and location of various service facilities should be so decided as to enable these centres to perform their service role efficiently. Further, the municipalities of the small towns and Panchayati Raj institutions should be brought into relations of mutual interaction.

The latter can be done only at the district level: the block is too small a unit for this purpose. The recommendation of the Sadiq Ali Report for providing for association of municipalities with the Zila Parishad in Rajasthan is evidence of recognition of this need (Government of Rajasthan, Jaipur, 1964, pp. 37-38). This association will become especially important when integrated area development is accepted as the object of local planning and development of both towns and villages is viewed as part of it.

A Case of Local Planning: The Wardha Plan

The Plan was drawn up jointly by the Gokhale Institute, Poona, the Regional Planning Institute, Wardha and the staff of the Wardha Zila Parishad. It illustrates some of the principles mentioned below:

(a) It is a district plan. The district was selected as the unit of planning for two reasons. First, the district institution, the Zila Parishad is the most important Panchayati Raj institution in Maharashtra. Second, the district is considered a more appropriate unit than the blocks for drawing up a plan of this kind. Plans for blocks and smaller areas fit into the framework of the district plan.

(b) An indication of resources likely to become available for execution of the plan was given by the State Government at the outset.

(c) The Plan is based on analysis of existing data, which were supplemented by surveys of socio-economic conditions and technical surveys for location of minor irrigation works, etc.
(d) The plan has been formulated by technical officers of the district and the special staff loaned by the institutes. The technical nature of the planning task has been fully realized in its formulation.
(e) The plan has been formulated with the coordinated efforts of the State Government, the Panchayati Raj institutions and the specialised institutes.
(f) The plan puts primary emphasis on resource development. Development of certain services (transport, welfare of backward classes, etc.) has been emphasized on account of special circumstances of the district.
(g) The plan stresses inter-sectoral relationships, though these have not been systematically worked out. Further, it recognizes that if a large industrial or other resource development project comes to be located in the district, major readjustments will be necessary in the plan.
(h) The plan includes a section on rural-urban relationships and development of towns as service centres. Significantly, the centres selected are *mandi* centres and not block headquarters, thus emphasising the economic rather than the administrative aspects of the relationships.

Efforts similar to the Wardha Plan can be made only in a few selected districts, where special arrangements can be made for institutional assistance. But these plans have considerable methodological value. They bring out the basic principles and the techniques of local area planning; the nature of work involved in it, and the place of local area plans in the National Plan. Appreciation of these will lead to more systematic and fruitful planning efforts in other areas.

APPENDIX-I

MAJOR PROJECTS AND RELATED INPUTS

A. Major Irrigation Project

(1) Associated Inputs

(i) Transport (road, rail) facilities needed for movement of equipment, supplies and personnel needed for the project, communication facilities.

(ii) Housing, water supply, social services (education of children, medical care) facilities for the project staff; creation of a township, if necessary.

(iii) Soil conservation measures in the catchment area.

(2) Complementary Inputs

(i) Land development and agricultural improvement: reclamation, clearance and levelling of land which is to receive irrigation; reorganization of agriculture, especially switching over from dry to irrigated farming; adoption of improved agricultural practices, *e.g.*, use of improved seed, chemical fertilizers, etc.

(ii) Supplementary minor irrigation—digging of wells, installation of lift irrigation devices, etc.; drainage and other steps to prevent water logging in the irrigated area.

(iii) Improvement of transport and marketing facilities.

Measures of category (*i*) require creation of services of technical assistance, supplies, etc., and also provisions for loans to cultivators for enabling them to take up land development or agricultural improvement measures.

(3) Derived Inputs

As the above measures take effect and agricultural production increase, the area will need agricultural processing industries, agro-industries (*e.g.*, manufacture of improved agricultural implements) and consumer goods industries. These may be called derived inputs, which derive from or follow the earlier developments.

B. Steel Plant

(1) Associated Inputs

(i) Facilities for mining of coal, iron-ore, limestone and construction materials.
(ii) Transport, rail and road, for carrying raw materials and intermediate and finished products.
(iii) Generation of power.
(iv) Supply of water to the plant and to the township.
(v) Urban development—construction of township to house industrial workers and those working in trades and services; organization of various essential services in the township.

(2) Complementary Inputs

(i) Rehabilitation of persons dispossessed of their lands.
(ii) Orderly absorption of immigrants and taking steps for ensuring smooth relations between them and the original residents of the area.
(iii) Training of craftsmen and other personnel for the plant.
(iv) Social education among tribal people with a view to ensure that they can derive adequate benefits from new economic opportunities within their area.
(v) Reorganization of local agriculture to meet the consumption needs of the larger population, especially for high value perishable products such as milk, vegetables, fruit, meat and poultry products.

(3) Derived Inputs

Industries, which depend upon raw materials supplied by the steel plant or on use of other facilities like power and transport created for it.

(i) Heavy engineering industries, *e.g.*, machine building, manufacture of transport equipment, fabrication of structurals, etc.
(ii) Heavy chemical industries, *e.g.*, manufacture of chemical fertilizers.
(iii) Manufacture of other construction materials.
(iv) Light engineering, light chemicals and various consumer goods industries attracted by the raw materials and other facilities available in the area.

APPENDIX-II

SCOPE AND CONTENT OF THE DISTRICT PLAN AS DEFINED IN THE SECOND AND THE FOURTH FIVE YEAR PLANS

A. Second Five Year Plan

"20. It was recognised that both at the district and at the State level three kinds of programmes sponsored on behalf of public authorities would be included in the plan, namely:

(a) Programmes initiated at the level in question, *e.g.*, taluka, district and State,
(b) Programmes initiated at lower levels and integrated with those in (a), and
(c) Programmes initiated at levels above and integrated with (a), for instance, schemes sponsored by the Central Government but executed through States or schemes sponsored by the State Government and implemented through machinery available in the district.

23. The main constituents of district plan are:

1. the community development and national extension programme,
2. social welfare extension projects,
3. agricultural production programme and allied activities in the field of rural development such as animal husbandry, soil conservation, etc.
4. development of cooperatives,
5. village panchayats,
6. village and small industries,
7. schemes for utilising effectively resources developed through State projects for irrigation, electricity, communications, industrial development and expansion of training facilities,

8. housing and urban development,
9. the programme of small savings,
10. aiding construction projects through labour cooperatives and shramdan,
11. programmes for the welfare of backward classes,
12. programmes in rural and urban areas relating to social services, especially expansion of education at primary and secondary levels, health units, health education, sanitation, malarial consciousness, family planning, etc.,
13. utilising and assisting voluntary organisations engaged in constructive social work,
14. land reform,
15. prohibition work, and
16. dissemination of information about programmes of national, state, regional and local development."

(Planning Commission: Second Five Year Plan, 1956, pages 156 and 158.)

B. Fourth Five Year Plan

"A district development plan should comprehend various activities envisaged in the State Five Year Plan for execution at the district level without respect to the nature of the sponsoring authority or the location of the budget provisions. Some activities undertaken in a district are provided for in the plans of the Zila Parishad and the Panchayat Samitis, others in the plans of Departments at the State level. These latter fall technically outside the field of Panchayati Raj institutions. The following are the principal sectors in which the local initiative and participation have to be carried as far as possible and can be developed around programmes embodied in the Five Year Plan:

(i) Agriculture (in its wider sense including animal husbandry, dairying, fisheries, poultry, horticulture, forestry, minor irrigation, etc.),
(ii) Co-operatives,
(iii) Village and small industries in processing industries,
(iv) Elementary and social education,
(v) Rural water supply and sanitation,

(vi) Rural health and medical services and family planning,
(vii) District and rural roads, including village approach roads (excluding National and State Highways),
(viii) Work programmes for the fuller utilization of rural manpower,
(ix) Development of focal points of growth like market centres, service centres, etc.,
(x) Social Welfare, including welfare of weaker sections, and
(xi) Voluntary organizations."
(Planning Commission, 1964, pp.80-81).

NOTES

1. *Indian Journal of Public Administration*, New Delhi, Vol. IX, No. 2, pp. 174-193, April-June, 1968.
2. Reference here is to the investment under the budget of the C.D. Block and to the concept which inspired the phasing of this budgetary pattern. It should be made clear, however, that the total quantum of investment and tempo of development activity (including both programmes included within the Community Development budget and others forming part of the development plans of the State) has been accelerated in nearly every area because of general acceleration of development activity under the Five Year Plans.

REFERENCES

Government of India, (1964): "Memorandum on the Fourth Plan", Planning Commission, New Delhi.
Government of India, (1961): *Third Five-Year Plan*, Planning Commission, Delhi.
Government of Rajasthan, (1964): *Report of the Study Team on Panchayati Raj*, Jaipur, 1964.
Wardha District Plan Frame (Unpublished).

5

Decentralized and District Planning under Economic Liberalization[1]

INTRODUCTION

The economic liberalization policy regime does not mean the end of planning. On the contrary, planning in India remains very much alive and continues to be the principal instrument of guiding the direction and growth of the national economy. The Eighth Five-Year Plan, 1992-97 was started in April 1992[2] and is being followed by other Five Years Plans.

The objectives, priorities and thrust areas of the Eighth Plan, its macro economic aggregates—level of public and private investments, rate of growth of GDP (total, sectoral and per capita), distribution of investment by sectors, programmes and major projects, target of increase in output in various sectors and financing—were decided by the National Development Council, which is presided over by the Prime Minister and has as its members chief ministers of all the states and Union territories and Central ministers of finance, commerce, industry, agriculture, etc., who are most concerned with economic development. Similarly, macro-economic and sectoral aggregates and allocation of public investment by sectors and projects have been or are being decided for the plans of States and Union territories which have been formulated within the framework of the national plan.

Besides its role as the central guide to economic development, national and state level planning is also the mechanism through which national goals and objectives of economic, social and political reforms are articulated. The statements on the goals and objectives, and on policies and programmes to achieve them, reflect a national consensus, arrived at through discussions in various fora. Thus, planning is also a major instrument of economic, social and political integration of the country.

Annual Plans

Annual plans are the annual components of the Five-Year Plans and are formulated every year by the same process of discussion between the Central government and the governments of States and Union territories. The discussions on the annual plan for 1992-93, the first year of the Eighth Five-Year Plan, were held during February and March 1992, and implementation of the plan had also begun in April 1992. The content of the annual plans is similar to that of the Five-Year Plan. However, trends in agricultural and industrial output, exports and imports, employment and availability of financial resources are given primary consideration in determining of the priorities and contents of the annual plan. Allocations for individual projects and programmes are decided keeping in view the variables mentioned above, as also progress on on-going projects and programmes, and on detailed preparation of new ones.

Economic Liberalization

Economic liberalization policies comprise industrial, trade and fiscal policies. Their central objective is to increase efficiency in the productive and service sectors of the economy by removing, or reducing progressively, the impediments to these. In case of the manufacturing sector, this objective is sought to be achieved by removing restrictions on location, capacity, output and pattern of equity participation of larger private sector industrial enterprises which had been imposed by the system of industrial licensing. The latter has been abolished for all but eighteen industries which include sensitive industries such as defense production and atomic energy.[3]

Economic liberalization policies also envisage greater private sector participation both in basic industries such as steel, coal and heavy engineering and in infrastructures such as power, transport and telecommunications (the outputs of which can be sold), which has been the preserve of the public sector since the mid-1960s. A number of public enterprises are proposed to be partly privatized, while several loss-making enterprises may be closed or sold. A number of private sector power generation projects have been approved in recent months and others are being examined. Mini and medium-sized pig iron and steel plants have all along been in the private sector. However, the private sector is also being encouraged to establish large steel plants with capacities of one million tons or more. A number of projects have been cleared by the concerned ministries while others are being examined. On the other hand, several public enterprises are proposed to be privatized, wholly or in part, and several loss-making enterprises may be closed. A National Renewal Fund has been established to take care of the interests of the effected workers.

A third objective of economic liberalization policies is to increase foreign investment in India both by transnational corporations and individuals, particularly non-resident Indians, with a view to increase the quantum of investment in the economy and also facilitate import of the most efficient industrial technology. The restrictions on such investment have been abolished and private foreign investment is being actively encouraged.

The trade policy package involved removing progressively the restrictions on imports and exports. The fiscal policies aim at reducing budgetary and balance of payment deficits. The budgetary deficit is sought to be reduced by curbs on expenditures, particularly non-developmental expenditures of the Central and the State governments and the losses of public enterprises. Reduction of the budgetary deficit will reduce the inflationary pressures generated by the large budgetary deficits particularly during 1988-89 to 1990-91 and devaluation of the Indian rupee in July 1991.

It is hoped that (a) these measures will help make Indian industrial enterprises more efficient and competitive in the export markets, (b) India's exports will increase progressively with reduction in the trade and payment deficits, and (c) the Indian consumer will be served with manufactures of improved quality at international or lower prices and more efficient infrastructures and other services.

Three important points have to be noted in this connection:

(i) The new industrial policy announced by the present government in July 1991, constituted a quantum leap in a process that had been started in 1979. One indication of the latter is provided by progressive decrease in the number of industrial enterprises that had been subject to licensing. A great majority of small and medium scale industrial enterprises were already outside the scope of industrial licensing.

(ii) The ELP package is being unfolded in stages. The budgets for 1991-92 (formulated in July 1991) and 1992-93 marked important stages in this process of unfolding. The import policies for the second half of 1991-92 and the first half of 1992-93 constitute similarly two stages in the unfolding of trade policies. Furthermore, the various statements in Parliament by the Finance Minister and the Prime Minister spell out their details and implications, which are elaborated further by the Governor of the Reserve Bank of India.

(iii) The price and trade policy packages would undergo further changes in the light of domestic and international developments. Two important factors militating against expansion of India's exports at present are the global recession and the economic collapse of the Soviet Union which was the most important market for India's exports.

The relationship between planning and economic liberalization is better understood if we keep in view the fact that planning in India is indicative planning for a mixed economy with a small public sector and large organised and unorganised private sectors. It is not central planning for a command economy in which the entire productive and distributive system is controlled by the state. The public sector in India aims mainly at providing physical and social infrastructure services—electricity, water, transport, telecommunications, medical and public health, education and training, social welfare, etc. The public sector industrial and mining enterprises are confined mainly to coal, steel, heavy engineering and the heavy electrical industries. And even in some of these industries, private sector enterprises were allowed to continue and expand.[4] The share of the private sector in steel, heavy engineering and heavy electrical industries, in transport, power generation and other infrastructures, the outputs of which can be sold, would increase progressively under economic liberalization. This is because private sector participation in these areas is not only being allowed but is also encouraged through various facilities and incentives provided to the prospective entrepreneurs.

Decentralized and District Planning

The central objective of decentralized and district planning is to provide basic services and satisfy urgently felt needs of the people, both rural and urban. It envisages their maximum participation in both formulation and implementation of the plans. Decentralized plans have also to be prepared within the overall framework of the national and state plans. Thus, their objectives, priorities, policies and programmes must be in conformity with those of the latter. Furthermore, their requirements of finance and manpower should be within the availability of these, from the local bodies and from the state governments. Overlooking this aspect would undermine the entire planning process because there would be difficulties and delays in approval of the plans by state governments and further delays and shortfalls in their implementation.

Plans for districts, community development blocks/talukas/mandals and villages are prepared for their respective jurisdictions by the Zilla Parishads, the intermediate level institutions (CD block/taluka/mandal) samitis and the village panchayats in predominantly rural districts. However, in about 150 districts, one-third of the total of 446 districts in the country, in which the proportion of the urban population is higher than the national average of 25.7 per cent (the actual proportions vary from 25 to 100 per cent), the municipal bodies—municipal corporations, municipal committees, cantonment boards, notified area committees, etc., have also an important role in planning for their respective jurisdictions.

Moreover, in the large metropolitan cities (with population of 500,000 or more) for which development authorities have been established, they have the principal role in development planning. Indeed, the long-term development plans prepared by the authorities have pre-eminence in the areas covered by them. The latter include besides the agglomeration of the large cities, considerable rural areas. The panchayats of the rural areas covered by the plans may not engage in any activity which constitutes a violation of the development plan drawn up by the development authority. The most common violation is sale by panchayats and/or individuals for residential, industrial, commercial or other uses of lands which had been reserved under the development plan for public purposes such as location of educational and medical institutions, parks and other recreation areas.[5]

History of Decentralized and District Planning

Formulation of district plans goes back to the mid-fifties when the Second Five-Year Plan was being formulated by the Planning Commission. The Commission asked the State governments to get district plans prepared through the Development Advisory Committees to be constituted specially for this purpose.[6] However, since the total expenditure projected in these plans was several times greater than the funds available for them, the plans were not implemented and the idea of preparation of district plans itself was given up.

But, there is no alternative to formulation of district plans in the radically changed context of the early 1990s. There is a national consensus among all political parties on revival or revitalization of both the Panchayati Raj institutions and urban local bodies which have remained under suspension for long periods in several states. Formulation of plans for their respective jurisdictions is, or should be, an important function of these institutions. In a number of states notably Karnataka, West Bengal and Kerala, Panchayati Raj institutions with greatly enhanced functions and resources were established during the 1980s and have been encouraged to formulate development plans for their respective areas. Elections to municipal bodies have also been held during the last two or three years in a number of states, including Uttar Pradesh and Haryana, where they had not been held for almost two decades and the municipal areas had been administered by administrators appointed by the state governments.

Plans for districts and lower level areal units must contain a programme for employment generation[7], keeping in view the magnitude of unemployment and under-employment. The programme will also contribute to alleviation of poverty by providing gainful employment and income to the poor. Such programmes should be undertaken in both the rural and urban areas.

The Process of Decentralized Planning: Planning from Below and Planning from Above

Plans for districts, villages and intermediate units such as talukas mandals or community development blocks can be formulated either through planning from below or planning from above. Planning from below involves preparation of plans by panchayats or villages or multi-village circles in consultation with the leaders of the villages concerned. They would be formulated by assessment of local needs, development potential, resources and constraints. Decentralized planning is most meaningful—it meets the urgently felt needs of the people best and can elicit their maximum cooperation through contribution of cash, labour, materials etc. in construction works and effective use of service facilities—if planning from below is the dominant process in it. But planning from below is not easy and it is time-consuming. Obtaining agreement of all the leaders and groups involved in preparation of the plan for a village or multi-village circle takes time. Furthermore, personnel from their technical departments have to be deputed to the panchayats to assist them in preparation of the plans. They must ensure that the plans keep in view the guidelines of their departments in respect of availability of finance and manpower and achievement of targets etc. Finally, the village or multi-village plans need to be modified and adjusted before they can be included in the plan for the CD block/ taluka/mandal. A similar process of adjustment of plans for these units has to be undertaken to formulate the district plan.

Planning from above means breakdown by districts and smaller units of state level targets of accomplishments, allocation of resources of finance, technical personnel, etc., and is done mainly by the district and lower level officials of various technical departments on the basis of their assessment of the needs and development potentials of the units within their jurisdiction. Thus, the agricultural development plans for districts and CD blocks would be prepared by the district and block level agricultural officers by breaking down, for their respective districts and blocks, the state level agricultural plan. A similar procedure would be followed by district and block level officials of industrial, educational, medical and public health, and social welfare departments. The plans would be prepared in consultation with the PRIs, of course. But they would be governed by the detailed directives for their preparation issued by the heads of the respective technical departments.

Planning from above has the following advantages:

(i) It is expeditious;
(ii) Technical personnel *viz.*, the district, block and lower level officials of technical departments are generally available;
(iii) There is no problem of adjustment of district and lower level plans with the state plan; and
(iv) Implementation of the plans is virtually assured.

Decentralized Planning Under Economic Liberalization

Decentralized planning and economic liberalization have such different objectives and levels of operation that, at first sight, it appears that economic liberalization would have little, if any, effect on decentralized planning. However, a little reflection will show that the effects are profound and far-reaching.

If economic liberalization policies are successful, they would lead to faster economic growth, particularly through more rapid expansion in the non-agricultural sectors—industries and services—which would mean larger employment in these sectors. The greatest spatial effects would be in the large metropolitan cities and their peripheral regions, which stretch long distances along the principal highways radiating from them. Expansion of industrial enterprises, particularly large and medium-sized enterprises, would take place mainly in the peripheral regions: enterprises would seek peripheral locations in order to avail of relatively lower cost of land while retaining the advantages of linkage with the cities, provided by their physical, economic and social infrastructures.

Most small and medium-sized enterprises would, however, continue to be concentrated in the metropolitan cities.[8] Small enterprises having backward and forward linkages with large enterprises could be located both in the cities and in the peripheral regions in the vicinity of large enterprises. Examples of the latter would be enterprises providing components and spares and repair and maintenance services to the larger enterprise, or those processing their outputs. Industrial expansion would mean corresponding or greater employment in the service sectors.

Effects on the Rural Areas

Manufacturing and service sector enterprises would draw, especially at the beginning, skilled labour and professional personnel mainly from the cities[9] and only unskilled labour from the surrounding villages. But with the spread of industrial and service skills in the rural areas, more and more skilled workers would also be drawn from them.

Employment in industries and services would mean higher incomes for the rural people which would lead, in turn, to higher and more diversified consumption and spread of urban life styles among them. The positive effects of these changes on consumption would range from quantitative increase and qualitative improvement in food such as milk, vegetables and fruit through acquisition of durable consumer goods such as gas stoves, refrigerators, and TV sets, to living in pucca houses having electricity, water and indoor toilet facilities. Other effects would include increase in literacy and education (including vocational and technical education), improvement in health and nutrition, primarily through use of modern medicine, greater attention to personal hygiene and weakening of traditional taboos and social restrictions. The negative effects would range from increase in drinking and use of drugs to prostitution, crime and other social evils.

Since industrial entrepreneurs would be under little obligation to locate in backward regions, regional disparities in economic development could increase in the short-to-medium terms. Over a longer period, however, industry would go to backward regions also partly to avail of the incentives offered by the state governments for locating there. There would also be greater rural-to-urban migration and combination of rural living and urban work in the peripheral regions of the metropolitan cities.

APPENDIX-I

That economic liberalization and planning can proceed simultaneously as illustrated by the following four news items appearing in *The Times of India*, New Delhi of March 8, 1992, p. 7.

1. Prime Minister's call to increase exports.
2. Government clears three major coal projects.
3. Outlay for Punjab (Annual Plan 1992-93) fixed at Rs. 1,500 crores.
4. Rs. 3,853 crores annual plan (1992-93) for U.P.

The first item relates to the Prime Minister's speech on the occasion of laying the foundation stone for a large private sector project which has a large potential for export promotion and import substitution. The second item relates to three major projects for expansion of output of coal for meeting the needs of coal-burning thermal plants. The last two items are self-explanatory.

PM's Call to Increase Exports (*The Times of India News Service*)

Nagpur, March 7: The Prime Minister, Mr. P.V. Narasimha Rao, today urged industrialists to increase their export targets.

The Prime Minister arrived here on a day's visit. He addressed a public meeting at Maudha, about 33 kilometres from here, after dedicating two industrial plants to the nation and laying the foundation stone of a third.

Mr. Rao said that though the present foreign exchange position was comfortable, it was not enough to meet the country's requirements.

He said petroleum products, fertilizers and edible oils were still imported. The country's production of these items was not enough to meet the requirements.

Mr. Rao arrived at Maudha by helicopter after landing at Nagpur airport and drove straight to the Rs. 23 crore Visakha Industries plant manufacturing synthetic blended yarn. The plant is already commissioned and this year would reach the export figure of $ 5 million.

From there, Mr. Rao arrived at the sprawling 120 acre Pennar Aluminium Company Limited which is putting up a Rs. 90 crore plant which will manufacture sophisticated value added aluminium products.

From Maudha, the Prime Minister flew to Kalameshwar where he laid the foundation stone of a cold rolling mill, a Rs. 250 crore plant of Nippon Denso Ispat Complex, a Mittal group company.

Incidentally, all the three plants are promoted by industrialists from the PM's home state, Andhra Pradesh.

Government Clears Three Major Coal Projects
(*The Times of India News Service*)

New Delhi, March 7: The government has cleared three major coal projects to be implemented at a total cost of Rs. 2,137.93 crore.

A new project approved by the government is the Kalinga Opencast of the South-Eastern Coalfields. The project, located in the Talcher coalfields in Orissa, will cost Rs. 485.77 crore and will have an annual output of eight million tonnes of coal when completed. Coal from this project will be supplied to coastal thermal plants.

The government has also cleared the expansion of Nyvelli lignite mine-I at a cost of Rs. 1,336.93 crore. With this expansion, coal output from this mine will go up to 10.5 million tones from the present level of 6.5 million tones per annum.

The third project concerns the extension of the service life of the 600-MW thermal power plant of the Nyvelli Lignite Corporation for another fifteen years. This project will cost Rs. 315.23 crore.

Coal production in the country during 1990-91 was estimated at 201.73 million tones. It is projected to go up to 306 million tones by the terminal year of the Eighth Plan.

The Union Budget for 1992-93 provides for an allocation of Rs. 14,998 crore for the energy sector of which the share of the coal sector is Rs. 2,683 crore.

Rs. 3,853 Crore Annual Plan for Uttar Pradesh (*The Times of India News Service*)

New Delhi, March 7, 1992: The annual plan of U.P. for 1992-93 has been fixed at Rs. 3,853 crore, Rs. 150 crore more than last year's plan in money terms.

The plan was finalised at a meeting yesterday between the Deputy Chairman of the Planning Commission, Mr. Pranab Mukherjee and the Chief Minister, Mr. Kalyan Singh, who gave an assurance that the state would mobilize additional revenue to the tune of Rs. 150 crore in 1992-93.

The additional tax effort will reflect on the 1992-93 budget to be presented by the State Finance Minister on March 12, 1992.

Outlay for Punjab Fixed at Rs. 1,500 Crore

New Delhi, March 7, 1992. P.T.I.: Punjab will have a plan outlay of Rs. 1,500 crore, including Rs. 90 crore as loan from financial institutions for 1992-93.

This was decided at a meeting here today between the Planning Commission Deputy Chairman, Mr. Pranab Mukherjee and the Chief Minister, Beant Singh.

The current year's revised plan outlay of the state is Rs. 1,000 crore.

In his introductory remarks, the deputy chairman stressed the need to complete the on going projects instead of taking up new projects.

Punjab, he said, had tremendous development potential and should be able to regain its position among the front ranking states.

The chief minister referred to the special problems of the state, especially those relating to power and irrigation, transport and education.

The meeting also discussed the crucial point in development like utilization of groundwater resources and afforestation.

NOTES

1 "Decentralized Planning in Multilevel Framework" Eds. Rakesh Hooja and B. Yerram Raju (1993), Rawat.

2. The two-year interval between completion of the Seventh Five-Year Plan,

1985-90 and beginning of the Eighth Plan was filled in by annual plans for 1990-91 and 1991-92.

3. The industries are listed in Annex II. p. 22 of the statement on industrial policy issued by the Ministry of Industry on July 24, 1991. Annex I of the statement gives the proposed list of eight industries to be reserved for the public sector. Annex III lists thirty-four industries for which there will be automatic approval of foreign technology agreements and for foreign quality participation. The statement contains a detailed survey of the industrial polices followed since Independence. The survey concentrates on explaining the progressive changes in the policies keeping in view the national priorities and needs. It also emphasized how the new industrial policy constitutes a continuation of the same process of evolution and why the changes incorporated in it are needed keeping in view national and international developments.
4. Along with establishment of five public sector steel plants, the two existing plants—the Tata's located at Jamshedpur and of the Indian Iron and Steel Company—were modernized and allowed to expand.
5. This practice is widespread and constitutes a serious impediment in the implementation of the second development plan for Delhi and the Regional Plan 2001 of the National Capital Region. The principal reason for the practice is high prices of land in the DMA, so much so that sales of even small areas of land by a Panchayat would bring amounts far in excess of the annual revenues of the panchayats.
6. In states like U.P., a Planning and Development Department was created to consolidate the district plan into a plan for the state and overseeing implementation of the district plan become the most important responsibility of the Planning Department.
7. The programmes, such as the national employment programme, which aimed at providing gainful employment and income to the landless and the marginal farmer and other rural poor, have been implemented for long periods. The Jawahar Rozgar Yojana started in 1989 constituted a major intensification of the programme. However, similar programmes have not been undertaken in the urban areas in most states despite the fact that the problems of unemployment and under-employment of the urban poor, especially recent migrants to the cities, are widespread. The programmes in the urban areas should concentrate on providing shelter and basic service facilities to the urban poor. The land development and housing programmes, particularly the slum improvement programme, are the most suitable for the urban areas.
8. The reasons for the concentration are explained V. Nath: Ubanization, Urban Development and Growth of Metropolitan Cities in India. 2007 (Chapter 2).
9. The author's field survey in 1990 of two new industrial centres, Bhiwadi (Rajasthan) and Dharu Heda (Haryana), located about 25 kilometres from Delhi and producing a wide variety of products for the Delhi market, revealed that nearly all the skilled workers and professionals commuted to work from Delhi and only unskilled workers came from the surrounding villages.

6

Regional Development in Indian Planning[1]

INTRODUCTION

Regional development began to receive attention in the western countries in the 1930s on welfare considerations. Specifically, the need was to relieve: (i) mass unemployment and distress in the depressed regions, such as the northern and western industrial regions of the UK, which had suffered severely during the depression, and (ii) poverty and backwardness in regions such as Appalachia in the US and the Italian South, which had been by-passed in the course of the economic development of these countries. Other considerations, such as development of natural resources, were added later. In recent years, because of the appearance of increasingly difficult economic, social and physical problems (including deterioration of the physical environment) related to large metropolitan cities and urban-industrial concentrations, attention has begun to be directed to regional development and related aspects of urban growth and industrial location. Regional development policies and programmes in most Western countries are motivated by one or both of the complimentary objectives of relieving distress or poverty in depressed or backward regions and tackling pressures of over development in the metropolitan regions.

However, with the rationalisation of the French Plans since 1962, significant advance has been made in the Western countries towards formally incorporating regional planning into the national planning process. The development is notable, not so much for its objective of diverting development from metropolitan Paris to the other regions of France, as for the planning concepts, structures and processes associated with it. The country has been divided into 21 planning regions; regional plans are drawn up and are integrated with the national plan; financial resources and operational procedures for implementation of the plans have been defined, and the effort has sparked some very productive thinking on regional development policies and strategies (Hansen, 1968, Chapter 4, pp. 74-101). In the UK, while regional development measures have been aimed at directing economic growth towards the depressed regions, regional planning is seen primarily as providing the spatial framework for physical and economic planning, which is more rational and more suitable than that provided by local government units (Planning Advisory Group, 1965).

Among the centrally planned economies, the Soviet Union and Yugoslavia, both federal countries are notable for their regional planning and for their development of distinctive concepts, techniques and institutions for it. In the Soviet Union, preparation of plans for the Republics is an integral part of the planning process. Since 1962 the scope and importance of the republican plans has increased greatly, because they now relate to all development programmes located within the Republics, instead of being confined to the programmes of the Republican governments. The Constitution of economic administration regions, and establishment of *Sovnarkhozy* (Regional Economic Councils) for planning and administration of industrial, constructional and related programmes in the regions, are other distinctive features of Soviet planning (United Nations, 1965, pp. 176-183). They have made possible regional decentralisation of planning and administration in the major investment-absorbing sectors, and have given recognition to economic regions (as distinct from political-administrative entities) as planning units and to industrial complexes as the nuclei of the planning regions. In Yugoslavia, while the main thrust of decentralisation in planning has been from the central level to the level of the commune, the regional level of the Republic is also important. Republican planning agencies are an important constituent of the planning structure; republican plans disposed of 16.9 per cent of the budgetary and planning resources in 1959 (Macesvich, 1964, p. 14).

The structure and processes of regionalisation of the national plan are well developed in India—thanks to the constitutional prerogatives and responsibilities of the State Governments in the areas of planning and development. Preparation of State plans and their integration with the national plan is a very important part of the planning process; total expenditure on the State plans formed about half of total public sector expenditure in the first three plans (Planning Commission, 1963, Tables 11 and 15). But the importance of State level planning has also had the effect of equating regional planning with it. As a result, policies for regional development and preparation of development plans for regions with special problems or promises —*i.e.*, backward regions, metropolitan regions, river valleys or other resource development regions—have not received the attention that they deserve.

The difficulties experienced by the Damodar Valley Corporation in undertaking integrated development of an inter-State, resource-rich, river valley region, resulted in the progressive dilution of the integrated regional development concept. Besides, the devolution of several functions of the Corporation to the respective State Governments emphasised the role of the States in "regional" planning, and discouraged attempts to look at regions beyond the framework of States (Hamilton, 1969, pp. 86-109).

But awareness of regional development problems particularly regional disparities in development, has existed among the planners since the beginning of planning: a reference to the need for reducing such disparities was made in the very first plan document, *viz.*, the Draft Outline of the First Five-Year Plan (Planning Commission, July 1951, pp. 42-43). Successive Five Year Plans have referred to the subject and to the related issue of dispersal of industries and other economic activities away from large cities. The Third Five-Year Plan contained a chapter on Balanced Regional Development, in which these issues were discussed in detail (Planning Commission, 1961, pp. 142-153).

This chapter examines whether this awareness on the part of the planners has been followed by formulation of adequate policies for meeting the problems, and whether progress in reducing regional disparities or in securing industrial dispersal has been significant. For this purpose, the policy statements in the plan documents have been summarised and selected data on levels of development, State plan expenditures, and rates of economic growth in the States, and some data relating to location of industries by size of towns have been presented. Such an analysis is of particular interest at this stage because several recent developments, notably the agitations for creation of a separate State of Telengana and location of a second petroleum refinery in Assam, as also the unresolved controversies over location of the fifth public sector steel plant and development of the waters of the rivers Krishna and Narmada, have emphasised the political and emotional overtones of regional development, and the possibility of the issue being taken from the economic seminar or political conference table to the streets. These developments indicate dissatisfaction with existing policies and programmes related to regional development, location of projects, and resource development and emphasise the urgency of adequate and appropriate policies and programmes.

Analysis of 'regional' levels of development and rates of growth is by States, on considerations of both availability of data and limitations of space. But it is recognised that in view of the very large size and known intra-State development disparities in several States such as UP, Maharashtra, Madhya Pradesh and Bihar, the analysis needs to be carried down to the divisional or district levels for a more precise delineation of regional disparities and for identification of regions most in need of special development efforts.

POLICIES AND STRATEGIES

According to Friedmann and Alonso, the regional development issue is particularly important in the early stages of economic development, when the tendency for concentration of development in the core areas is strong and when the political pressures exerted by the peripheral regions for diversion of development to them create tensions. The issue becomes less important in mature industrial economies, because the spread effects of development from the core regions are strong, regional differences in location costs and welfare get reduced and the dominant spatial interactions are between systems of cities (Friedman and Alonso, 1965, pp. 3-6).[2] Myardal agrees that the 'spread' effects are stronger than the 'backwash' effects in mature economies, and regional disparities in development tend to be reduced in them, but he gives greater importance to the tendency of free market forces to accentuate regional disparities and emphasises the role of public policies and programmes in reducing disparities (Myardal, 1957). Detailed case studies to support these hypotheses are few; (Perloff, 1960, Table 64, p. 187, and Table 125, p. 276)[3] but the limited success of the efforts to reduce north-south disparities in Italy

(Schachter, 1967, pp. 398-407) or divert economic growth from Paris to the other regions in France (Hansen, 1968, Chapter 4, p. 73) attests to the strength of concentrating tendencies and weakness of spread effects, even in mature economies. Moreover, the view that the problem is transitional, and will be solved as economic maturity is reached, is unhelpful, particularly in large countries such as India, in which size, social and cultural diversity, and highly developed feelings of regional identity greatly add to the tensions resulting from regional disparities in development or differential growth rates. It is an imperative of successful planning in these countries that the people of every region feel that they have adequate opportunities of participation in the planning process and that regional distribution of the benefits of the plans is equitable. But it is difficult to carry conviction on the latter score, if development continues to be concentrated in a few regions, such as the metropolitan cities, and the disparities between them and the other regions continue to increase.

It is often thought that regional development involves a choice between regional welfare and national welfare, and the sacrifice of national welfare for regional welfare. It is argued that location of projects in less developed regions on considerations of regional welfare rather than of techno-economic efficiency (as judged from the overall national view) will reduce national welfare, because it will reduce benefit/cost ratios of projects (by increasing costs or time of completion, or by reducing efficiency of operation) and thus slow down economic growth. This view was expressed in the Indian context by Lefeber who favoured concentration of major development projects in the metropolitan regions and advocated for the backward regions community-development and local works programmes based on utilisation of low-cost rural labour and other locally available resources (Lefeber, pp. 18-29).

The Planning Commission, while specifically rejecting concentration of development in the metropolitan cities, would appear to agree with basic position of Lefeber, *viz.* of subordinating regional welfare to national welfare and deciding locations of projects on techno-economic considerations (see below). However, economists like Marglin take the view that regional welfare is important enough to be given separate consideration in the evaluation of location of projects. Marglin has developed techniques of quantification of regional benefits and of their incorporation in the benefit/cost analysis of projects (Marglin, 1967, pp. 23-29). Lewis's rejection of metropolitan concentration and advocacy of dispersal of development to medium sized towns is derived more from the social inefficiency of the metropolitan cities as locations for projects, than from the primacy of regional welfare. He argues that the apparent advantage of the metropolitan cities is based on the fact that the costs are borne by the public agencies or by the community (in terms of residential congestion, reduced availability of urban services, etc.) and not by the enterprises—and that if these costs were fully internalised, locations in metropolitan cities would not appear so efficient (Lewis, 1962, p. 177). The issue of location in large cities or small and medium-sized towns is closely connected with regional development, because the large cities are the developed regions, and dispersal of industries from them to reduce regional disparities will be primarily to small or medium-sized towns. The complex of infrastructures and services needed for modern industrial projects can only be created in such towns; regional development will ensue from spread of growth from the towns to the regions.

On the strategy of regional development again, two views are of particular interest. One of these, following Francois Perroux's 'development role' concept, emphasises the role of large projects in the development of regions (Hansen, 1968, pp. 105-16). The growth-inducing effects of the projects are believed to flow from the employment and income provided by them directly and by the enterprises attracted to the regions because of backward or forward linkages with the projects (indirect effects). The other view, advocates expansion of economic and social overhead capital in the backward regions on the ground that the handicap of these regions and their unattractiveness for industrial location is due primarily to inadequacy of such capital, so that removal of the handicap would make the regions attractive for industrial location (Hansen, p. 22). In India, the Planning Commission had taken the latter view and has rejected location of large projects in backward regions as a regional development strategy. Nevertheless, at the political level, regional development is often identified with location of large projects. Apart from the recent agitations for location of the fifth steel plant in Andhra Pradesh and of the petroleum refinery in Assam, demands for removal of regional disparities, especially by members of Parliament, are often accompanied by pleas for location of large projects in backward regions.

REGIONAL DEVELOPMENT IN THE PLANS

As mentioned above, a brief reference to the need for reducing regional disparities was made even in the Draft Outline of the First Five-Year Plan issued in 1951. Reference in the Second Five-Year Plan was also brief but the principal policy and the related issue of industrial dispersal was clearly stated (Planning Commission, 1956, pp. 36-37 and 48). The Third Plan chapter on 'Balanced Regional Development' may be regarded as the major policy statement on regional development and related issues in the Plan documents. In it, the policies outlined earlier were elaborated and reiterated, and experience with them was reviewed. In the Fourth Five-Year Plan, an interesting development is noticeable. The Draft Outline, issued in 1966, contained no reference to regional development for reducing regional disparities. The phrase used was 'urban and regional development' and the discussion related only to urban development (Planning Commission, 1966). But in the Approach to the Fourth Five-Year Plan document, issued in May 1968, references to regional development and to related issues of industrial dispersal and of reducing metropolitan concentration are dispersed throughout the 36 pages, occupying perhaps as much as two pages (Planning Commission, 1968). They indicate a concern and a preoccupation with these issues, which is quite unusual for Plan documents. In the Draft of the Fourth Five-Year Plan, issued in 1969, references to these issues occur in the chapters on 'Approach and Policy', and 'Industry and Minerals' (Planning Commission, 1969, pp. 17-19 and pp. 240-241). There is reference also to development of backward areas under State plans, and to a provision of Rs. 497 million (1.4 per cent of the total State plan outlays) for the purpose (Planning Commission, 1969, p. 347).

The following summary is based primarily on the Third Plan chapter. Statements in the Draft Outline of the First Plan, the Second Plan, the Approach to the Fourth Plan, and the Draft of 1969 have been utilised to the extent necessary. The task of summarising is facilitated by the remarkable continuity of approach on the issues in the plan documents. Even limitation of resources is mentioned in almost all the documents. But the statements in the 1968 and 1969 documents, display much clearer recognition of the strength of the concentrating tendencies and the difficulties of correcting regional imbalances or securing industrial dispersal, than do the earlier statements. References to the measures needed to achieve objectives are also more specific.

(i) The principal policy objective is balanced regional development. The phrase has not been explained adequately, though its principal operational connotation is reduction of regional disparities in development.

(ii) The scope for action for reducing regional disparities is limited because of limited resources. But as development proceeds and larger resources become available, the benefits of development will extend increasingly to the less developed regions.

(iii) The basic resource-development and social-service activities—in agricultural development, community development, irrigation (major and minor), education, rural works and other employment-creating programmes—which are being undertaken under the Plans throughout the country will benefit the less developed regions.

(iv) The disadvantage of the less developed regions, particularly for location of industries, is due to lack of developed infrastructure facilities, such as power, transport and water supply. This disadvantage will be removed progressively.

(v) Location of large (basic, capital goods or producer goods) industries should be governed by techno-economic considerations, such as proximity to sources of raw materials. Since many of the public sector industrial projects are being located in backward regions because raw materials are located in them, these regions will benefit.

(vi) To the extent that industrial location is not determined by techno-economic considerations, however, balanced regional development should be aimed at. Concentration of industries in developed industrial areas should be avoided. Expansion of capacity of existing industrial units located in the cities, is unavoidable; but care must be taken as far as possible to set up new units away from large cities. In the licensing of private sector units, the claims of the underdeveloped regions are kept in view and locations in such areas are suggested to industrialists.

(vii) Regional patterns of development should be fostered in case of consumer goods and processing industries. Development of village and small-scale industries, which are spread throughout the country, will also promote dispersed industrial development. Industrial estates should be located increasingly in small and medium-sized towns.

(viii) Large projects should be thought of as nuclei of regional growth and related and complementary activities should be undertaken in the regions where they are located. It is noteworthy, however, that the activities mentioned include agriculture, education, training and small and medium-scale industries. Large-scale industries, related to the projects through backward or forward linkages, or development of industrial complexes round the projects, are not mentioned.

LEVELS OF DEVELOPMENTAL AND RATES OF GROWTH OF STATES

Some selected data on levels of economic development and rates of growth, for India and 14 States, are given in Table 6.1. The States of Jammu and Kashmir and Nagaland are not included, because data for several indicators of development or of growth rates were not available for them. Haryana is included under Punjab, because all the data relate to the period before the formation of Haryana. The indicators of development are:

(i) Per capita income;
(ii) Proportion of urban population to total population;
(iii) Proportion of male workers in manufacturing industries to all male workers;
(iv) Proportion of population living in districts at the two higher (top and second) levels of development;
(v) Literacy rate for population in age groups of five years and above.

Per capita income data are compiled by the State Statistical Bureaus, and have been made available by the Central Statistical Organisation; the other data on levels of development are from the 1961 Census. Data on proportions of population living in districts at different levels of development are from the Census publication, "Levels of Regional Development in India" (Census of India, 1964).

Table 6.1: Levels of Development and Rates of Growth—India and 14 States

Rank	State	Per Capita Income in 1964–65 (rupees, at current prices)	Proportion of Urban Population to Total Population in 1961 (per cent)	Proportion of Male Workers in Manufacturing Industries to all Male Workers in 1961 (per cent)	Proportions of Population Living in Districts at Different Levels of Development (per cent)				Literacy (5 years and above)	Total Rank Score	Investment under First Three Five–Year Plans		Rate of Growth of Population 1951–61 (per cent)	Compound Rate of Growth of Agricultural Output, 1952–53 to 1964–65 (per cent, per year)	Increase in Value-Added in Industry, 1955–65 (rupees per capita)	Compound Rate of Growth of Per Capita Income 1955–56 1964–65 (per cent per year)
					Bottom	Third	Second	Top			Expenditure under State Plans (rupees, per capita)	Central Investment (rupees, per capita)				
(1)	(2)	(3)	(4)	(5)	(6)	(7)	(8)	(9)	(10)	(11)	(12)	(13)	(14)	(15)	(16)	(17)
1.	Maharashtra	524	28.22	10.22	4.62	22.37	20.39	52.6	35.1	14	210	12.2	23.60	2.93	67.86	2.00
2.	Tamil Nadu	416	26.69	7.43	–	–	38.59	61.41	36.4	14	165	24.6	11.85	4.17	34.43	1.57
3.	Gujarat	429	25.77	8.80	–	12.30	45.04	42.66	36.2	16	224	20.2	26.88	4.55	66.74	1.66
4.	West Bengal	388	24.45	12.39	3.90	33.96	4.14	58.00	34.5	25	182	93.5	32.97	1.94	76.41	1.30
5.	Punjab	576	20.13	5.88	5.33	8.77	7.57	78.33	28.8	25	288	14.7	25.86	4.56	25.20	1.22
6.	Kerala	370	15.11	9.96	–	10.51	79.24	10.25	55.1	25	187	14.9	24.76	2.27	17.45	0.98
7.	Mysore	352	22.33	5.11	4.67	29.99	41.87	23.97	29.8	36	211	12.7	21.57	3.54	28.06	1.31[3]
8.	Andhra Pradesh	406	17.44	3.43	7.83	36.46	44.21	11.50	24.6	39	172	15.8	15.65	2.71	12.67	0.33[2]
9.	Assam	394	7.69	2.67	4.83	37.17	40.94	17.06	24.6	46	177	23.2	34.45	1.17	17.27	0.41
10.	Rajasthan	400	16.28	2.46	15.21	40.01	20.58	24.20	18.1	51	217	7.0	26.20	2.74	8.33	0.88
11.	Madhya Pradesh	387	14.29	3.03	25.77	41.27	16.61	16.28	20.5	54	183	144.3	24.17	2.49	12.54	1.02
12.	Uttar Pradesh	288	12.85	3.42	50.12	9.16	20.12	20.60	20.7	56	126	9.7	16.66	1.66	10.80	0.76[4]

(Contd.)

(*Contd.*)

(1)	(2)	(3)	(4)	(5)	(6)	(7)	(8)	(9)	(10)	(11)	(12)	(13)	(14)	(15)	(16)	(17)
13.	Orissa	304[1]	6.32	1.37	53.64	42.04	4.32	–	25.2	59	189	195.5	19.82	2.48	19.71	1.20
14.	Bihar	272	8.43	2.97	32.55	45.35	8.84	13.26	21.8	61	136	48.6	19.89	2.97	16.20	2.60
	INDIA	422	17.97	5.56	19.66	25.02	24.60	30.72	28.3	—	180	NA	21.51	3.01	28.80	1.64
Co–efficients of rank correlation with index of development													0.16	0.43	0.77	0.34

Notes: Jammu and Kashmir and Nagaland are not included due to non-availability of data for several indicators; Haryana is included in Punjab.

[1] 1963-64

[2] 1955-56 to 1960-61

[3] 1956-57 to 1964-65

[4] 1960-61 to 1964-65

Sources:

Columns 3 and 17: Central Statistical Organisation, Government of India: "Estimates of Total and Per Capita Net Domestic Product for Different States." (Mimeographed) New Delhi, 1968.

Columns 4, 5, 10 and 14: Registrar General India: Census of India, 1961, Paper Number 1 of 1962. Final Population Totals. New Delhi, 1962.

Columns 6-9: Registrar General, India: "Census of India, 1961", Volume I India Part I (A-i) Text: 'Levels of Regional Development in India, New Delhi, 1964, p. 19.

Column 12: Compiled from figures on actual public sector outlay in States and Union Territories given in Planning Commission, Government of India: "Selected Plan Statistics." New Delhi, 1963. pp. 38-39.

Column 13: Compiled from figures of Central investment in States given in, Peccee: "Imperatives of Central Assistance Policy", *Economic and Political Weekly*, Bombay, Volume III, Number 40, October 5, 1968. p. 1529.

Column 15: Economic and Statistical Adviser to the Government of India, Minister of Food and Agriculture: Growth Rates in Agriculture, New Delhi, 1966, p. 37.

Column 16: Industries and Minerals Division, Planning Commission.

The levels of development of the States are indicated by a composite index of development, constructed by giving equal weight to each indicator in the following manner. The States were first ranked according to the value of each indicator. The five rank-values of each State were then added to obtain its total rank score, and the States were arranged in ascending order of rank score, those with the lowest score being considered the most developed. The States are arranged in this fashion in Table 6.1, and their total rank scores are given in Column 11 of the Table. Maharashtra and Tamil Nadu, with rank scores of 14 each, share the top position, followed by Gujarat, West Bengal, Punjab and Kerala. These six States have been considered relatively developed, while the remaining eight have been considered less developed. Division of the States into two groups of seven each would have been more logical: but the six: eight distribution was decided, because the rank score values showed a discontinuity at this point[2].

Data on growth rates, presented in Columns 14 to 17 of Table 6.1, relate to population, agricultural output, per capita value-added in industry, and per capita income. Data on growth rate of agricultural output have been published by the Economic and Statistical Adviser to the Ministry of Food and Agriculture. Similar data are available in case of industrial output, though growth rates could be calculated from time-series data on indicators of industrial growth, such as industrial employment, value-added in industry or consumption of electricity, which are available. But calculation of the growth rate from the time-series data would have given the highest figures for States such as Orissa and Madhya Pradesh, for which the base-year figures are very low. In order to get over this difficulty, the indicator selected is 'per capita increase in value-added in industry'. The figures are derived by dividing the figures of net increase in value-added in industry between 1955 and 1965 by the 1961 (which is the approximate mid-period) population of each State.

It is necessary to mention that the figures relating to per capita income are rather unsatisfactory. The introductory note of the CSO relating to these figures states that "owing to the differences in concepts, methodology, and source materials used, the figures for different States are not strictly comparable". Figures on growth rate of per capita income are even less satisfactory than those on the level of per capita income. They are derived from figures of income at constant prices. But different base years have been used for calculation of constant price figures in different States. Secondly, whereas for most States, the period is 1955-56 to 1964-65, for three States it is shorter, and for two, UP and Andhra Pradesh, it is as short as five years. These differences of time-period and base-year, add to differences in concepts and methods of estimation and greatly reduce the value of these figures.

The relationship between the level of development and rates of growth have been analysed in two ways:

(i) by calculating the co-efficient of rank correlation between the levels of development of each state (as given by the composite index) and each of the four growth indicators, and
(ii) by counting the number of developed and less developed States, which rank among the first six, and the last eight in case of each growth indicator. The co-efficients of rank correlation are given at the bottom of Columns 14 to 17 in Table 6.1; the results of the counts are given in Table 6.3.

GROWTH RATES

Population

The rate of growth of population during 1951-61 was 21.51 per cent for all India, with inter-State variation from 34.45 per cent in Assam to 11.85 per cent in Tamil Nadu. The six developed States had four of the first six ranks in order of growth rate. The highest rate was however for Assam, a State which is in the less developed group, while the lowest was for Tamil Nadu, which is at the top of developed group. The co-efficient of rank correlation with the index of development is 0.16 and is not significant at five per cent level.

Per capita Income

The compound rate of growth for the period, 1955-56 to 1964-65, was 1.64 per cent for all India, with inter-State variation from 2.60 per cent in Bihar to 0.33 per cent in Assam. The high figure for Bihar appears to be due to an underestimation of income in the base year. Excluding Bihar, the other States have growth rates of two per cent or under, with rates for eight States ranging between one and two per cent. The Developed States had four of the six ranks in order of the rate of growth; but the co-efficient of rank correlation with the index of development is 0.34 and is not significant.

Agricultural Output

The rate of growth of agricultural output for the period 1952-53 to 1964-65 was three per cent annually for all India, with inter-State variation from 4.6 per cent in Punjab and Gujarat to 1.2 per cent in Assam. As in case of growth of per capita income, the relatively developed States have done rather better than the less developed ones; the former have four out of the six first ranks. The coefficient of rank correlation with the index of development is 0.43 and is not significant.

Increase in Value-added in Industry

The all-India value of the indicator is Rs. 28.8, with inter-State variation from Rs. 76.4 in West Bengal to Rs. 10.1 in UP. The more developed States have done significantly better than the less developed ones; five out of the first six ranks are taken by them. The co-efficient of rank correlation with the index of development is 0.77 and is significant at five per cent level.

INVESTMENT UNDER THE PLANS

As mentioned above, the Planning Commission has placed emphasis on expansion of social service and infrastructure facilities, agricultural improvement, development of irrigation, etc. in the backward areas, in order to reduce their handicap for development. Expenditure on all these activities is included primarily under State plans. Central investment being mainly in large projects in industry, transport, communications etc. Accordingly, a comparison of levels of State plan expenditures is of interest because it will indicate whether any preference has in fact been given to the less developed States in undertaking such development activities. Figures of per capita State plan expenditure under the first three Plans are given in Column 12 of Table 6.1. They show a broadly similar level of expenditure in most States: 11 out of the 14 States had expenditures ranging between Rs. 165 and Rs. 225. The highest figure, Rs. 288, is for Punjab which is among the more developed States, while the two lowest figures,

Rs. 126 and Rs. 136, are for UP and Bihar, which are near the bottom according to our index of development.

Figures of Central investment under the three Plans, given in Column 13 of the Table 6.1, show a much larger range of variation—from Rs. 195.5 in Orissa to Rs. 7.0 in Rajasthan. The high figures for Orissa, Madhya Pradesh, West Bengal and Bihar are due to location in these States of the steel and heavy industry complexes. Location of the complexes has been decided on techno-economic considerations, principally by location of iron ore and coal, and not on regional development considerations. But since three of these four States are backward, the investment may be considered to contribute to the development of backward regions.

Figures of per capita State plan outlay proposed for the Fourth Plan, given in Table 6.2, show somewhat larger inter-State variation than the figures of State plan expenditure under the first three Plans. The range of variation, from Rs. 190 in Punjab to Rs. 73 in West Bengal is not larger, but the States are distributed throughout the range instead of being concentrated in a part of it. Secondly, the outlays for most of the developed States are considerably higher than those for the less developed ones: five of the first six ranks are taken by the former. The differences in outlays are due to differences in levels of both Central assistance and the States' contributions to financing the State plans. Central assistance varies from Rs. 137.6 per capita in case of Assam to Rs. 48.1 per capita for Maharashtra; but is between Rs. 48 and Rs. 65 for as many as 10 States. The States' contributions vary much more, from Rs. 111.1 in Maharashtra to Rs. 3.4 in Assam. Some less developed States will receive considerably more Central assistance than others; but others, including the most populous ones, UP and Bihar, will not be the beneficiaries of higher assistance. Moreover, it is clear from Table 6.2 that higher Central assistance cannot compensate for low contributions of the State Governments, because with the exception of Assam all States with higher outlays (having the first six ranks) have higher levels of State contributions, while all the State with low outlays have low contributions. The level of States' contributions depends upon the capacity and/or willingness of the States Government to raise resources for development. The Governments of the developed States have higher capacity, because higher per capita income and location of industrial and commercial enterprises within the States offers opportunities for raising resources. But such opportunities may not be utilised, as is obviously the case with West Bengal.

Table 6.2: Per Capita State Plan Outlay and Central Assistance under the Fourth Five-Year Plan

State	*State Plan Outlay (Rupees, per capita)*	*Central Assistance (Rupees, Per capita)*	*State's Contribution (Rupees, per capita)*	*State Plan Outlay as Percentage of Per Capita income of 1964-65*
(1)	*(2)*	*(3)*	*(4)*	*(5)*
1. Maharashtra	159.2	48.1	111.1	30.4
2. Tamil Nadu	125.4	50.5	74.9	30.1
3. Gujarat	166.2	58.3	107.9	38.7
4. West Bengal	73.0	48.2	21.8	18.0
5. Punjab	190.0	65.1	102.5	29.0
6. Kerala	119.1	80.6	38.5	32.1
7. Mysore	109.7	57.9	51.8	31.1
8. Andhra Pradesh	82.1	54.6	27.5	20.2
9. Assam	141.0	137.6	3.4	35.8
10. Rajasthan	89.0	82.0	7.0	22.3
11. Madhya Pradesh	85.8	63.2	22.6	22.2
12. Uttar Pradesh	102.9	56.9	46.0	35.7
13. Orissa	82.0	72.7	9.3	27.0
14. Bihar	75.1	57.5	17.6	27.6
India	108.4	62.5	45.9	25.7

Source: Planning Commission: "Fourth Five-Year Plan", 1969-74. Draft, p. 61. The total figures of outlay and central assistance given in the Draft have been divided by the estimated 1971 population of each State, to obtain per capita figures of Columns 2 and 3.
Figures of column 4 have been derived by dividing those of column 2 with per capita income figures given in Column 3 of Table 6.1.

The figures in the last column of Table 6.2, showing per capita State plan outlays as percentages of per capita income, are interesting. The range of inter-State variation is from Rs. 38.7 per cent (Gujarat) to 18.0 per cent (West Bengal), but for 10 out of 14 States the ratios are between 27 and 36 per cent. Since the future level of development is dependant upon current investment, the fact that the ratios are not significantly higher in the less developed States than in the developed ones (they are in fact lower in several cases), indicates that the disadvantage of the former will not be reduced as a result of State plan investment during the Fourth Plan.

Table 6.3: Distribution of Relatively Developed and Less Developed States According to High and Low Rank Values of Growth Indicators and State Plan Expenditures and Outlays

		Total number	*Relatively Developed States*	*Less Developed States*
Total Number		14	6	8
Growth Indicators				
Population	H	6	4	2
	L	8	2	6
Per capita income	H	6	4	2
	L	8	2	6
Agricultural production	H	6	4	2
	L	8	2	6
Value added in industry	H	6	5	1
	L	8	1	7
State plan Expenditure in first three Plans	H	6	3	3
	L	8	3	5
Outlays under Fourth Five-Year Plan	H	6	5	1
	L	8	1	7

Note: H = High, L = Low

Since the above analysis of State plan expenditures under the first three Plans and outlays for the Fourth Plan does not give evidence of higher levels of investment in the less developed States, the conclusion is justified that accelerated development of social service, infrastructure and related activities, which the Planning Commission had visualised as the principal means of overcoming the handicaps of the backward regions, will not, in fact, have occurred during the period of the first four Plans. Indeed, the handicap of States such as Bihar, UP, Andhra Pradesh, and Madhya Pradesh will have increased further because of low levels of investment in them. The current formulae for distribution of Central assistance for State plans do provide for larger assistance to the less developed States; but it is clear from the figures of outlays for the Fourth Plan that higher Central assistance cannot, in most cases, compensate for low capacity/willingness of the Government of these States to raise resources for development.

INDUSTRIAL DISPERSAL

Analysis of trends in industrial dispersal is handicapped by inadequacy of data. Data relating to industrial growth (investment, increase in industrial employment, or of value of output) are not available by size of towns. Some data which throw some light on the subject are given in Table 6.4. They relate to distribution by size of towns of:

(i) licences for establishment of new manufacturing units or for expansion of existing units, issued during 1952-64,
(ii) employment in functioning industrial estates in 1963, and
(iii) investment in public sector industrial units in the first three Plans.

Table 6.4: Urban Growth and Industrial Dispersal

	Cities with Population			*Towns with Population*		
	1 million and above	*100,000 to 1 million*	*All Cities*	*50,000 to 100,000*	*20,000 to 50,000*	*Below 20,000*
1. Growth rate of population, 1951-61, (per cent)	34.8		48.0	27.6	40.5	7.2
2. Distribution of industrial licences, 1952-64, (per cent of total)	41.4	23.4	64.4	6.9	10.9	17.8*
3. Employment in functioning industrial estates, 1963, (per cent of total)	NA	NA	68.9	15.6	4.0	11.5*
4. Public Sector industrial units started during the first three Plans Number of units			33	3	26*	
Per cent of total investment	6.6	19.1	25.7	1.8	72.6*	

* Including rural.

Source: Line 1: "Census of India, 1961."
Lines 2-3: Town and Country Planning Organisation, Government of India, Background paper on "Coordination of Industrial Development and Location with Urban and Regional Planning and Development". New Delhi, 1966 (Mimeographed).
Line 4: Industries Division, Planning Commission.

The deficiencies in the data need to be mentioned. The industrial licences data relate only to the number of licences issued, and not to the number utilised; the difference could be sizeable. Second, they do not give any quantitative details, such as on investment, about the licences. The employment data relate only to the factories established within the industrial estates; the factories located outside the estates are excluded.

The data bring out the strong tendency of private sector industry to concentrate in cities, especially the large, metropolitan cities. More than two-thirds of the employment in industrial estate factories was in factories located in city industrial estates. Similarly, nearly two-thirds of all industrial licences were issued for manufacturing units proposed to be located in the cities, units with proposed locations in the metropolitan cities accounting for over 40 per cent of the total. Public sector industrial development has not been concentrated in cities to the same extent: nearly three-fourths of the total investment has been in units located in small towns of rural areas (green-field location). The high proportion is due to the large investment in the steel and heavy industry complexes, which have had green-field locations. But most of the other units have been located in the cities. Finally, figures on growth rates of towns of different sizes during 1951-61, given in line 1 of the Table 6.4, show significantly higher rates for the cities than for the smaller towns.

CONCLUSION

The brief analysis indicates that economic growth during the 1950s and early 1960s was probably somewhat more rapid in the developed States than in the less developed ones. The tendency for more rapid growth in the developed areas was particularly marked in the industrial sector; this is brought out both by the State data on increase in value of industrial output, and the available data, by size of towns, on distribution of industrial licences and employment in industrial estates. The principal advance towards industrial dispersal, or industrial development in backward regions was represented by the green-field location of a number of large public-sector industrial complexes in the backward States of Bihar, Orissa and Madhya Pradesh, though the primary rationale of such locations was techno-economic (*i.e.*, proximity to raw·material sources, and the need to choose a green-field location to meet the large requirements of land for the factory and the township), and regional development or industrial dispersal considerations were incidental if at all. The planners had specifically rejected location of large projects on regional development considerations, and insisted that the primary criterion for such locations should be techno-economic efficiency (as judged from the point of view of national welfare). They had visualised that the handicaps of backward areas would be removed through expansion of social service and infrastructure facilities, development of agriculture, irrigation, etc. Analysis of State plan expenditures—from which such developments are financed—does not, however, show higher expenditures in the backward States. Indeed, the most recent trend appears to be towards significantly lower outlays in the poorer, backward States.

The reasons for these trends must be found partly in the area of policy, and partly in the areas of formulation and implementation of programmes. Reduction of regional disparities has not been considered important enough to influence either locational decisions relating to large public sector projects or to merit large special provisions for development of backward areas. Indeed, comparative indifference to the regional development issue, evidenced by the failure to define backwardness and delineate backward areas or even to assemble adequate data on regional rates of growth, is more apparent than attention to it by way of references in the various plan documents. Industrial dispersal, especially prevention of industrial concentration in the metropolitan cities, was accepted as a policy objective in 1956. But acceptance has not been followed, either by use of industrial licensing as an instrument of dispersal, or by effective public sector programmes to stimulate industrial development away from the large cities. Indeed, reference to negative and positive measures needed to secure industrial dispersal, appears for the first time in the 1968 document, "Approach to the Fourth Five-Year Plan". Even the industrial estate programmes, which could have been used as an instrument of industrial dispersal, have not been used for this purpose.

NOTES

1. *Economic and Political Weekly*, Vol. V, Nos. 3, 4 & 5, Annual Number, January 1970.
2. The study shows that, between 1880 and 1950, there were no major changes in the rank order of regions of the United States by per capita personal incomes: the Far West and the Middle Atlantic remained the richest regions and the South East and the South West the poorest. But the spread between the incomes of the richest and the poorest region decreased, from more

than 4:1 in 1880 to 5:2 in 1920, to less than 2:1 in 1950. (Table 69, p. 187, and Table 125, p. 276). Industrial concentration also declined between 1910 and 1950, and there was spread of industry to the new regions (Far West) as well as to the impoverished South East and South West: the proportions of manufacturing labour force and value-added in manufacture in all these regions increased, while those in the older industrial regions, New England and Middle Atlantic, decreased (Tables 102 and 103, p. 252). The results appear to support the Friedmann and Alonso thesis of strength of spread effects and reduction in inter-regional disparities with economic maturity.

3. The Working Group on Identification of Backward Areas. (Pande Group, Government of India, Planning Commission, February 1969) has used a similar method of ranking of States in industrial backwardness.
Seven indicators of industrial development used were: per capita income, contribution of industry and mining to total product, per capita electricity consumption, length of surfaced roads, and railway lines per capita and per unit of area. The States were ranked according to their total rank scores. The ranking revealed the following order of industrial backwardness—Nagaland, Jammu and Kashmir, Orissa, UP, Assam, MP, Rajasthan, Bihar, AP, Kerala, Haryana, Punjab, Maharashtra, Gujarat, Tamil Nadu, and West Bengal—which is very similar to the ranking evolved for this chapter.

REFERENCES

Friedman, J. and Alonso, W. (1965): *Regional Development and Planning-A Reader*, MIT Press, Cambridge and London.

Govt. of India, (1964): *Census of India*, 1961, Vol. I, Part I (A-1), New Delhi.

Hamilton, Richard E. (1969), "Damodar Valley Corporation: India's Experience with the TVA Model", *Indian Journal of Public Administration*, Vol. XV, New Delhi.

Hansen, Niles M. (1968): *French Regional Planning*, Indiana University Press.

Lefeber, L. (1964): Regional Allocation of Resources in India, in Rosenstein Rodan, P.N. (1964): Ed., *Pricing and Fiscal Policies,* George Allen & Unwin Ltd., London.

Lewis, John P. (1962): *Quiet Crisis in India*, The Brookings Institution, Washington.

Macesvich, G. (1964): *Yugoslavia, The Theory and Practice of Development Planning*, University Press of Virgina, U.S.A.

Marglin, S.A. (1967): *Public Investment Criteria*, MIT Press, Cambridge and London.

Myardal, G. (1957): *Economic Theory and Underdeveloped Regions*, London.

Perloff, H.S. (1960): *Regions, Resources and Economic Growth*, Johns Hopkins Press, Baltimore.

Planning Advisory Group, (1965): *The Future of Development Plans*, HMSO, London.

Planning Commission, '*Third Five Year Plan*', 1961.

——, '*Approach to the Fourth Five Year Plan*', May 1968.

——, '*First Five Year Plan – A Draft Outline*', July 1951.

——, '*Fourth Five Year Plan – A Draft Outline*', 1966.

——, '*Fourth Five-Year Plan*' 1969-74 – Draft 1969.

——, '*Second Five Year Plan*', 1956.

——, '*Selected Plan Statistics*', 1963.

Schachter, G. (1967): Regional Development in the Italian Dual Economy, *Economic Development and Cultural Changes*, Vol. 15, Number 4.

United Nations, (1965): *Planning for Economic Development, in Centrally Planned Economies*, Vol. II, Part 2, New York.

7

Regional Planning in the National Plan[1]

INTRODUCTION

This chapter presents the principal issues relating to regional planning in India. It is divided into two parts. Part I describes the issues, the thinking relating to them, and the experience with some regional-planning policies, during the period of the three plans. Part II describes the politico-administrative structure within which planning is done in India, and the contribution of regional planning techniques to improving efficiency of planning through this structure. The question of planning-regions has been discussed briefly, and the regions which can be easily incorporated within the politico-administrative structure, and some others which may need to be added for particular planning purposes, have been mentioned.

I. LOCATION OF ECONOMIC ACTIVITIES—BALANCED REGIONAL DEVELOPMENT

A national plan has certain overall goals, which are stated in terms of growth-rate or rate of increase in national income, increases in employment and output in agriculture, industry and other sectors of the economy, expansion of power, transport and communications, housing and various social services. These goals are achieved through development activities—factories, dams, power stations, roads, schools, hospitals, etc. Regional planning is concerned with the locational aspects of planned development—where the factories, power stations, or schools, are to be located, where the increases in agricultural and industrial output are to take place, and what combination of development activities is to be located in a particular region. It is also concerned with the development of different regions of a country. The two are inter-related, because the decisions relating to location of projects made by the government or by businessmen are the major factors in the economic growth of regions.

The issues of location of economic activities and economic growth of regions are of central importance in planning for developing countries like India; their importance arises from economic, social and political considerations. Capital is very scarce in these countries, and maximizing returns from investment is an important consideration in planning. Locational decisions have the same effect on economic growth as decisions relating to choice of techniques; a wrong decision leads to lower returns from investment and slower economic growth, in the same way as does a decision to use inefficient techniques. Planners are therefore interested in knowing the best places for location of plan projects. But the strictly economic consideration of return on investment, which is the principal factor guiding locational decisions by an individual entrepreneur, has to be balanced by the planners against many other considerations, social, and political. The return to the employer (which may be the government itself) may be the highest when a factory is located in a large city. However, this has to be viewed by them against the economic and social costs of further concentration of economic activities in the city. The factory in the city may give a higher return, but this advantage may be neutralized by the very high costs of providing housing, water supply, transport and other services for the workers. An individual employer can afford to overlook these costs (if he is not required to contribute to them), but the planers cannot, because investment on housing and urban services has to come out of the same pool of national resources from which the factory is financed. Data on comparative costs of creating housing and essential urban services in Indian cities and towns of different sizes given in Tables 7.1 and 7.2, show that the differences in unit costs between the large cities and the small towns are so large that these costs have to be taken into consideration when deciding the location of industries and other economic activities.

The difference may, in fact, be greater than that indicated by these figures. Unit costs are rising progressively in large cities, because

Table 7.1: Cost of Providing Housing in Urban Centres of Different Sizes

	*Cost per dwelling unit**
In a four-storey tenement on an expensive site at maximum density (primarily in Bombay and Calcutta)	Rs. 6,000 to 7,500
In a two or three-storey structure on moderate priced land	Rs. 4,000 to 5,000
In a one-storey structure on cheap land, in smaller towns or in the outlying fringe of larger cities	Rs. 2,500 to 3,500

**Source*: Wurster, C.B. 'Urban Living Conditions, Overhead Costs and the Development Pattern', Turner, R. (Ed.), *India's Urban Future*, University of California Press, Barkeley and Los Angles, 1962, p. 284, (Based on materials provided to the author in 1959 by the Ministry of Works, Housing and Supply, Government of India.)

Table 7.2: Costs of Provision of Urban Services*

Major heads of development	*Cost per capita (Rupees)*					
	Class A Special (Metropolitan cities with population above two millions—Kolkata, Mumbai, Delhi)	*Class A (Cities with population between 500,000 and 2 millions)*	*Class B (Cities with population between 100,000 and 500,000)*	*Class C (Towns with population between 50,000 and 100,000)*	*Class D (Towns with population between 20,000 and 50,000)*	*Class E (Small Towns with population below 20,000)*
Water supply (including head works, treatment plants, etc.)	65.00	47.00	39.00	30.00	22.00	18.00
Sewerage (including sewage disposal)	75.00	65.00	55.00	45.00	34.00	28.00
Construction of roads and paths	81.00	70.00	41.00	29.00	21.00	16.00
Construction of storm water drains	41.00	29.00	26.00	22.00	20.00	17.00
Provision of street lighting	30.00	25.00	22.00	20.00	19.00	14.50
Total Cost Per Capita	**307.00**	**249.00**	**193.00**	**153.00**	**121.00**	**96.00**

**Source*: Augmentation of Financial Resources of Urban Local Bodies, Report of the Committee of Ministers constituted by he Central Council of Local Self Government, Nov. 1963, p. 116.

land prices are going up, service lines have to be constantly extended, and more difficult and more expensive projects have to be undertaken to meet the demands of expanding populations. On the other hand, the total costs (as distinguished from unit costs) of providing housing and services would be greatly reduced in the case of factories located in small towns (or any other place having easy access to the countryside) if the number of people for whom these facilities have to be provided is much less then the total number of employees. This will happen if a substantial proportion of the work force consists of commuters. These people will continue to live in their old houses in villages or small towns, and new housing and other services will not have to be created for them. They can themselves improve their old houses, or build new ones, in course of time. Water supply, transport and other services can be improved by the village communities, of course, with some financial assistance from the government. In this way, heavy investment by the government or the employers or by both is replaced by much lower investment over a period of time by individuals and village communities.

Social and political considerations also focus attention on the issue of location of economic activities. The present economic pattern of the developing countries is characterized by marked differences in levels of development between the cities and the other areas. Manufacturing industries and other modern economic activities are concentrated in and around large cities, while the rest of the economy remains predominantly agricultural and rural. In the case of India, 40 per cent of the workers in large-scale factory-establishments were concentrated in 1961 in the metropolitan areas of seven cities—Kolkata, Mumbai, Delhi, Chennai, Hyderabad, Bangalore and Ahmedabad—each of which had a population of a million or more. Metropolitan Kolkata and Greater Mumbai with only 2.3 per cent of the population of the country, had nearly 30 per cent of the factory workers.[2]

The process of economic growth does not automatically lead to reduction in these disparities. On the contrary, according to Friedmann and Alonso, there is in the early stages of economic development a strong tendency towards further concentration of economic activities in large cities. They call it the tendency of the 'center to grow at the cost of the periphery' (Friedmann and Alanso, 1964, p. 3). This tendency arises mainly from the fact that cities of the developing countries are centres of government and business, entrepreneurs and officials are concentrated in them, and that the facilities needed by modern manufacturing industries—modern transport and communications, banking, insurance and advertising, supply of imported goods including imported machinery and spare parts, skilled labour capable of handling modern machines and attuned to the rhythm and discipline of industrial life—are available mainly in them. Moreover, modern amenities desired by the entrepreneurs and business executives—modern housing, western-style schools, up-to-date hospitals, cinemas, restaurants, nightclubs, etc.—are also available only in the cities. Indeed, the cities are modern enclaves in a traditional agricultural-rural society, and all modern people and economic activities tend to concentrate in them.

But concentration of industries and other modern economic activities in the cities increases the disparities between them and the rest of country—disparities in income and patterns of consumption, and the even more significant disparities in values, attitudes and modes of social and economic inter-action. Indeed, a dual society, in which there is a growing polarization between the cities and the rural areas, begins to emerge. These trends have important political and social implications, to which the planners must give serious thought. The central objective of planning in the developing countries is to bring about social changes which will substitute modern, dynamic, growth-oriented attitudes, production techniques and patterns of socio-economic inter-action for traditional static ones. The principal method of bringing about such social changes is by providing opportunities to an increasing number of people to participate in modern economic activities. Rapid expansion of transport and communications and various social services, rural electrification, etc., find a prominent place in the plans of developing countries, partly on account of their direct, immediate benefits, and partly for their indirect, long-term effect in accelerating social change. Dispersal of modern economic activities is equally necessary for accelerating social change, because it is only by participating in them that people acquire knowledge of modern techniques and attitudes. Therefore, social and political considerations apart, even on purely economic consideration of growth strategy—the total investment required to attain a given rate of economic growth by the community—a policy of dispersal of economic activities from the metropolitan cities to smaller urban centers in the hinterland deserves serious consideration.

The Government of India has favoured the policies of industrial dispersal and balanced regional development, from the beginning of planned development. These were stated as important objectives of the industrial policy of the Government in the Second Industrial Policy Resolution of 1956 and in the Report on the Second Five-Year Plan. (Planning Commission, 1956, pp. 36, 37, 48 and 416).[3] The Report on the Third Five-Year Plan reiterates these objectives. These policies have considerable support from economists and regional planners. Prominent among those who favour dispersed development is John P. Lewis, who has made a powerful plea for location of industries and other economic activities, away from the large cities, in medium-sized and small towns (Lewis, 1962, Chapter 7). But the opposite view, favouring concentration in metropolitan cities and other industrially advanced areas, is also held by some economists. Lefeber has argued for such concentrations on the ground that it will maximize returns on investment and accelerate economic growth, while location in less developed areas will give lower returns and retard the growth process. He has advocated, as a counter part to this policy, a programme of rural works and expansion of social services in the depressed and backward regions in order to utilize their idle manpower and other resources (Lefeber, 1964).

The Central Government and the State governments in India can influence location of industries by their powers of control over location of industrial units of the private sector, by providing fiscal and other incentives for location in particular areas and not in others, and by their own decisions on location of industrial units of the public sector. Under the industrial licensing powers which they have under the Industrial (Development and Regulation) Act, 1951, they can refuse permission for location of units in particular areas. Among measures for influencing location, the most important is establishment of industrial estates and industrial areas. In these areas, developed land with facilities of electric power and water supply (industrial sheds also in industrial estates) are made available to industrialists on attractive terms. Considering the shortages of water and power in most cities, and the very high cost of land and the difficulties of acquiring it, one can say that these are the major advantages for industrialists. The programme for industrial estates and industrial areas can be a powerful instrument for influencing location of industrial units. Decisions relating to location of industrial units in the public sector are, of course, entirely subject to Government policies. However, as the following analysis of location of new industrial units during the period of the three plans reveals, the policies of industrial dispersal have had only limited success so far.

II. LOCATION OF NEW INDUSTRIAL UNITS

Units in the Private Sector

An analysis of location of industrial units licensed under the Industries (Development and Regulation) Act, 1951, during the period 1952-64, has been made recently by the Town and Country Planning Organization (T.C.P.O.), New Delhi (T.C.P.O., Unpublished, p. 19). The results are summarized in Table 7.3.

It will be seen that 64.4 per cent of the units have been located in and around the cities, and as many as 41.4 per cent have been located in cities with population of a million or more. On the other hand, only 17.8 per cent of the units have been located in the rural areas or in small towns with population of 20,000 or less. Nearly two-thirds of all the units are in the four groups of industries—metals and metal products, machinery and equipment, transport equipment, and chemical and allied products. These are the fastest-growing industries, and it is noteworthy that preference for location in large cities is particularly marked in their case. 75 per cent of the units in these industries are located in the cities, and 53 per cent are located in the 'million+cities'. A more detailed analysis contained in the T.C.P.O. paper reveals that 39.1 per cent of the units in the 'machinery and equipment' group and 40.6 per cent of the units in the 'chemical and allied products' group have been located in metropolitan Kolkata and Greater Mumbai alone.

A similar picture emerges from the analysis of distribution of employment in the factories located in the industrial estates (Table 7.4).

Nearly 70 per cent of the total employment is in the factories of industrial estates located in the cities. This concentration in the cities is most interesting because in establishment of industrial estates, while the primary object is encouragement to small-scale industries, dispersal of industries and rural industrialization are important secondary objectives. A number of industrial estates have been located in rural areas, and others should, according to the Report on the Third Plan, be located "as far as possible near small and medium-sized towns" (Planning Commission, 1961, p. 449).

Table 7.3: Distribution of New Units and Units Licensed for the Manufacture of New Articles in Selected Groups of Industries (1952-64)

Industry group	*No. of units*	*Distribution by size of cities* — *Cities with population of* — *1 million and more*	*500,000 to 1 million*	*200,000 to 500,000*	*100,000 to 200,000*	*Total of cities*
1. Metal and metal products	535	244 (45.5%)	42 (7.9%)	47 (8.8%)	45 (8.4%)	378 (70.7%)
2. Machinery and equipment (excluding transport, but including electrical)	1018	577 (54.7%)	82 (8.1%)	91 (8.9%)	48 (4.7%)	798 (76.4%)
3. Transport equipment	259	145 (56.0%)	11 (4.2%)	23 (8.9%)	14 (5.4%)	193 (74.5%)
4. Chemical and allied products	530	270 (50.9%)	21 (4.0%)	48 (9.1%)	49 (9.2%)	388 (73.2%)
Total of four groups	2342	1236 (52.8%)	156 (6.7%)	209 (8.9%)	156 (6.7%)	1757 (75.1%)
Total all Industries	3618	1497 (41.4%)	207 (5.7%)	363 (10.9%)	264 (7.3%)	2331 (64.4%)

Soruce: I.C.P.O.

Table 7.4: Distribution of Employment in Functioning Industrial Estates Located in Cities and Towns of different Sizes (1963)

Size of city/town	*Total No. of functioning industrial estates*	*Employment*	
		Total No.	*Per plant*
I (Above 100,000)	47	19,252	68.85%
II (50,000—100,000)	20	4,358	15.58%
III (20,000—50,000)	168	1,128	4.03%
IV (10,000—20,000)	7	1,225	4.38%
V (5,000—10,000)	4	405	1.45%
VI (Below—5,000)	12	1,502	5.37%
VII Village	1	94	0.24%
Total	107	27,964	100.00%

Source: T.C.P.O., *op. cit*., pp. 23-24.

Location of Industrial Units of the Public Sector

The distribution of the industrial units of the public sector (excluding defence establishments) established in the first three Plans is given statewise and by classes of towns in Table 7.5.

Table 7.5: Location and Investment of Public Sector Industrial Units started during the First Three Plans, by Size of Towns

(*In crores*)

All units		*Units located in*							
Total No of Units	*Invest-ment in crore*	*Metropolitan cities (Population one million and above)*		*Medium-size towns (Population between 50,000 & 100,000)*		*Other cities*		*Small-town or green-field location*	
		No.	*Invest-ment*	*No.*	*Invest-ment*	*No.*	*Invest-ment*	*No.*	*Invest-ment*
62	1770.52	12	116.12	21	338.34	3	31.30	26	1284.76
Per cent of Total Investment									
	100.00		6.6		19.1		1.8		72.6

It will be seen that the largest investment (72.6%) of the total has been in industrial units having small-town or green-field location. But this group consists of a few very large units, mainly the steel plants and the petroleum-based industries. The next largest investment is in units located in the medium-sized cities. Industrial units having green-field location are large, while those located in large cities are comparatively small. This proves the point made by many economists that only the large units which can create their own infra structure facilities can choose a green-field location and that the smaller units have to be located in urban centres with developed infrastructure facilities.

From the above analysis, it would appear that the units in the private sector, large-scale or small-scale, have a marked preference for location in or around large cities. No such preference is visible in the case of units in the public sector; but even in their case, only the large units have been able to choose small-town or green-field locations.

The most notable dispersal of industries so far has been from the central areas of cities to their peripheral regions in suburbs, or in satellite industrial towns. In the case of Mumbai, for instance, industrial development in the period immediately after Second World War, was concentrated in the suburbs, but it has now spread to the mainland area opposite Mumbai Island. The entire mainland area up to the Western Ghats has been affected by industrial and urban development. From the other side of the Ghats, Pune is expanding westwards. Industrial and urban growth in the Delhi region has already extended far beyond the area of Delhi State into the Punjab and U.P. Location of public industrial units has contributed to this process in the case of some cities such as Chennai, Hyderabad and Bangalore.

In each of these cities public sector industrial units were located in the peripheral regions, industrial townships grew round them, and the areas between the townships and the cities have been gradually urbanised.

A variant of these developments, which is of interest for future policies, is industrial and urban growth in the Coastal Gujarat area between Ahmedabad and Surat, and the Central Punjab area between Amritsar and Ludhiana. In both these areas, industrial growth has spilt over from the cities to the small towns and even to villages located along the highways, with the result that entire regions are being steadily industrialized and urbanized. There are undoubtedly some differences between the developments in the two areas. In Gujarat, the typical factory is a large or medium-sized unit, established by an industrialist having sufficient capital. In the Punjab, on the other hand, most factories are very small units run by artisans, whose main assets are their own skill and determination to succeed. The factories are poorly capitalized; they do not have modern equipment and often face many problems. But in both areas, dispersed industrial development has become a reality because of certain common features. Transport and communications are good; electric power and water are easily available; educational and medical services are well developed; literacy and health standards are comparatively high; villages and towns are relatively modern, and workers with the necessary skills, awareness of the requirements of modern industry, and willingness to do industrial work are readily available. Finally, as the workers continue to live in their old, small-town or village homes and come to work on bicycles or by public transport, the employers are not burdened with the need to provide housing and other facilities for them. These advantages more than compensate the disadvantage of locating factories away from the big cities.

Continued concentration of industries in or near the big cities demonstrates the strength of the concentrating forces; their location in ever-widening, peripheral regions of metropolitan cities, and in the two regions mentioned above, point to the directions in which dispersal is likely to be achieved. More important, it brings out the essential requisites of industrial dispersal, *viz.*, well-developed infrastructure, and a population having skills and enterprise.

Instruments of Regional Growth—Large Projects, Economic Policies, Development of the Economic Infrastructure and Institutional Reforms

Discussion of regional development in India is dominated at present by the question of location of large, public sector projects, especially the industrial units. Interest in the location of these projects is connected with the belief that they provide large employment (a direct relation between investment and employment is assumed), which generates a growth-process in the regions in which they are located. Interest in the location of public sector projects is understandable in a democracy. It will grow in future, the role of some projects in initiating regional economic growth is seen and with greater experience with the democratic process, the politico-economic nature of the decisions relating to their location becomes better known. It is already much greater than it was 10 years ago because a number of projects are now in operation, and because there are now both in the Central and the State legislatures a number of young leaders, who are interested in economic development of their areas.

A large project can become the starting point of vigorous economic growth in its region if it is followed by other developments in industry, agriculture and transport, and if social and economic conditions in the region are propitious for such growth. A steel plant can become such a growth-nucleus, if various ancillary or derived-product industries (steel-fabricating industries, engineering industries, manufacture of chemicals and various consumer goods) get established in its vicinity. An irrigation project can be a similar growth nucleus, if it leads to a large increase in agricultural output which in turn stimulates development of commerce and establishment of various agricultural processing industries or consumer goods industries. The Planning Commission had such developments in view when it called large projects, the 'nuclei of regional growth' (Planning Commission, 1961, p. 449). But the projects themselves provide employment only to a limited number. The largest industrial projects in the public sector, the three steel plants, employed between 13,000 and 17,000 workers each at the one-million stage when total investment in each of them was more than 2,000 million rupees. The irrigation and power projects provide employment primarily at the construction stage; employment at the operational stage, after the dams, canals and powerhouses have been completed, is quite small.

But the connected developments take place when the requisites for them exist in the region, the foremost among these are good facilities of transport and communications, and when social and economic conditions in the region are favourable. An irrigation power project will lead to agro-industrial development, if effective use of irrigation waters by the farmer leads to a large increase in agricultural production, and if availability of power leads to establishment of a large number of industries. Such agro-industrial development is taking place, as mentioned above, in the Central Punjab area, following availability of irrigation and power from the Bhakra Nangal Project. It occurred earlier in the Coimbatore area of Chennai as a result of the Pykara Project and in a few other areas. But it has not occurred in all areas of irrigation or irrigation-power project. In the areas of a number of older projects while prosperous agricultural communities have been established, the further step of industrial development has not been taken. The irrigated areas of Western U.P. and the Krishna-Godavari delta in Andhra Pradesh are examples.

In the areas of several of the new projects, the irrigation water itself is not being utilized adequately. The numerous examples include the Chambal area in Rajasthan—Madhya Pradesh, the Hirakud area in Orissa and the Tunghabhadra area in Mysore—Andhra Pradesh. The causes of such differential response are not fully understood, though in each case a number of reasons are cited in explanation.

Economic policies and social and institutional factors, though they do not attract the attention that large projects do, often have an equal or greater influence on economic growth of regions. The policies of equalizing steel prices throughout India or of power rates throughout the area of a state have far-reaching implications for regional growth. The policy of equalizing steel prices, followed since 1955, has reduced significantly the advantage of location of the steel fabricating industries and the engineering industries near the steel producing centers of Eastern India. It may on analysis be found to have been the main factor in stimulating growth of these industries in South India, Maharashtra, Gujarat and the Punjab. Equalization of power rates eliminates the advantage of location of industrial units close to power-generating centres. Both these policies are being used as instruments of industrial dispersal and development of backward regions.

Strengthening the economic infrastructure, expansion of social services, and social and institutional reforms are the most important means of stimulating regional growth. The advantage of cities rests mainly on a very high level of development of the infrastructure. Moreover, in the two regions, Coastal Gujarat and the Central Punjab, in which dispersed industrial and urban growth, desired by the planners, is actually taking place, the most notable characteristics are developed infrastructure, comparatively high levels of education and skills, and concentration of entrepreneurs. The latter two are a consequence of the first.

The importance of developed infrastructure and the social factors is brought out, negatively by the backward areas. Most of them are areas of former princely states, or areas of British provinces in which the feudal *Zamindari* system of land tenure prevailed, or areas inhabited predominantly by primitive tribal people. The princely states areas which are inhabited by the tribal people (parts of Orissa and Madhya Pradesh) are the most backward among them. In all the backward areas, social services and facilities of transport and communications are significantly less developed than in the other parts of the country. Moreover, growth-inhibitive institutions, values and attitudes are much stronger in these areas than elsewhere, because their social, economic and political evolution had been retarded[4] Planning Commission, 1964, pp. 8-10). These handicaps of the backward areas must be removed through rapid expansion of the infrastructure and institutional reforms before a self-propelling growth-process can get under way in them. In the absence of these measures, even location of large projects can have only a limited influence on their growth. It will create modern, urban-industrial enclaves in a primitive, peasant or tribal society. The steel town of Jamshedpur located in the backward tribal area of Chhotanagpur Bihar remained such an enclave for almost 50 years. And the new steel towns located in the same macro-region will remain similar enclaves, until social progress in the region enables the tribal or other rural population of the region to participate in industrial and service occupations in large numbers.

Regional Resource Development—Optimum Pattern of Development of Regions

While regional planning is concerned with stimulating growth in backward regions, it does not aim at producing uniform, or even similar, patterns of economic activity in different regions of a country. Such a connotation of 'balanced regional development' would be erroneous, because it is a basic postulate in regional planning that the patterns of economic development—the nature of economic activities, the distribution of population among primary, secondary and tertiary activities and between rural and urban areas—will be different in different regions of a country, depending upon differences in natural resource endowment, locational advantage and other factors. Thus, Eastern India, with its rich resources of coal, iron ore, limestone, and other minerals, is particularly suitable for development of steel industry and various engineering and chemical industries. Ports and other transport centers offer favourable locations for a variety of industries, including those based on the processing of bulky, imported materials such as petroleum. The potential for increasing agricultural output also varies greatly in different parts of the country. It is the highest in fertile plain areas which have the advantage of assured moisture (supplied either by abundant rainfall or by irrigation facilities), because investment in improved seed, chemical fertilizers, pesticides and other improvements yields the best results in them.[5] On the other hand, most areas in the Himalayas, or areas of low and uncertain rainfall such as Western Rajasthan, have a limited potential for agricultural development. Such areas are also not suitable for location of most industries on account of poor communications and distance from markets. They can advance only through exploitation of their distinctive advantages. In the Himalayan areas these advantages are distinctive climate and landscape, and resources of forests and waterpower. Their temperate climate makes these areas particularly suitable for production of temperate fruit and vegetables. Himachal Pradesh is concentrating on production of apples and seed potatoes with conspicuous success. The tourist industry, based on the climate and landscape of these areas, is already growing rapidly, and has an immense potential for further growth in the future when economic development in the country will make it possible for large numbers of people to travel on vacation. Industries based on forest raw materials, other local materials such as wool, or on local skills, have also considerable possibilities of expansion. The dry areas should similarly concentrate on exploitation of their particular advantages, *e.g.*, for development of the pastoral industries. But the growth of most areas with environmental handicaps will be slower than that of other parts of the country, and this fact should be clearly recognized.

It is the object of the regional plans to indicate for each region its optimum pattern of development, and for the nation an economic map showing which activities should be located in which region, and how activities located in different regions should be related. Such an economic map, showing regional specialization in economic activities, and regional input-output relationships, is the spatial expression of a national plan.

Economic and Social Goals of Regional Plans

It will be useful to make a distinction here between the economic and the social goals of the regional plans. The former relate to the patterns of economic activity in regions; the latter, to the levels of economic and social welfare of their people. The two sets or goals are, of course, related: changes from agricultural to industrial employment and from rural to urban living, for instance, are generally accompanied by rise in income and levels of consumption. But it would be useful to state here as a general principle, however difficult it may be to translate it into practice, that while regional plans should provide for different patterns of economic activity in different regions, they should aim at achieving in all regions, the national goals in education, medical care and social welfare and the national minima in per capita income and consumption. If regional plans succeed in achieving their social goals, much of the political pressure for uneconomic location of projects, on grounds of 'balanced regional development' or 'accelerating growth in backward regions' will be relieved. Leaders from backward regions desire location of large projects in them mainly because they feel that these projects will mean higher levels of income and social welfare for their people. More important, the very expansion of social services and infrastructure facilities in the backward regions will raise their development potential and make them more attractive for location of industries.

Inter-Regional Migration

Free inter-regional migration is essential for progress towards attaining, in each region, the national goals of economic and social welfare. The migrants from stagnant regions can obtain higher incomes by moving to regions of rapid growth; their departure from the stagnant regions may raise marginal productivity and wage-levels in them. Freedom here refers to removal, not of legal restraints (there are none in India), but of the more important social impediments to free mobility of people in a traditional society. Migration policies have particular importance in India, because of the particular pattern of distribution of population and natural resources. The Coal-Steel Belt of Eastern India and other areas of peninsular India, which are rich in resources of minerals and power, and in which agricultural production can also be increased considerably through more purposeful exploitation of their resources of land and water, are thinly populated. On the other hand, some very densely populated areas, such as the plains of Bihar and Uttar Pradesh, have relatively limited natural resources. The Coal-Steel Belt has attracted large numbers of immigrants in recent years after location in it of several industrial, mining and power projects, and migration into the region will continue as its industrial potential is developed. Metropolitan cities are also major centres of immigration. On the other hand, the densely populated plains of U.P. and Bihar have long been the areas of emigration, and may continue to be so. Regional and national plans should visualize the direction and magnitude of inter-regional and intra-regional flows of people, just as they would visualize those of flows of goods. They should also include the policy-measures needed for direction of these flows. Thus, the plan for the Coal-Steel Belt should contain adequate programmes for absorption of immigrants and establishment of satisfactory relations between them and the local tribal people. These programmes are especially necessary, because the tribal people can be easily exploited by unscrupulous traders, contractors and others. If adequate safeguards are not provided for the protection of the tribal people, serious tensions such as have already developed in some industrial centres in the region, will develop between them and the outsiders.

Changing Technology and New Patterns of Urban and Regional Growth

The development potential of different regions—locational advantages, natural resources or the economic significance of these—changes over time, with changes in technology, discovery of new sources of raw materials or power or exhaustion of old sources, changes in income and patterns of consumption and other factors. In the nineteenth century the coalfields were the most suitable places for location of the iron and steel, engineering and various other industries. The advantage of location near supplies of coal was so great that the coalfields of Great Britain, Western Europe and U.S.A. became major industrial regions. A similar development took place somewhat later in the Soviet Union, Japan and many other countries. But in recent years, exhaustion of some of the best coal deposits and changes in technology leading to progressively greater use of petroleum, hydro-electricity and nuclear energy as industrial fuels have significantly reduced the advantage of location in the coal fields. Advances in petro-chemical technology have introduced a variety of new products and given completely new orientations to the chemicals, textiles and several other industries. The chemicals industry, formerly dependent on coal-based derivatives, used to be located in coal-fields; but with increasing dependence on petroleum as the basic raw material, it now seeks locations which have the best combination of advantages with reference to petroleum supplies and distribution of products. Technological advances in generation and transmission of power and development of road transport have also introduced significant new elements in location of industry. As the unit cost of power generation falls sharply with increase in capacity of the generating station and power can be transmitted over long distances at low costs, it is becoming economic to serve the power needs of large regions from a few giant, central stations. One result of this development is that the price of power is the same over large areas and proximity to energy sources—coalfields or hydro-electric power sites—ceases to be a significant locational advantage for industries. Development of road transport, with its door-to-door delivery, means that industries need not be located along railway lines or be clustered round railway junctions. Both these developments give much greater freedom to entrepreneurs in locating their factories. They can consider other locational advantages, and very often the advantages of labour (skilled, efficient or free from trouble), cheaper land, lower taxes or even a congenial environment for living prove decisive in their decisions. The large firms are especially well-situated to take these factors into account in location of their regional or branch factories: they have their own well-developed channels of marketing of products and supply of raw materials and can locate new factories at any place which offers such advantages.

As against these decentralising factors, new concentrating factors have appeared, as a result of which concentration of industries and other economic activities (and of population) in the metropolitan cities of the industrially advanced countries has not only continued, but is also increasing. In Great Britain, economic growth in the years after Second World War has been more rapid in the South East (in the London-Midlands conurbation) than in other parts of the country (Self, 1957, pp. 131-33). In Japan and the Netherlands, to mention only two other examples, the most rapidly growing areas are the central metropolitan areas—the Tokyo Bay area in Japan and the Randstad—Holland area in the Netherlands.This development together with emergence in every industrially advanced country of gigantic conurbations has brought a new interest in regional planning. The interest centres on the one hand on dispersal of economic activities from the rapidly growing, but increasingly congested metropolitan areas and on the other on stimulating growth in the slow growing or depressed regions. Governments in a number of countries are taking steps to achieve one or both of these objectives through various fiscal and other measures. In U.K., the inter-connected nature of the steps needed to reduce concentration in the South East and stimulate development in the depressed industrial regions of the North and the West has been perceived for a long time, and the British Government, has since the end of Second World War, taken several measures to achieve these two objectives. In the immediate post-War years, emphasis was on control measures; but later it shifted to financial incentives (Self, 1957, pp. 128-30). In Japan and the Netherlands, where regional measures have begun to be taken more recently, the emphasis is on dispersal from the central metropolitan areas. In Italy, on the other hand, interest in regional planning has been focused since the 1930s on accelerating growth in the depressed South. In U.S.A., similarly, regional planning and area development have been associated with stimulating growth in the depressed regions such as the Appalachian mountain areas.

In all industrially advanced countries, the regional aspects of city planning have assumed importance with dispersal of urban settlement in recent years. The metropolitan areas of all large cities now extend over hundreds of square miles, and in some case such as the London-Midlands region and the Atlantic Sea-Board of the United States, gigantic conurbations extending over thousands of square miles have appeared. In this situation, the municipal areas of cities have become increasingly irrelevant as units of planning and attention has had to be focused on units which are adequate in size and which express all the relations which have to be kept in view in planning. These units are metropolitan regions or larger areas in which are included, besides the municipal areas of the central cities, large numbers of suburbs, satellite towns and other urban communities. The New York metropolitan region, for instance, covers 6900 square miles in three States and includes the areas of 550 separate municipal governments (Chinitz, 1965, p. 134). The city-region relationship is also being given increasing attention, as cities are getting linked more closely with surrounding areas in the hinterland and the need for dispersal of economic activities from the central areas of cities to the peripheral regions and further into the hinterland, makes a study of the existing and probable future trends in economic activity in the entire hinterland an essential part of metropolitan planning.

These changes, technological and socio-economic, provide to planners in developing countries, a unique opportunity and a challenge. The old factors of industrial location, which led to creation of the present industrial regions in the advanced countries, have no longer the same significance. Factor costs are changing rapidly, new products and new economic activities are assuming importance and the settlement pattern is in a state of flux. As a result, planners everywhere have much greater flexibility in industrial location and greater opportunities of stimulating growth in slow-growing regions. Planners in developing countries can learn from the experience of the developed countries and adopt various measures for diverting growth from congested large cities and regions to the less developed regions. They can go further and through imaginative and bold exploitation of the new techno-economic possibilities, create new urban and industrial location patterns which avoid the high costs of urbanisation and are in accord with the social conditions of their countries. They have this opportunity because urbanisation is still in its early stages in their countries.[6] Finally, by careful planning, they can ensure that large numbers of people can obtain industrial and other non-agricultural employment without leaving their village or small town homes. This development will avoid the high cost of creation of housing and other services in the urban centres. It will also accelerate rural modernization and economic growth by bringing into the rural areas new incomes, ideas and knowledge of new techniques, and widening the world-view of the rural people.

The Politico-administrative Structure for Regional Planning in India—States, Districts, Blocks, Towns and Villages

Planning in any country must be done primarily with its politico-administrative divisions as the units, because the political and administrative institutions needed for formulation and execution of plans are already established round them. In India, states, districts, blocks, towns and villages are such units. Under the federal Constitution of India, planning and development are concurrent responsibilities of the Central Government and the State Governments. The Central Government has responsibility for overall economic and social policies, and for planning in transport and communications, basic industries and some other sectors. The State governments have the primary responsibility for agriculture and other aspects of rural development, irrigation, power, education, health and other social services, housing, urban development, etc. This division of responsibilities is indicated in the list of Central and State subjects in the Constitution of India; its effect on planning is reflected in the figures of distribution of public sector outlays between the Center and the States, (Table 7.6).

Table 7.6: Distribution of Public Sector Outlays of the Centre and the States in India—The Second and the Third Plan

(*Percentage*)

Sl. No.	*Head of Development*	*Second Plan*		*Third Plan*	
		Centre	*States*	*Centre*	*States*
1.	Agricultural Programme	1.0	12.5	3.0	15.2
2.	Community Development and Co-operation	0.9	11.4	–	7.7
3.	Irrigation	2.9	18.0	0.1	15.3
4.	Power	0.7	20.3	2.3	26.8
5.	Industry	38.1	5.8	40.9	5.0
6.	Transport	43.7	8.1	40.0	7.0
7.	Social Services	10.7	22.4	8.4	20.7
8.	Miscellaneous	2.0	1.5	4.5	1.5
	Total	100.0	100.0	100.0	100.0

Source: Goyal, S.K., Working paper on Area Planning, Indian Institute of Public Administration, New Delhi, 1965 (Unpublished).

There is constant consultation between the Central Government and the State governments in the formulation of the national and state plans, and of policies in all sectors of development. At the time of formulation of each Five-Year Plan, overall goals in agriculture, irrigation, power, education, health and other sectors, for which the primary responsibility is of the states, are decided first at the national level (though these decisions are based on assessment of past progress and possible future trends furnished by the state governments), and the State governments then formulate their programmes within the framework of these goals. On the other hand, even though major industries and transport and communications are the responsibility primarily of the Centre, the state governments have a considerable influence in decision-making in respect of individual projects. The competitive claims of the states for location of major projects is one aspect of their interest. The last fifteen years of planning have seen evolution of an institutional structure for consultation between the Central Government and the state governments in the planning process and of certain patterns of inter-action. The National Development Council, in which the Chief Ministers of all the States are represented, the Central Cabinet, the Planning Commission, the State Cabinets and the State Planning Boards are principal constituents of the institutional structure. Consultations between the Central Government and the State governments at the time of formulation of Five-Year Plans and annual plans, and the sharing of costs of various schemes between the Centre and the States are patterns of interaction which have either evolved during this period or have been greatly strengthened (Planning Commission, 1964, pp. 43-50).

Most states of the Indian Union are quite large both in area and in population. Their areas range from 10,000 square miles to 1,25,000 square miles, and their populations are, with the exception of Nagaland, and Jammu and Kashmir, between 15 millions (Kerala) and 75 millions (U.P.). An adequate organization for formulation and execution of plans can therefore be established at the state level. Secondly, the areas of many states are co-terminous with the linguistic regions of the country so that there are among their people developed feelings of cultural-linguistic identity. But most states are so large that there are significant differences in physical conditions, natural resource endowment and levels of economic development within their areas, and it is useful, for many purposes of planning, to divide them into smaller, more homogeneous units.

The principal administrative unit below the state level is the district. The district is also a fairly large unit: most districts are between 2000 and 5000 sq. miles in area and have populations between 1 and 2 millions.[7] The organization of the departments of the state governments is reproduced at the district level, as each department has a representative in the district.

Districts are divided into smaller administrative units—talukas or tehsils and community development blocks. The talukas or tehsils (different names are used in different states) are the old units of revenue administration; but the community development blocks began to be formed only after the inception of the community development programme in 1952. But the block has become already the principal unit for planning and execution of all rural development programmes. The primary unit of rural settlement, the village, is the smallest unit for planning and execution of development programmes. Each panchayat or village council formulates development programmes for its village or villages—very small villages are grouped together into area of one panchayat.

There has been a long tradition of decentralization of decision-making in planning and execution of development programmes at the district level. The principal executive officer in the district, the Collector, has always had considerable initiative and co-ordinating responsibilities in this field. These were re-emphasized after the inception of the community development programme, under which the Collector was made the leader of the team of the district officers of development departments and was designated as the District Development Officer. Since 1959, democratic Panchayat-Raj institutions, having responsibility for planning and execution of development programmes, have been established at the district and block levels. The district institution, the *Zilla Parishad*, is primarily a co-ordinating body in most states, though in some states, such as Maharashtra and Gujarat, it has, in addition, important executive responsibilities. The block-level institution, the *Panchayàt Samiti*, is an executive body with a responsibility of executing programmes of community development and related rural development, within the block area. The panchayat, as mentioned above, has similar responsibilities at the village level.

The need for formulation of plans of districts (and smaller units) has been recognized from the beginning of planned development. The Report on the Second Five-Year Plan in particular, contained a detailed discussion of the content of such plans and the principles, methods and problems of their formulation (Planning Commission, 1956, pp. 155-59). But the importance of these plans has increased with the establishment of *Panchayat Raj* institutions. Formulation of the district plan is being given particular attention because the district is considered to be a sufficiently large unit for drawing up an integrated development plan. Moreover, it is felt that officials and non-officials of the requisite calibre are available at the district level for drawing up the plan. The Memorandum on the Fourth Five-Year Plan gives an important place to the district plan in the scheme of planning (Planning Commission, 1964, pp. 79-83).

The institutional and administrative arrangements for the planning and execution of development programmes at state, district and lower levels, provide the mechanism for relating at successively smaller-area levels, the national goals, priorities and targets in planning on the one hand, and local needs, development potential and aspirations on the other. The plan of each state is drawn up within the framework of the goals, investment magnitudes and physical achievement targets of the national plan; but it reflects in its details—the financial and physical magnitudes of different sectors and the projects included in it—the development potential of the state, and the needs and aspirations of its people. Similar two-way communication operates between the state and the district, and the district and the lower-level units, in the formulation of development plans.

State, district, and blocks are administrative regions. They need to be supplemented by other regions for particular purposes of regional planning; these may range from multi-state macro-regions to small areas, such as the metropolitan area of a city. The patterns of inter-action between the Centre and the States, or between States, may also need to be supplemented in various ways. However, it is well to reiterate that the States, districts and the smaller units must remain basic units for formulation and execution of most development programmes.

Vertical and Horizontal Integrating of Plans—Contribution of the Regional Method

The vertical inter-relation of plans of different areal units and horizontal integration of sectoral programmes into a plan for each unit can be made more effective and rational through the application of regional-planning techniques. Such inter-relations are worked out at present primarily in financial terms. The result is that the distribution of outlays among different sectors of the National and State plans (and among different schemes within the same sector) is often reproduced somewhat mechanically in the plans of smaller units, and there is a corresponding mechanical breakdown of targets of achievement. Horizontal integration is confined even more to financial terms: the district and block plans tend to be mere aggregations of sectoral plans for the respective areas. It is obvious that with such planning-practice, adequate attention cannot be given to meeting particular needs and problems of particular areas of exploiting their distinctive development potential. The need for basing local development plans on detailed surveys of local resources and assessment of local needs, and providing in them appropriate inter-sectoral relationships, has been recognized from the time of the Second Five-Year Plan, but in actual practice emphasis has remained on sectoral planning and integration mainly in financial terms. However, such planning-practice is proving increasingly inadequate now. One reason for this is that the content of local plan is changing gradually. Whereas in the early years of planning, local plans were concerned mainly with agricultural development and creation of basic service facilities—schools, primary health centres, approach roads, co-operative societies, etc.—there is now much greater emphasis on industrial and urban development programmes. This shift in the content of the local plans needs to be accompanied by a shift in the methods of planning. It is now necessary to draw up for each district, an integrated plan of development which would show, besides the financial and physical magnitudes, the location of major economic activities in the district. The plan should give particular attention to development in each district of a number of growth-centres and establishment of effective communication between them and the rural areas. The growth-centers will be medium-sized or small towns—district or block headquarters towns, *mandi* towns, small towns which function as service centres for a group of villages in their vicinity. The constellation of service facilities needed for rural modernization should be developed in each growth-centre, and they should receive first preference for location of industries and other modern economic activities. In this way, they can serve as focal points of growth within the district, and links between the policies of industrial dispersal and rural modernization. A beginning with the preparation of regional plans of this kind should be made in the districts which are receiving large investments on account of location of major plan-projects, or those selected for special development efforts, such as the intensive agricultural development programme.

Regional-planning techniques can also make for more adequate and more effective linking of plans of different regions by visualizing production magnitudes in each region, and inter-regional flows of goods and services. This is another aspect which has received too little attention in Indian planning so far. The production specialization of different states (or other regions) and inter-state movement of goods have not been worked out in the Indian plans so far. One result of this failure is that development of the distinctive potential of particular states does not often receive adequate attention, and the state governments in their anxiety to confirm to patterns of sectoral outlays in the national plan, take up development activities for which they have much less advantage in preference to others for which they would have much greater advantage. Let us illustrate this with the example of planning for two major sectors of development—irrigation and power. It is essential that each state gives adequate attention to these sectors in its development plans. But it is not necessary that the outlays on irrigation and power in the plan of each state should correspond to the outlays in the national plan; nor is it necessary that each state should try to develop all its irrigation and power resources, irrespective of unit costs. On the contrary, efficient resource utilization requires that different states give different emphasis to irrigation and power programmes—State A concentrating on irrigation, and State B on power—depending upon their advantages for development of these. The Central Government should encourage such differential emphasis: indeed, it has the primary responsibility in this respect because the finances for undertaking large projects are provided largely by the Central Government.

Regional planning is associated by some people with such inter-state action: they feel that it furnishes an intermediate level of planning between the Centres and the States. There is in India considerable experience of inter-state co-operation in programmes of development of water resources, power generation and others. The inter-state river-valley projects, undertaken in recent years, are outstanding examples of such co-operation. The prime requirements of such co-operation—subordinating parochial interests of particular states or local areas and focusing attention on integrated resource development of the region—as well as the various issues and problems involved—allocation of waters among different areas and different users, sharing of costs between the states concerned—are all very well understood. However, the long time taken and the difficulties experienced in arriving at agreements in some cases, such as development of the Krishna and the Narmada river systems, illustrate the difficulties in securing inter-state co-operation in democratic societies. Similarly, in the case of power generation programmes, there is considerable and continuing experience of inter-state action. The power system of every state is linked with those of its neighbours, and the economic issues of pricing as well as the techno-administrative problems of operation of inter-state power systems are well understood. Formation of regional power grids has been advocated for some time; the regional grids are visualized as a step in the formation, eventually, of a national power grid.

However, the area of inter-State action, especially action between neighbouring States will become progressively larger with economic growth. Rural modernization, industrial and urban development and expansion of transport and communications, will open continually new areas of inter-State cooperation, ranging from taxation to regulation of traffic.

Supplements to Administrative Regions

1. *Zones or macro-regions*:—Since the reorganization of the states of India in 1956, an institutional arrangement for inter-state action has existed in the form of Zonal Councils. These Councils have been constituted for each of the five zones of the country—Northern, Central, Eastern, Southern, and Western. Each zone consists of two or more states and adjoining Union Territories. The institution of the Zonal Councils could be used for planning and co-ordinated execution of programes of inter-state interest much more effectively than has been done so far. Zones also provide a useful conceptual framework for macro-regional division of the country: most macro-regional divisions are variations on the zonal scheme[8] (Government of India, 1965, p. 85). Macro-regional schemes are useful for planning in sectors, such as basic industries and transport which are the responsibility of the Centre, and for regional economic and social analysis. They can be very useful for planning flows of basic commodities—foodgrains, agricultural raw materials, coal, iron and steel, cement, petroleum products—and for deciding location of large industrial units keeping these flow-patterns in view. The concept of such macro-regions has been best developed in the U.S.S.R. which has been divided into a number of 'major economic regions', each based on one or more major industrial complexes. However, the related Soviet concept of self-sufficiency at 'major economic region' level has distinct limitations in India, because of the particular distribution of its mineral resources. As the bulk of the coal and iron-ore deposits of India are located in Eastern India, in the Coal-Steel Belt, concentration of the iron and steel industry in this region, and large-scale movements of coal and steel from it to other regions of the country should remain an important feature

of the Indian economy. Ignoring these facts and attempting to achieve macro-regional self-sufficiency would result in distortions in the pattern of industrial development, which could prove very costly.

Macro-regional schemes are useful for economic and social analysis because they make possible presentation of data on regional differences within a large country in terms of a relatively small number of units. In the U.S.A., the Census Divisions are now used extensively for this purpose, and the practice is growing in India[9] (Perloff and Isard, 1960).

2. *Divisions*: Most states of India have such large contrasts in physical and socio-economic conditions within their areas that it is useful to divide them into a number of smaller, more homogeneous units—the divisions. These units, each consisting of a few districts, provide to state-planners a useful frame of reference, both for comprehending the diversity within the state and for indicating the directions along which sectoral programmes should be modified to suit local needs. They indicate to local planners the most essential areas of inter-district co-operation. The divisions can be adopted as units for preparing outline regional plans which would serve as guides for preparations of district plans. The work on preparation of such divisional plans is most advanced at present in Maharashtra. The importance of the division as a planning unit will increase progressively in future, as emphasis in planning shifts to intensive agricultural and resource development activities. It appears also that in many states, the division will be accepted as the most suitable unit for planning for urbanization.

Other Planning Regions

Zones or macro-regions, and divisions may be regarded as supplements to the administrative regions, because they interpose additional units in the structure of administrative regions. With these supplements, this structure provides a regional framework extending from the macro-level of the zone to the extreme micro-level of the village.

But the administrative regions are not suitable for many planning purposes, because they do not express the relationships which are most relevant for these. Thus, the municipal area of a large city does not express (in most cases) the relationships which have to be kept in view in planning for its growth, and the much larger metropolitan area, which includes besides the municipal area, suburbs, semi-urban areas and even rural areas having close socio-economic relationships with the city, has to be adopted as the planning-unit. For water-resource development, similarly, the river basin is the most suitable unit. Industrial regions and backward regions are other examples of regions which have to be especially demarcated for particular purposes. The number and nature of such regions will vary with planning-needs. However, from the scope and objectives of planning in India at present, it appears that metropolitan areas, river basins, industrial regions and backward regions are the most important extra-administrative regions. The nature of the administrative and institutional arrangements needed for formulation and execution of plans for these regions and of the relationship of the agencies established for them with the existing political and administrative structures, raises important issues which are outside the scope of this Chapter.

CONCLUSION

Regional planning is concerned with the spatial aspects of planned development. Regional economic analysis reveals differences in growth-rates of regions and the reasons for these differences, and points to be measured—location of industries and other economic activities, strengthening the infrastructure, and social and institutional reform—needed to reduce inter-regional disparities. Regional-planning techniques contribute to formulation of plans which ensure that each region contributes to the national growth process in accordance with its natural and human resources and its locational advantages, and in so doing reaches its own optimum development. Industrially advanced countries are turning to regional planning to meet the problems of metropolitan growth, accelerate development of retarded or depressed regions, and to reduce inter-regional disparities. The need for regional planning is equally urgent in developing countries in which contrasts between the metropolitan cities and hinterland regions are equally striking. There is a strong tendency for further concentration of economic activities in metropolitan cities, and this tendency has important social and political consequences. Well-defined policies of regional planning have to form part of the national plans if the disparities between the metropolitan cities and hinterland areas are not to be widened, and if the benefits of planned development are to reach all areas.

In large federal countries, such as India, in which planning has to be undertaken at different area-levels, ranging from the national to the local, and political and administrative structures at each level have to participate in the planning process, regional planning techniques can make a major contribution towards more effective and more efficient integration of plans for different areas. The need for such integration is becoming increasingly urgent in India as emphasis in planning shifts with economic growth from development of agriculture and creation of basic social service facilities to industrial and resource development activities, and from basic, simple activities to more complex and specialized activities.

APPENDIX-1

Appendix Table (Source for Table 7.5)

Location of Public Sector Industrial Units started during the First Three Plans, by Size of Towns

Name of the State	*All units*		*Units located in*							
	No.	*Investment in crores*	*Metropolitan cities (Population one million and above)*		*Other cities*		*Medium–size towns (Population between 50,000 & 100,000)*		*Small–town or green–field location*	
			No.	*Investment in crores*	*No.*	*Investment in crores*	*No.*	*Investment in crores*	*No.*	*Investment in crores*
(1)	*(2)*	*(3)*	*(4)*	*(5)*	*(6)*	*(7)*	*(8)*	*(9)*	*(10)*	*(11)*
Andhra Pradesh	7	56.98	4	44.66	3	12.32	–	–	–	–
Assam	2	27.50	–	–	1	13.00	–	–	1	14.50
Bihar	5	200.75	–	–	4	159.75	–	–	1	41.00
Gujarat	1	32.00	–	–	–	–	–	–	1	32.00

(Contd.)

(Contd.)

Name of the State	All units		Units located in							
	No.	Investment in crores	Metropolitan cities (Population one million and above)		Other cities		Medium-size towns (Population between 50,000 & 100,000)		Small-town or green-field location	
			No.	Investment in crores	No.	Investment in crores	No.	Investment in crores	No.	Investment in crores
(1)	(2)	(3)	(4)	(5)	(6)	(7)	(8)	(9)	(10)	(11)
Kerala	7	26.24	–	–	6	26.09	–	–	1	0.15
Maharashtra	2	42.48	1	37.28	1	5.20	–	–	–	–
Madhya Pradesh	7	442.61	–	–	2	66.88	–	–	5	375.73
Madras	6	82.71	3	14.11	1	22.30	1	8.30	1	38.00
Mysore	4	24.69	3	18.69	–	–	1	6.00	–	–
Orissa	3	403.84	–	–	–	–	–	–	3	403.84
Punjab	3	40.60	–	–	–	–	–	–	3	40.60
Rajasthan	2	6.00	–	–	2	3.00	–	–	1	3.00
Uttar Pradesh	5	62.90	–	–	1	29.80	1	17.00	2	16.10
West Bengal	8	321.22	1	1.38	–	–	–	–	7	319.84
Total:	62	1800.52	12	116.12	21	338.34	3	31.30	26	1284.76

NOTES

1. *Artha Vijnan*, Vol. 9, No. 1, March 1967, Gokhale Institute of Politics and Economics, Poona
2. Based on analysis of figures given in 'Large Scale Industrial Establishments in India' (Annual); published by the Central Statistical Organization, Government of India.
3. The text of the Industrial Policy Resolution is given in the Plan on pages 43 to 50.
4. This point has been emphasized by a Team appointed by the Planning Commission to study development-needs of certain backward districts of Eastern Uttar Pradesh.
5. This fact is now being given increasing recognition in planning for agricultural development in India. In the early years of planning, attention was focused on creation of the basic administrative and institutional structures for agricultural extension, credit and supplies, in all areas of the country. However, after these structures had been created, emphasis shifted progressively to intensive effort in areas having the most favourable environmental and socio-economic conditions for increasing production. In 1960, 15 districts having these advantages were selected for intensive agricultural development; the object was to secure rapid increases in output through concentrated application of inputs. The principle of concentrated effort in favourable areas has been progressively extended by selecting extensive production areas for all important crops. Secondly, in all recent policies, the trend is towards concentration of all available inputs—chemical fertilizers, pesticides, high-yielding seeds—in the intensive production areas.
6. "The strongest centripetal force operating on behalf of metropolitan-centred location commonly is said to be the pull exerted by the already concentrated markets that exist in the largest cities. But, in the case of a country at as early a stage of industrialization as India now is, it actually begs the whole longer-run locational question to put much stock in this argument. For so much of the total locational outcome is yet to be settled that the question at issue virtually comes down to this: What will the territorial disposition of demand be in the Indian economy of 1970 and 1980? At this stage, the planners still are modeling with wet clay, as it were, most of which has not yet been put in place… But so much of the modelling remains to be done that very soon the emergence of a new pattern would begin to be reinforced and facilitated by the very centripetal and intertial forces that are now alleged to obstruct it."
7. Some districts of Bihar have larger population of up to 4 millions. On the other hand, most of the districts of Rajasthan, Madhya Pradesh, and Jammu and Kashmir are very small.
8. One such scheme is that used by the Energy Survey Committee, which divides the country into the following six Energy Regions: (i) Northern:

Punjab, Himachal Pradesh, Delhi, Rajasthan and Jammu & Kashmir; (ii) Central: U.P. and Madhya Pradesh; (iii) Eastern: Bihar, West Bengal, and Orissa; (iv) Assam: Assam, Tripura, and Manipur; (v) Southern: Andhra Pradesh, Mysore, Madras, and Kerala; and (vi) Western: Maharashtra, and Gujarat.

9. Almost the entire analysis in these two well-known recent studies is in terms of census divisions. In India the data of a number of countrywide studies and surveys are being presented by Zones or macro-regions. The National Sample Survey of the Government of India, and the surveys conducted by the National Council of Applied Economic Research, New Delhi, are some of these.

REFERENCES

Chinitz B.(1965): *A Metropolitan Region. Scientific American*, Vol. 213, No. 3, New York.

Friedmann, J. and Alanso W. (1964): Ed., *Regional Development and Planning—A Reader,* M.I.T. Press, Cambridge, Mass.

Government of India, (1965): *Report of the Energy Survey of India Committee*, New Delhi.

Isard, W. (1960): *Methods of Regional Analysis*, M.I.T. Press, Cambridge Mass.

Lefeber, L. (1964): Regional Allocation of Resources in India, in Rosenstein Rodan P.N. (1964) Ed., *Pricing and Fiscal Policies,* George Allen & Unwin Ltd., London.

Lewis, John P. (1962): *Quiet Crisis in India*, The Brookings Institution, Washington.

Perloff, H.S. (1960): *Regions, Resources and Economic Growth*, Johns Hopkins Press, Baltimore.

Planning Commission, Government of India,

—— *Second Five Year Plan 1956.*

—— *Memorandum on the Fourth Five-Year Plan*, October 1964.

——, '*The Planning Process*', 1964.

——, '*Report of Joint Study Team*', Uttar Pradesh (Eastern Districts) 1964,

Self, Peter (1957): *Cities in Flood*: *The Problems of Urban Growth*, London, Faber and Faber Ltd.

Town and Country Planning Organization (T.C.P.O.): New Delhi, '*Background paper on Co-ordination of Industrial Development and Location with Urban and Regional Planning and Development*' (Unpublished).

8

Levels of Economic Development and Rates of Economic Growth in India: A Regional Analysis[1]

INTRODUCTION

Regional disparities in levels of economic development and rates of economic growth are an important feature of the economies of many countries. The most common disparity is between the cities and the remaining areas: the core-periphery dichotomy of Friedmann and Alonso. (pp. 3-6) In several countries, such as U.S.A., Italy and France, the northern regions are significantly more developed than the southern ones so much so that Hirschman uses the terms North and South to designate, respectively, rapidly growing and lagging regions. (Hirschman, 1961 p. 187). In U.K. on the other hand, the Southern regions especially the South, East and Midlands, are more developed and have been experiencing since the 1930s more rapid growth than the Northern and Western regions because the traditional industries of the latter have experienced chronic stagnation. The persistence of stagnation or backwardness in particular regions leads governments to undertake programmes for their economic development or growth; such programmes have been undertaken in all the four countries mentioned above. Geographers are interested in precise delineation of regional disparities in economic development and growth because besides being the subject of developmental or welfare programmes, they are among the most important manifestations of areal differentiation resulting from human activity.

In India, the planners have been conscious of the existence of large inter-regional disparities in development and of the need to reduce them. Balanced regional development has been accepted as the objective of planning, and policies, such as dispersal of industries from large cities and creation of social and economic overhead capital in the less developed regions in order to enable them to overcome their handicap for development and have been advocated in the Five Year Plans to achieve it (Planning Commission, 1961 Chap IX pp. 142-152). But systematic analysis of regional differences in economic development or economic growth and identification of less developed or slow-growing regions have not been undertaken by the planners. Even the preliminary step of evolving suitable criteria for identification of backward areas was entrusted to a Working Group (Planning Commission, 1969) only in 1968, 18 years after the initiation of planning. The Group indicated in its report six criteria for identification of backward districts and classified the states according to industrial backwardness with the help of 8 indicators (Planning Commission, 1969 pp. 13 and 16-17) But it is interesting to note that neither the Working Group nor the Planning Commission has delineated backward areas on basis of either set of criteria: this task has been left by the Commission to the State Governments (Planning Commission: Draft 1969 pp. 346-347).

The object of this chapter is to bring out, with the help of readily available state-and-district-level data, the regional patterns of economic development and economic growth within India. Analysis of level of economic development has been made for both states and districts, but analysis of growth rates has been made only for states because district level data, on which such analysis could be based, are not available. A part of the state-level analysis has appeared in a recent article by the author in the *Economic and Political Weekly*, Mumbai (Nath, V. Jan 1970).

METHODOLOGY

Comparison of economic development or economic growth of different areal units (countries, regions, etc.) involves (i) selection of suitable indicators of development/growth, and (ii) evolving suitable methods of combining data for several indicators, if more than one indicator is selected. Selection of the indicators depends, in turn, on their suitability as measures of development/growth and availability of adequate and accurate data on them. One approach is to use one or very small number of carefully selected indicators; the other is to use a large number of indicators and construct composite indices based on them. Per capita income is the most commonly used single indicator: it is being used in both international and inter-regional comparisons of economic development and historical analysis of economic growth. Its popularity is due to its comprehensiveness and simplicity. But several difficulties, such as (i) deficiencies in population and national income data, especially for the under-developed countries, (ii) differences between the internal purchasing power and external exchange rates of currencies—international comparisons of per capita income are generally made in terms of the U.S. dollar, and (iii) the tendency to under-estimate the value of goods and services produced and consumed within the households (home-produced food and owned housing in agricultural households), lead to dissatisfaction with per capita income as a measure of economic development and to a search for other measures. The most notable among the latter are attempts to compare 'real income', and to construct 'levels of living' indices. Beckerman's work on international comparisons of real incomes (Backerman, 1966) and the level of living indices developed by Bennet (1951 pp. 632-49) and the U.N. Institute of Research in Social Development (U.N. 1966) are examples of these. The multi-indicator approach to measurement of economic development is illustrated also by the Atlas of Economic Development in which data on 43 indicators (including per capita income) were presented for 95 countries. (Ginsburg, 1961). In Part VII of the Atlas, Brian Barry (1961) tried to identify with the help of regression analysis four basic patterns of economic development, relating respectively to technology, demography, income and external relations, and size. Use of multi-indicator indices gets over the second and the third difficulty listed above for per capita income; but it does not eliminate the first difficulty of deficiency of data because data for many indicators are as difficult to obtain as those for national income. Some economists try to steer a middle course between the single-indicator and the multi-indicator approaches to measurement of economic development, and use besides per capita income a few carefully selected indicators, such as per capita consumption of energy, distribution of labour force among primary, secondary and tertiary sectors, literacy rate, the number of doctors or hospital bed per thousand of population, etc. (Zimmerman, 1965).

Use of per capita income for intra-national (inter-state and inter-district in India) comparisons of economic development presents fewer problems than for international comparisons: the problem of difference between the internal purchasing power and the exchange rate of currencies is non-existent, and those arising from differences in consumption patterns in different countries, or large consumption of home-produced goods and services in the rural sectors of the developing countries, are much smaller. The principal difficulty is deficiency of data. In case of India, district-wise data on per capita income are not available (National Council of Applied Economic Research, 1963), and state-wise estimates, compiled by state statistical bureaus, are not strictly comparable because of differences in methods of estimation followed by the different bureaus (Central Statistical Organization). Data on growth of income suffer from the further limitation that different base years have been adopted by different bureaus for calculation of income at constant prices and the data are not available for the same period for all the states. After a preliminary examination of the available data, it was decided to calculate for this paper, growth rates of per capita income for the decade 1955-56 to 1964-65. But the calculation had to be limited to shorter periods of 5 to 9 years in case of 3 states and could not be made at all in case of one state, Jammu and Kashmir. Finally, there is the problem of annual fluctuations in total and per capita income. These are large because, agricultural output, which contributes nearly half of the total output, fluctuates greatly from year to year under the influence of the monsoons. The difficulty is overcome by using 3 or 5 years average figures instead of single year figures of income: 3 years (1963-64 to 1965-66) average figures have been used here (Col. 3 of Table 8.1).

The levels of economic development of states have been measured in two ways: (a) on basis of per capita income, and (b) through use of a composite index of economic development, based on the following four indicators besides per capita income:

Table 8.1: Levels of Economic Development and Rates of growth—India and 15 States*

Rank order	*Name*	*Per capita income (3 year average, 1963–66, Rupees at current prices)*	*Proportion of urban population to total population in 1961 (per cent)*	*Proportion of male workers in manufacturing industries to all male workers in 1961 (per cent)*	*Proportions of Population living in districts at different levels of development, in 1961* Bottom	Third	Second	Top	*Literacy rate (excluding 0–4 age group) in 1961 (per cent)*	*Total Rank score*	*Rate of growth of Population 1951-1961 (per cent)*	*Compound rate of growth of agricultural production 1952–53 to 1964–65 (per cent, per year)*	*Increase in value added in industry, 1955–65 (Rupees, per capita)*	*Compound rate of growth of per capita income 1955–56 to 1964–65 (per cent per year)*
1	*2*	*3*	*4*	*5*	*6*	*7*	*8*	*9*	*10*	*11*	*12*	*13*	*14*	*15*
1.	Maharashtra	478	28.22	10.22	4.62	22.37	20.39	52.62	35.1	13	23.60	2.93	67.86	2.00
2.	Tamil Nadu	400	26.69	7.43	–	–	38.59	61.41	36.4	15	11.85	4.17	34.43	1.57
3.	Gujarat	462	25.77	8.80	–	12.30	45.04	42.66	36.2	17	26.88	4.55	66.74	1.66
4.	West Bengal	465	24.45	12.39	3.90	33.96	4.14	58.00	34.5	20	32.79	1.94	76.41	1.30
5.	Kerala	341	15.11	9.96	–	10.51	79.24	10.25	55.1	25	24.76	2.27	17.45	0.98
6.	Punjab[1]	473	20.13	5.88	5.33	8.77	7.57	78.33	28.8	26	25.86	4.56	25.20	1.22
7.	Mysore	373	22.33	5.11	4.67	29.99	41.87	23.97	29.8	33	21.57	3.54	28.06	1.31[3]
8.	Andhra Pradesh	386	17.44	3.43	7.83	36.46	44.21	11.50	24.6	41	15.65	2.71	12.67	0.33[2]
9.	Assam	393	7.69	2.67	4.83	37.17	40.94	17.06	33.0	47	34.45	1.17	17.27	0.41

(*Contd.*)

(*Contd.*)

1	2	3	4	5	6	7	8	9	10	11	12	13	14	15
10.	Madhya Pradesh	325	14.29	3.03	25.77	41.27	16.61	16.28	20.5	56	24.17	2.49	12.54	1.02
11.	Uttar Pradesh	306	12.85	3.42	50.12	9.16	20.12	20.60	20.7	56.5	16.66	1.66	10.08	0.76[4]
12.	Rajasthan	314	16.28	2.46	15.21	40.01	20.58	24.20	18.1	58	26.20	2.74	8.33	0.88
13.	Bihar	265	8.43	2.97	32.55	45.35	8.84	13.26	21.8	63	19.89	2.97	16.20	2.60
14.	Jammu & Kashmir	302	16.66	2.85	67.50	17.98	–	14.52	13.0	63	9.44	N.A.	N.A.	N.A.
15.	Orissa	306	6.32	1.37	53.64	42.04	4.32	–	25.2	66.5	19.82	2.48	19.71	1.20
16.	INDIA	372	17.97	5.56	19.66	25.02	24.60	30.72	28.3	–	21.51	3.01	28.80	1.64
											0.14	0.35	0.77	0.40

* Coefficient of Correlation

* Coefficients of rank correlation with total rank score (Col. 11): Nagaland is excluded because of non-availability of data for several indicators.

1. Includes Haryana, 2. 1955-56 to 1960-61 3. 1956-57 to 1964-65. 4. 1960-61 to 1964-65

Sources:

Cols. 3 and 17 : Central Statistical Organization, Government of India: Estimates of total and per capita net domestic product for different States. (Mimeographed) New Delhi, 1968.

Cols. 4, 5, 10 & 12 : Registrar General, India: Census of India, 1961, Paper No. 1 of 1962. Final Population Totals, New Delhi, 1962.

Cols. 6-9 : Registrar General, India: Census of India, 1961. Vol. I, India Part I (A-i) Text: Levels of Regional Development in India, New Delhi, 1964, p. 19.

Col. 13 : Economic and Statistical Adviser to the Government of India, Ministry of Food and Agriculture: Growth rates in Agriculture, New Delhi, 1966. p. 37.

Col. 14 : Industries and Minerals Division Planning Commission.

(i) proportion of urban population to total population in 1961;
(ii) proportion of male workers in manufacturing industries to all male workers in 1961 (Sharma, 1963 pp. 433-45);
(iii) proportions of population living in districts at the two higher levels of development (top and third) as estimated in the 1961 Census publication, Levels of Regional Development (Census of India 1964 p. 19); and
(iv) literacy rate in 1961 of the population, 5 years old and over.

The composite index was constructed as follows. The states were first ranked according to the value of each indicator. The five rank values for each state were then added to obtain its total rank score. The states were then arranged in ascending order of the score, that with the lowest score being considered the most developed and placed on top and that with the highest score being placed at the bottom. The states are listed in this way in Table 8.1; data for individual indicators are presented in Columns 3 to 10 of the table, while the total rank scores are shown in Col. 11. Maharashtra with the lowest rank score of 13 is at the top, while Orissa with the highest score of 66.5 is at the bottom. Nagaland is excluded because data for several indicators were not available for it and Haryana is included under Punjab. It may be mentioned that the Working Group on Identification of Backward Areas appointed by the Planning Commission adopted a similar method of ranking states according to indicators of "industrial backwardness" and obtaining an overall rank value for each state by adding the rank values of individual indicators. The indicators of the Working Group and the ranking of states made by it are shown in Appendix I. The similarity between the rankings of the Working Group and of this paper may be noted.

Analysis of economic growth has been made with the help of data on growth rates of population, agricultural output, per capita value added in industry, and per capita income (Cols. 12 to 15 of Table 8.1). Data on growth of population are from the Census of 1961, and those on growth of agricultural output are from a publication of the Economic and Statistical Adviser to the Ministry of Food and Agriculture (March 1966, pp 29). Similar data on growth rates of industrial output by states, are not available, though the rates could be calculated from time-series data on indicators such as industrial employment, value added in industry and consumption of electricity, which are available. But since calculation of industrial growth rates from the time-series data would have given the highest figures for states, such as Orissa and Madhya Pradesh, for which the base-year figures are very low, the indicator selected is per capita increase in value added in industry. The figures are derived by dividing the figures of net increase in value added in industry between 1955 and 1965 in each State by its 1961 (approximate mid-period) population. The relationship between the level of economic development and rates of economic growth has been analysed by calculating coefficient of rank correlation between the total rank score given in column 11, and each of the four growth rates. The calculation was not made for Jammu and Kashmir because data for 3 out of the 4 growth rates were not available for it. The coefficients of rank correlation are given at the bottom of Columns 12 to 15 in Table 8.1.

State-level analysis is particularly inadequate for delineation of regional differences in economic development or growth in India because most states are very large in size. Uttar Pradesh, the largest, had a population of 73.75 million in 1961, and an area of 294,000 sq. kilometres. Moreover, there are marked differences in levels of economic development among different regions of several states, such as between the western and eastern regions of Uttar Pradesh, or among the different regions of Maharashtra. Accordingly, state-level analysis has to be supplemented by analysis at the next administrative level, the district. But for district-level analysis, the problem for data is much greater than for state-level analysis. Analysis of growth rates of districts has not been attempted in this chapter because of lack of data: the data on levels of development is taken from the 1961 Census publication, mentioned above. This analysis is based on 35 indicators of economic development. The method involves division of indicators into five groups and division of districts into quartiles and octiles according to their cumulative scores for each group of indicators.The end result is a classification of districts into four levels of development—first or lowest, second, third and fourth or top—each having an approximately equal number of districts (Census of India 1964, pp. 9-14). The geographical distribution of districts at different levels of development is shown in Fig. 8.1, which has been reproduced from the publication, and their numbers, state-wise, are given in Table 8.2. The distribution of the population of each state among districts at different levels of development is given, as mentioned above, in Columns 6 to 9 of Table 8.1. It may be noted that whereas the number of districts in the different development levels does not differ much (Table 8.2), the proportion of population living in districts of the top level, is much higher than the proportion in the districts of the lowest level—30.72 per cent as against 19.66 per cent. This is because the more developed districts, many of which contain cities, are more populous than the less developed, mainly rural districts.

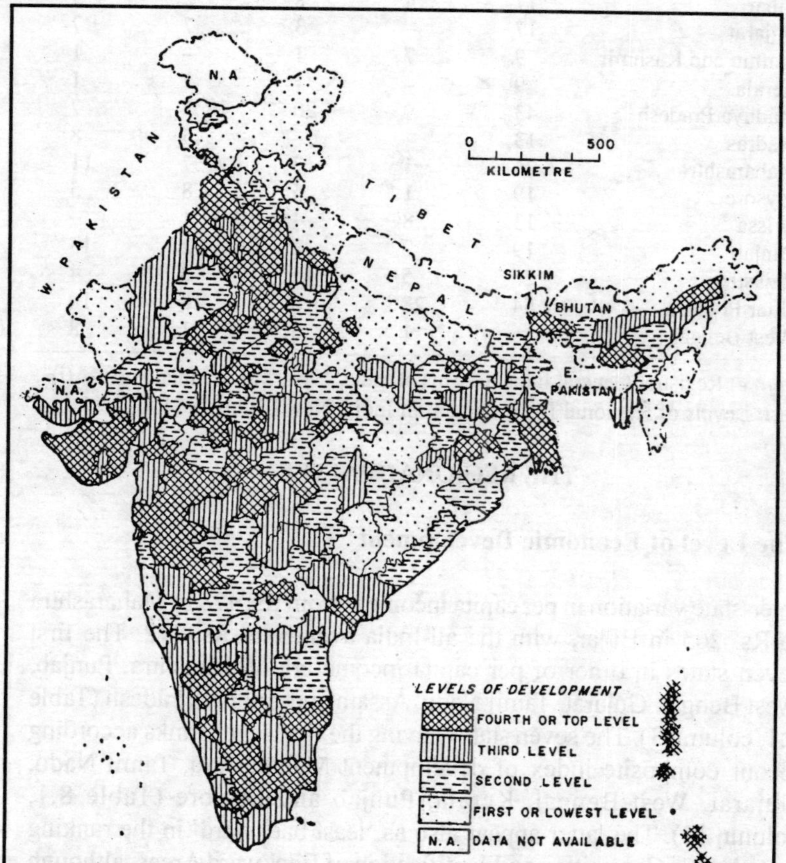

Fig. 8.1: Levels of Development.

Table 8.2: Distribution of Districts by Levels of Development in Each State

State	Total	Level of Development			
		Bottom	Second	Third	Top
1	*2*	*3*	*4*	*5*	*6*
Total	327	79	88	76	84
Andhra Pradesh	20	2	7	9	2
Assam	11	2	4	3	2
Bihar	17	4	8	2	3
Gujarat	17	–	3	7	7
Jammu and Kashmir	9	7	1	–	1
Kerala	9	–	1	7	1
Madhya Pradesh	43	9	20	7	7
Madras	13	–	–	5	8
Maharashtra	26	1	7	7	11
Mysore	19	1	5	8	5
Orissa	13	8	4	1	–
Punjab	19	2	2	2	13
Rajasthan	26	5	11	6	4
Uttar Pradesh	54	28	6	10	10
West Bengal	16	1	6	1	8

Source: Registrar General India: Census of India, 1961, Vol. I. India. Part I-A(i) *Text*: Levels of Regional Development in India, New Delhi, 1964. p. 25.

THE REGIONAL PATTERN

The Level of Economic Development

Inter-state variation in per capita income is from Rs. 478 in Maharashtra to Rs. 265 in Bihar, with the all-India average at Rs. 372. The first seven states in order of per capita income are Maharashtra, Punjab, West Bengal, Gujarat, Tamil Nadu, Assam and Andhra Pradesh (Table 8.1, column 3). The seven states having the first seven ranks according to our composite index of development Maharashtra, Tamil Nadu, Gujarat, West Bengal, Kerala, Punjab and Mysore (Table 8.1, column 11). The latter appear also as 'least backward' in the ranking done by the Committee on Identification of Backward Areas, although the ranks of individual states are somewhat different. These seven states may be considered as relatively developed, and the remaining eight states as less developed. It may be noted that the two most populous States of India, U.P. and Bihar, whose combined population formed

27.7 per cent of the all-India total in 1961, are both in the less developed group and are also near the bottom according to the ranking in Table 8.1. Further, it may be noted that six out of the seven relatively developed states, all except West Bengal, are southern or western states, while the eastern and north-central states are, with the exception of West Bengal, all in the less developed group.

The geographical distribution of states with levels of per capita income above and below the all-India average, and of relatively developed and less developed states are shown in Figs. 8.2 and 8.3. *The maps point to a dichotomy in economic development between the Western and Southern states on the one hand, and the eastern and north-central states on the other*. The dichotomy emerges more clearly from Fig. 8.1, which shows that most of the districts in the two higher levels of development—top and third—are located in the west or south of India. Indeed, it is possible to identify, in spite of some gaps, a band of relatively developed districts, which extends from Punjab in the north to Tamil Nadu and Kerala in the South. In contrast, most of the districts of the north-central and eastern states of India are at one of the two lower development levels; the map shows a solid mass of such districts, which is broken only by the relatively developed urban-industrial districts of West Bengal and Bihar, the districts of the North Bengal-Assam plain, or by an occasional city-district, as in U.P.

Growth of Population

The rate of growth of population during 1951-61 was 21.57 per cent for all India, with inter-state variation from 34.45 per cent in Assam to 9.44 per cent in Jammu and Kashmir. (Table 8.1 Col. 12) The seven relatively developed states had four of the first seven ranks according to the rate of population growth; but the highest rate was for a state of the less developed group. The coefficient of rank correlation with the index of economic development is 0.14 and is not significant at 5 per cent level.

Growth of Agricultural Output

The compound rate of growth of agricultural output during the period 1952-53 to 1964-65 was 3.01 per cent annually for India with inter-state variation from 4.56 per cent in Punjab to 1.17 per cent in Assam.

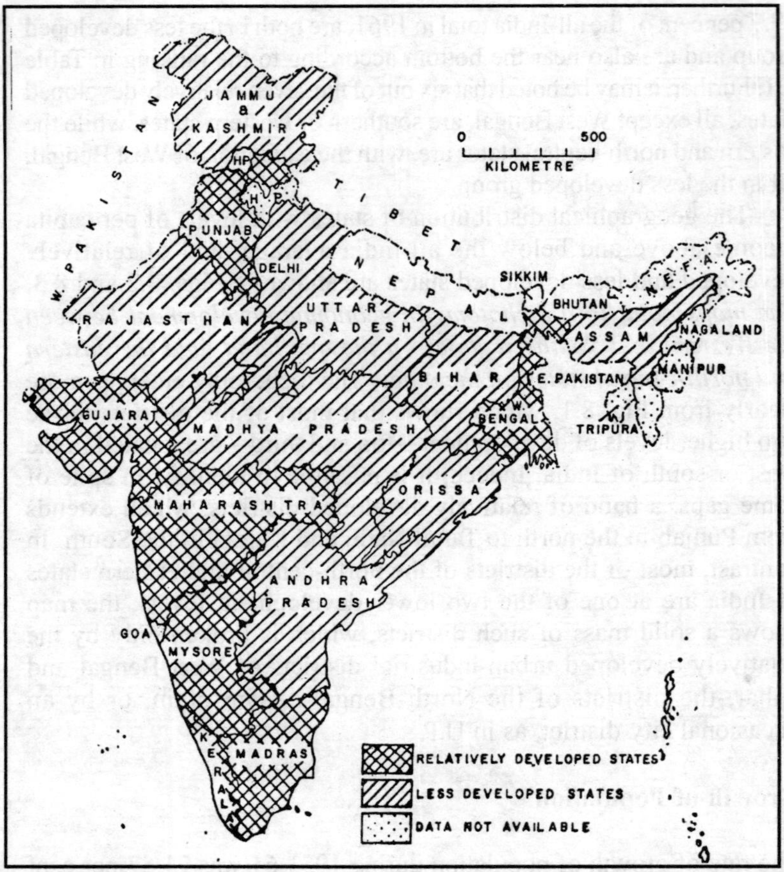

Fig. 8.2: States with Par Capita Income, above and below All India Average, 1963-66.

Five out of the 7 first ranks were among the relatively developed states but the coefficients of rank correlation with the index of economic development, 0.35, is not significant. (Table 8.1 Col 13) The geographical distribution of states having the first seven ranks according to rate of growth of agricultural output is shown in Fig. 8.4. The regional dichotomy, mentioned above, is apparent from this map also because, with the exception of Bihar, the figure for which is in doubt (Census of India 1955), all the states included among the first seven, are western or southern states.

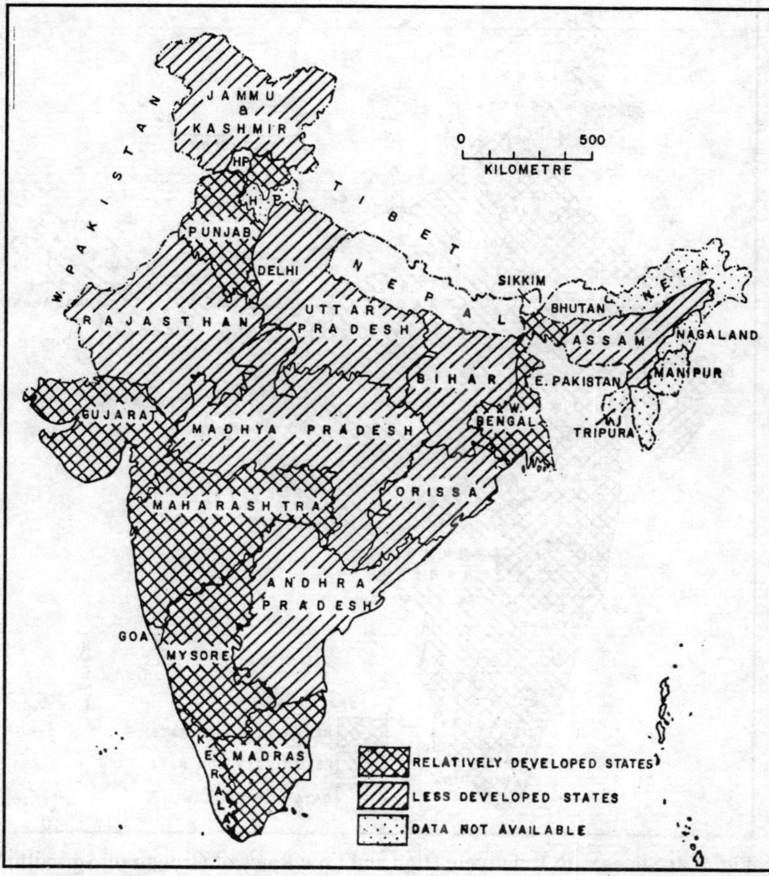

Fig. 8.3: Relatively Developed and Less Developed States.

Increase in Value added in Industry

The all-India average figure for the indicator was Rs. 28.8 with inter-state variation from Rs. 76.4 in West Bengal to Rs. 8.33 in Rajasthan. Six out of the seven first ranks were in the relatively developed states. The coefficient of rank correlation with the index of development, 0.77, is significant at 5 per cent level. Further, six of the seven first ranks were taken by western and southern states (Table 8.1 Col. 14).

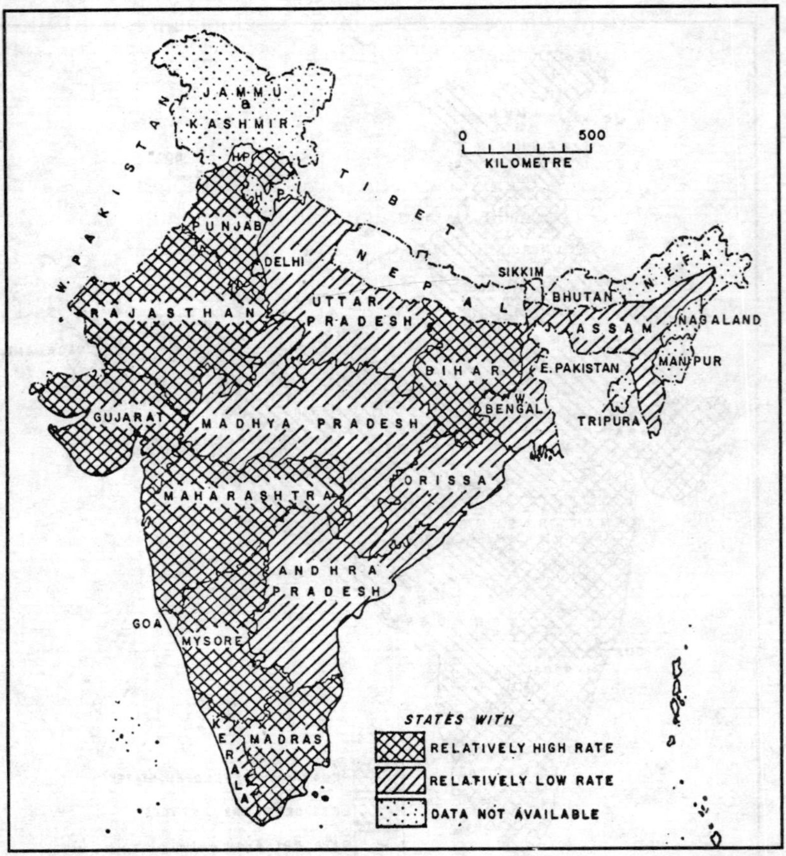

Fig. 8.4: States with Relatively High and Low Rates of Growth of Agricultural Production 1952-53 to 1964-65.

Growth of Per Capita Income

The compound rate of growth of per capita income during the decade 1955-56 to 1964-65 was 1.64 for all-India, with inter-state variation from 2.60 per cent in Bihar to 0.33 per cent in Andhra Pradesh. The high figure for Bihar may be ignored because it is related to deficiencies in data on agricultural output in the base year. Excluding it, the rates were 2 per cent or lower for all states, with rates for 8 states ranging between 1 and 2 per cent. The relatively developed states again had six out of the 7 first ranks, but the coefficient of the rank correlation with index of economic development is 0.40 and is again not significant (Table 8.1 col. 15).

A Regional Dichotomy in Development and Growth

The above analysis points to emergence of a dichotomy in economic development between the western and southern regions of India on the one hand, and the eastern and north-central regions on the other: the dichotomy is noticeable in state-level analysis, but is brought out more clearly by district-level analysis. Regional analysis of growth trends is handicapped by limitations of data—the deficiencies of data on growth of per capita income are particularly serious. Moreover, a time-span of 10-15 years is too small to arrive at meaningful conclusions on growth. Even so, it is noteworthy that most of the western and southern states had higher rates of both growth of agricultural output and increase in value added in industry, than most of the eastern or north-central states.

The next step would be to correlate the regional patterns of economic development and growth with various physical and socio-economic variables in order to identify the variables which have the most influence on the patterns. Such correlation will be of interest to geographers, other social scientists and development planners; but it is outside the scope of this paper which is aimed primarily at identifying the patterns. A few comments may be made however, in passing and only to indicate the need for further work in this extremely interesting field. First, most mountainous or hilly districts, in the Himalaya and in Peninsular India, are at the bottom or second level of development, indicating the unfavourable influence of mountain or hill topography on development (Fig. 8.1). Second, the majority of the districts at the two higher development levels—top and third—are in the 40—100 cm. annual rainfall zone. The north-south band of relatively developed districts, to which reference has been made above, is located almost entirely west of the 100 cm. rainfall line, and indeed has approximately the same location as the "famine and scarcity belt" of India, which had been identified by British Indian administrators on basis of experience of famines and scarcities for over 150 years before Independence (Census of India, 1955). Why the relatively dry regions of India, which were subject to frequent famine and scarcity until recently, should appear as relatively developed while most of the Gangetic Plain which has much more favourable conditions of moisture, soil and crop-security, and the mineral rich region of Bihar-Orissa-East Madhya Pradesh (the coal-steel belt of India) should appear less developed, is a question which deserves careful investigation. The explanations appears to be primarily socio-cultural and historical. Most parts of the Gangetic plain had the *Zamindari* system of land tenure which is known to have been more exploitative and initiative-inhibiting than the peasant-proprietor-like tenures, which prevailed in the western and southern states. The mineral-rich region has a large population of backward, tribal people and its resources have not yet been developed adequately: indeed, significant industrialisation, which could raise economic levels within the region appreciably began only in the late 1950s. It may be mentioned in this connection that a correlation analysis made by the author of the rates of growth of agricultural output and productivity in 14 states of India during 1952-53 to 1964-65 with rainfall, irrigation and various other socio-economic variables showed significant correlations, only with indices of urbanisation and social development (Nath, 1969). It is interesting to mention also that the historical rates of growth of agricultural output have also been lower in the eastern and north-central regions than in the western and southern ones: Blyn's analysis of agricultural growth rates during the period 1891-92 to 1946-47 shows significantly lower rates for the United Provinces and Greater Bengal than for Greater Punjab, Bombay-Sind and Madras (Blyn, 1966). Comparative data for selected provinces of British India, for the period 1891-92 to 1946-47 and the states of the Indian Union for the period 1952-53 to 1964-65 are given in Table 8.3, in order to bring out the regional patterns of agricultural growth rate in the two periods. It is true that the data for individual provinces/states for the two periods are not strictly comparable, because of extensive boundary changes after Independence. But the broad similarity in the regional patterns in the two periods deserves to be noted. It would be interesting, of course, to undertake a more detailed analysis for districts whose boundaries have not changed since 1891-92, delineate regional growth patterns more precisely, and bring out continuity or discontinuities in them. Such an analysis would be similar to the analysis of growth of population and cropped area during 1891-1951, undertaken for 61 districts whose boundaries had not changed during the period for the 1951 Census Report and may produce equally interesting results: the Census analysis had led to the interesting conclusion about decline of cultivation per capita only after 1921.

Table 8.3: Rates of Growth of population and crop output British India 1891-92 to 1946-47 and Indian Union 1952-53 to 1964-65

British India and Regions 1891-92 to 1946-47[1] *Average trend rate of change per year 10 reference decades*					*Indian Union and States*[2] *Rates of Growth: (Compound per year)*				
Region	*Population*	*All crops*	*Food-grains*	*Non-foodgrains*	*States*	*Population (Decade 1951-61)*	*All crops*	*Food-grains*	*Non-foodgrains*
British India	0.67	0.37	0.11	1.31	Indian Union	21.50	3.01	2.50	3.99
Greater Bengal	0.65	–0.45	–0.73	0.23	West Bengal	32.79	1.94	1.14	3.77
United Provinces	0.40	0.42	0.35	0.92	Bihar	19.78	2.97	3.05	2.40
Madras	0.80	0.98	0.42	2.37	Uttar Pradesh	16.60	1.66	0.85	3.61
Greater Punjab	0.93	1.57	1.10	2.40	Madras	11.85	4.17	4.17	4.17
Bombay-Sind	0.71	0.86	0.27	1.44	Andhra Pradesh	15.65	2.71	3.21	1.60
Central Provinces	0.58	0.48	0.29	0.97	Maharashtra	23.60	2.93	2.20	4.38

Source: 1. Blyn 1966 Tables 5.2 and 5.8.
2. Ministry of Food Agriculture 1966 page 29.

CONCLUSION

This analysis should be regarded as preliminary and the findings highly tentative. The principal handicap is limitation of data, and it is hoped that it will be reduced progressively. For state-level analysis, more adequate and reliable data on growth of per capita income are urgently needed. But since state-level analysis is not adequate for precise delineation of the regional patterns of economic development or growth, it is necessary (i) to make estimate of district income as early as possible, and (ii) to continue, expand and improve in the Censuses, the work on levels of development of districts which was begun in 1961.

APPENDIX I

The indicators of the Working Group were:

(i) per capita income, average of 1963-64 to 1965-66;
(ii) contribution of industry and mining to per capita income;
(iii) industrial workers engaged in registered factories, per lakh of population, 1966;
(iv) per capita annual consumption of electricity;
(v) length of surface roads in kilometres per lakh of population;
(vi) per 100 sq. kilometres of area;
(vii) length of railway line in kilometres per lakh of populations;
(viii) per 100 sq. kilometres of area.

The ranking of states in order of economic development, made by the Working Group is given below.

Reverse of ranking in order of industrial backwardness:

Rank No.	*State*
1.	West Bengal
2.	Tamil Nadu
3.	Gujarat
4.	Maharashtra
5.	Punjab
6.	Haryana
7.	Mysore
8.	Kerala
9.	Andhra Pradesh
10.	Bihar
11.	Rajasthan
12.	Madhya Pradesh
13.	Assam
14.	Uttar Pradesh

(*Contd.*)

Rank No.	State
15.	Orissa
16.	Jammu & Kashmir
17.	Nagaland

NOTE

1. *National Geographical Journal of India*", Vol. XVI, Part III-IV. September-December, 1970.

REFERENCES

Beckerman, W., "International Comparison of Real Incomes." *Development Center of the Organization for Economic Cooperation and Development*, Paris, 1966.

Bennet, M.K., "International Disparities in Conception Levels." *The American Economic Review*, XLI September 1951.

Blyn, G., *Agricultural Trends in India, 1891-92 to 1946-47*. University of Pennsylvania Press, Philadelhpia, 1966.

Brian Barry, *Atlas of Economic Development*, Chicago 1961, Part VII.

Census of India 1951, Publication, Appendices to the Census Report (Vol. I India Part 1-13) Manager of Publications, Delhi, 1955.

Census of India, 1961, Vol. 1, India Part I (A-I) Text. "Levels of Regional Development", New Delhi 1964.

Census of India, Vol. I Part I-A Report, Manager of Publications, Delhi, 1954, ch. IV.

Central Statistical Organization, "Estimates of Total and Per Capita Net Domestic Product for Different States."

Fourth Five Year Plan, 1969-74, Draft, 1969.

Friedmann, J. and Alonso, W., *Regional Development and Planning—A Reader*, The MIT Press, Combridge, London, 1965.

Ginsburg, N., *Atlas of Economic Development Part III,* The University of Chicago Press, Chicago, Part III, 1961.

Hirschman, A.O., *The Strategy of Economic Development*, Yale, 1961.

Ministry of Food and Agriculture; Economic and Statistical Adviser, "Growth Rates in Agriculture 1949-50 to 1964-65". New Delhi, March 1966, (Mimeographed).

Nath, V., "Regional Development in Indian Planning." *Economic and Political Weekly*, Bombay, Vol. V. Nos. 3, 4 and 5. Annual Number Jan. 1970, pp. 247-260.

Nath, V., "Growth of Indian Agriculture–A Regional Analysis." *The Geographical Review*, New York, Vol. 50 No. 3, July 1969, pp. 348-72.

National Council of Applied Economic Research, New Delhi, "Inter-District and Inter-State Income Differentials 1955-56." Occasional Papers No. 6, 1963.

Planning Commission: Government of India.

—— Report of the Working Group, "Identification of Backward Areas", New Delhi; February 1969.

Sharma, P.S., "A Note on Agricultural Workers in 1961 Census." Census of India 1961, Paper No. 1 of 1962 Registrar General of India, New Delhi, 1963, Appendix III.

Third five Year Plan, 1961.

United Nations Institute of Research in Social Development: *"The Level of Living Index"*, Geneva, September 1966.

Zimmerman, L.J., *Poor Lands, Richland—The Widening Gap,* Random House, New York, 1965.

9

Regional Disparities in Economic and Social Development in India[1]

INTRODUCTION

This chapter advances the hypothesis that there are five macro regions in India among which there are striking differences in physiographic and agro-climatic conditions, availability or otherwise of natural resources, economic motivations of the people and consequent differences in levels of economic and social development and per capita income.

A second hypothesis is that these differences are due in large part to trends in economic, industrial, agricultural and social development during the last half a century as a result of which some of the states which were backward earlier are now among the most developed. The differences have developed largely on account of the ways in which people of different regions have availed or failed to avail of the opportunities for economic development that have arisen on account of investment plans and economic or social policies of the governments of India and of the states and technological changes in agriculture, industries or services sectors. The propensity to migrate to other parts of India or abroad in pursuit of higher income and policies of the state governments to promote or fail to promote economic development or social change have been factors in influencing the rates of economic development and social change in different states and regions.

The five macro-regions are:

1. *Southern India*: Comprising the states of Tamil Nadu, Andhra Pradesh, Karnataka and Kerala and the union territory of Pondicherry.

2. *Western India*: Comprising the states of Maharashtra, Gujarat and Goa and the Union territories of Daman, Diu and Dadra-Nagar Haveli.
3. *North-western India*: Comprising the states of Punjab and Haryana, the National Capital Territory of Delhi and a strip of land 100-150 kilometres in width extending from Dehra Doon in the north to Gautam Buddh Nagar and Buland Shahr in the south in western Uttar Pradesh.
4. *North Central and Eastern India*: Comprising the rest of Uttar Pradesh, north and south Bihar, West Bengal and coastal Orissa.
5. *Central India*: Comprising Madhya Pradesh, inland Orissa, Chhotanagpur region of Bihar and forested areas of Maharashtra, Gujarat and south eastern Rajasthan. Agro-climatic conditions in Rajasthan vary from forested hills and valleys in the south to well watered plain in the centre to semi-desert and desert in the west.
6. *Not classified*: Assam and the seven hill states of the north east, with large populations of tribal people; Himachal Pradesh and Jammu and Kashmir.

I. Southern India

Tamil Nadu, Andhra Pradesh, Karnataka, Kerala and Pondicherry are included in it.

These states have higher levels than the national averages of:

(i) Proportion of urban/total population (Table 9.1),
(ii) Proportion of workers in factories/proportion of population (Table 9.2),
(iii) High yields of principal crops—rice, sugarcane and cotton in the principal producing areas,
(iv) Higher average and female literacy rates than the national averages (Table 9.1),
(v) Lower and falling rates of population growth than the national averages (Table 9.1),
(vi) Higher proportion of electrified villages than the national averages (Table 9.6), and
(vii) Lower proportions of population below poverty line than the national average (Table 9.4).

Table 9.1: Rates of Population Growth, Literacy and Infant Mortality

State and Region	*Population (millions)*	*Population Growth*			*Literacy (1991)*		*Mortality (1996)*
		Growth Rate of Population		*Per cent of urban population*	*Average Literacy rate (%)*	*Female Literacy rate (%)*	*Infant mortality rate (per 1000 children)*
		1971-81	*1981-91*	*1991*			
1	*2*	*3*	*4*	*5*	*6*	*7*	*8*
I. Southern Region							
Andhra Pradesh	66.3	23.1	23.8	26.9	45.1	33.7	66
Karnataka	44.8	26.8	20.7	30.9	56.0	44.3	53
Kerala	29.0	19.2	14.0	26.4	90.6	87.0	13
Tamil Nadu	55.9	17.5	15.0	22.0	63.7	52.3	54
II. Western Region							
Goa	1.17	26.7	16.0	41.0	77.0	68.2	n.a.
Gujarat	41.2	27.7	20.8	34.5	60.9	48.5	62
Maharashtra	78.3	24.5	25.4	38.7	63.0	50.5	48
III. North Western Region							
Punjab	20.2	23.9	20.3	29.5	57.1	49.7	57
Haryana	16.3	28.8	26.3	24.6	5.3	40.9	68
Delhi	9.4	55.5	51.6	889.9	76.1	68.0	–
IV. North Central and Eastern Region							
Bihar	86.4	24.0	22.4	13.1	38.5	23.1	72

(Contd.)

Table 9.1: (*Contd.*)

State and Region	*Population (millions)*	*Population Growth*			*Literacy (1991)*		*Mortality (1996)*
		Growth Rate of Population		*Per cent of urban population*	*Average Literacy rate (%)*	*Female Literacy rate (%)*	*Infant mortality rate (per 1000 children)*
		1971-81	*1981-91*	*1991*			
1	*2*	*3*	*4*	*5*	*6*	*7*	*8*
Orissa	31.7	20.1	20.2	13.4	48.6	34.4	95
Uttar Pradesh	139.0	25.5	25.2	19.8	41.7	26.0	85
West Bengal	6.0	23.2	24.6	28.5	57.7	47.2	55
V. Hilly, Forested and Desert							
Madhya Pradesh	66.1	25.3	26.8	23.2	43.5	28.19	97
Rajasthan	43.7	33.0	28.0	22.9	38.8	20.8	86
VI. Not Classified							
Assam	22.3	23.6	23.6	11.1	53.4	43.7	75
Himachal Pradesh	5.1	23.7	19.4	8.7	63.5	52.5	62
Jammu & Kashmir	7.7	29.6	23.5	23.8	n.a.	n.a.	–
Al India	84.3	24.7	23.5	25.7	52.1	39.4	72

Sources:

Cols. 2 to 4: Census of India 1991: Paper No. 1, Provisional Population Totals, Census Commissioner and Registrar General of India, New Delhi.

Col. 5: Tata Consultancy Services: Statistical outline of India 1998-99, Mumbai, Table 93, p. 51.

Cols. 6 & 7: Census of India, 1991, Paper No. 1. Provisional Population Totals, Registrar General and Census Commissioner, India, p. 62.

Col. 8: Tata Consultancy Services: Statistical outline of India 1998-99, Mumbai, Table 93, p. 15.

Yields of the principal food crop-rice have increased significantly since the early 1970s as a result of extensive use of dwarf, very high yielding varieties of rice, produced under conditions of assured and adequate water supply along with judicious use of organic manure, chemical fertilisers, pesticides and improved implements. The irrigated areas have increased progressively partly due to more efficient use of water from canals from the principal rivers and partly due to extensive use of electric or diesel driven pumps on wells.

Table 9.2: Population of workers in factory industries and Proportion of population of all India in selected states

Region and states	*Proportion in factory industries in state (per cent) in 1995-96*	*Proportion of value added in factory industries (per cent)*	*Proportion of population/ national total (per cent in 1991)*
I. Southern Region			
Andhra Pradesh	11.8	7.0	8.0
Karnataka	5.1	4.8	5.3
Tamil Nadu	12.3	10.2	6.6
II. Western Region			
Gujarat	9.5	12.6	4.9
Maharashtra	15.1	23.7	9.3
III. North Western Region			
Punjab	4.7	2.9	2.4
Haryana	N.A.	N.A.	2.0
IV. North Central and Eastern Region			
Bihar	3.3	3.8	10.2
Uttar Pradesh	8.9	8.4	16.3
West Bengal	8.2	4.7	8.0

Source: Tata Consultancy Service: Statistical Outline of India 1998-99, Mumbai 1998, p. 88. Percentages calculated from absolute figures.

Yields of sugarcane and cotton, the other important crops of the three states (excluding Kerala) have also been increasing progressively due to extension of irrigation, use of improved varieties of seed and better farm management. Increase in yields of plantation crops in Kerala has been less noteworthy.

A number of large cities, Chennai and Coimbatore in Tamil Nadu, Hyderabad and Visakhapatnam in Andhra Pradesh, Bangalore and Mangalore in Karnataka and Kochi in Kerala have emerged as major industrial centres. Employment in factory industries has increased progressively as new factories have located in the environs of these centres. The industries range from production of processed foods, textiles (in Coimbatore and Mysore), garments, a variety of consumer goods, consumer durables (refrigerators, air conditioners, TV receivers, electrically operated kitchen gadgets and motor vehicles) to building materials. The latest addition in all the three states except Kerala are information technology industries. Bangalore is the principal centre of these industries, the turnover of which is in billions of dollars and is increasing rapidly. Chennai and Hyderabad are also emerging as centres of the I.T. industries.

Tamil Nadu

The environs of Chennai have been favoured since the 1960s for location of factories manufacturing motor vehicles—trucks, buses, passenger cars, motor bicycles and scooters. Two factories, one for manufacture of buses and trucks and the other for manufacture of two-wheelers were established in the late 1950s. Their capacity has increased steadily. A Korean company has established in the 1990s a factory for manufacture of passenger cars in a suburb of Chennai.

Coimbatore is the centre of cotton textile industry which developed there following production of high quality cotton in the area irrigated by a canal from Pykara river. It is now a multi-industry centre with manufacture of textile, garments and textile machinery as the principal industries.

Chennai benefited greatly from the flight of capital from Kolkata in the late 1960s due to militancy of trade unions in Kolkata. Its principal advantage is a disciplined labour force, willing and able to learn industrial skills quickly and free from militant trade unionism. Furthermore, because of location closest to Singapore and Hong Kong, it is likely to be favoured as an industrial centre for establishment of industries by Singapore and Hong Kong based Indian industrialists.

Just over half of the cropped area in Tamil Nadu is unirrigated and the subsistence farmers produce sorghum or millets as the food crops and oil seeds, preferably groundnut as the cash crop. But there are pockets of prosperity in the lands, irrigated by Kaveri river and in the areas irrigated by wells fitted with electric or diesel driven pumps in which high yield rice is the principal crop. Sugarcane is a second crop in and around Coimbatore.

Although Chennai and Coimbatore are the principal industrial centres in the state, there are smaller centres such as Madurai, Tiruchirapally and Salem. The principal cottage industry is weaving of cotton and silk textiles by handloom and power looms. The state government has taken effective measures since the 1950s for protection of these industries on which millions of poor handloom weavers depend for their livelihood. As a result cotton and silk sarees made in Tamil Nadu have a ready market all over India. Certain kinds of handloom cloth have an export market also.

The values of most of the indicators of social development are higher than the national averages and have been rising steadily. Growth rate of population and infant mortality rate are lower than the national level and have been falling. Adult and female literacy rates are higher than the national average. However per capita income and proportion of population below the poverty line are close to national averages (Tables 9.3 and 9.4). A part of the reason for industrial development in the state is that the state government has since the 1960s taken effective measures to promote it.

The educated Tamil Brahmins, deprived of opportunities for white collar jobs in their home state have since the late 1920s been migrating to work in these jobs in Delhi, Mumbai, Kolkata and other large cities. They are also among the top ranking professionals – lawyers (jurists), physicians, teachers and scientists. In recent years, large numbers have joined as executives in Indian public sector and private companies as well as Indian branches of multinational companies. The best among them, have risen to the highest positions in all these fields. The latest trend among Tamil Nadu and Bangalore-based software specialists is to migrate to the Silicon Valley in California, the largest centre of information technology industries in the U.S.A., in which salaries for software specialists are much higher than in India.

Karnataka

Bangalore, the capital of Karnataka is today one of the fastest growing industrial centres in India. The industries located in and around it include:

(i) Hindustan Aircraft, established during Second World War for servicing and repair of aircraft which has diversified into manufacture of small trainer aircraft;
(ii) Manufacture of telephone receivers and other telecommunication equipment;
(iii) Manufacture of a variety of consumer goods and consumer durables—from textiles and garments to air conditioners;
(iv) Manufacture of precision machine tools and watches;
(v) Computer software and other information technology industries; and
(vi) Manufacture (or assembling initially from imported kits but progressively from domestically manufactured components) of passenger cars and heavy trucks for the regional and national markets.

The initial advantages of the city were a salubrious climate and well developed infrastructures (it was once a city of gardens) and a disciplined labour force. These have largely disappeared and it is now a busy, highly polluted city with serious deficiencies of infrastructures (adequate water supply, well maintained roads and an international class airport). The presence of two institutes of science and of a large number of men and women trained in the sciences has led to development of computer software and other information technology industries from the 1970s. The turnover of these industries is in hundreds of millions of dollars and is increasing by the year (Table 9.2-A).

Table 9.2-A: Electronics production profile

	1993-94	*1997-98*
Electronic hardware (in crore Rs)	14,070	22,100.0
Increase (per cent per year)		14.5
Computer software (in crore Rs)	15,785	32,070.0
Increase (per cent per year)		25.5

Source: Tata Consultancy Services: Statistical Outline of India, 1998/99, Table 80, p. 79.

The strip of about 175 kilometres between Bangalore and Mysore city is well irrigated from a canal from the river Kaveri. It produces large crops of rice and high yield sugarcane and has a number of rice and sugar mills. Climatic conditions are most suitable for rearing of silk worms on mulberry leaves. This has led to rearing of silk worms and weaving of silk cloth as remunerative cottage industries. Mysore city has a large mill manufacturing silk textiles. Thus, there is a sizeable class of people of middle income groups—professionals and white collar workers, well paid skilled industrial workers and well-to-do farmers among which there is a large market for manufactured consumer goods and consumer durables—from processed foods through refrigerators and air conditioners to two-wheeler scooters and passenger cars.

Another emerging industrial centre in Karnataka is Mangalore situated along the south-west coast. It is a port and has a petroleum refinery. The uplands between Karnataka and Kerala have plantations of coffee and tea. While the planters are rich, the workers in the estates are poor.

The rest of Karnataka is poor and backward. Rainfall is low and variable. Millets, cotton and oilseeds are the principal crops but yields vary with the vagaries of the monsoon. There are few industries. The values of most of the indicators of social development are not very high. Per capita income, growth rate of population, the proportion of workers in factory industries/proportion of national population, adult and female literacy rates, infant mortality rate and proportions of villages having access to electricity and safe and adequate drinking water are somewhat higher or at par with national averages.

Kerala

Kochi with a deep water harbour, a ship yard and a naval base, a petroleum refinery and an international air port is the largest industrial centre in Kerala. There is a high propensity to migrate to the Gulf countries in Kerala, south west Karnataka and Goa. These areas receive several thousand million dollars every year in remittances from migrants. The remittances have helped the families of migrants to raise their level of living and improve, enlarge or rebuild the family house and/or farm. The migrants use a variety of imported consumer durables. But the demand for them has not led to development of industries manufacturing them. There is large migration of residents of Kerala, South West Karnataka and Goa to work as white collar workers in Mumbai, Delhi and various cities in South India. Nurses from Kerala work in hospitals in India and abroad. Thousands of educated women work as teachers in schools run by churches throughout India. However, remittances home of these workers have also not sparked significant industrial development in the state. The industries in Kerala remain confined to handloom weaving, processing of coir, cashewnut (locally grown or imported) and shell fish for export and domestic consumption and manufacture of brassware. The reasons for lack of industrial development in the state need to be investigated.

Production of rice and the plantation crops of Kerala—coconuts, rubber, coffee and spices has been increasing steadily but not spectacularly. Kerala has also a large potential for development of winter tourism. Its sunny, storm-free beaches, good rail and air connections with the rest of India and two airports are its main attractions. Its handicrafts could have a large market among domestic and foreign tourists.

The values of indicators of social development—adult and female literacy rate, growth rate of population, infant mortality rate, proportion of villages having electricity and located within 2 kilometres of motorable road are very high in Kerala and only marginally lower in Goa and Mangalore. Indeed Kerala has been held up as a model state by the UNDP in having achieved high values of social development despite not having very high per capita income.

Andhra Pradesh

There is a large number of rice and sugar mills in coastal Andhra Pradesh. The region receives dependable irrigation from canals from Godavari and Krishna rivers. Some areas in coastal Andhra Pradesh are the principal producers in the country of flue cured tobacco which is used in manufacture of cigarettes. Large quantities are exported and the rest is used in manufacture of cigarettes within India. Hyderabad has a large factory manufacturing cigarettes. Other factories are located in various other cities in different regions of India.

Hyderabad, the capital of Andhra Pradesh, is the principal industrial centre in the state. It has in its environs, a number of defence related industries, a factory of Bharat Heavy Electricals, an undertaking of the Government of India which manufactures machinery for generation, transmission and distribution of electricity; machine tools, refrigerators and other consumer durables.

Visakhapatnam in the extreme north-east, on the border with Orissa is the other industrial centre in Andhra Pradesh. It has a shipyard and a large steel mill. However, it is too far from the rest of Andhra Pradesh to have much impact on its economy.

Values of most of the indicators of economic or social development—growth rate of population, literacy rate, female literacy rate, infant mortality rate, per capita income, proportion of population below the poverty line, percentage of villages electrified or within two kilometres of motorable road are not high. One reason for this is that Telengana, which constitutes more than half of Andhra Pradesh, is a backward region.

II. Western India

Maharashtra, Gujarat and Goa and Union Territories of Daman, Diu and Dadra-Nagar Haveli form this region.

Maharashtra and Gujarat are the most industrialised states in India. They have 25 per cent of the population but 36 per cent of the employment in factory industries (Table 9.2). Both states benefited from flight of capital from the Kolkata Metropolitan District (including both Kolkata and Howrah) in the late 1960s due to militancy of trade unions in the CMD. In this period, many non-Bengali owners and managers of factories had to go through a period when they were harassed and felt unsafe. Many Gujarati entrepreneurs closed their factories in the CMD to reopen them in coastal Gujarat or in the environs of Mumbai.

Coastal Gujarat has been called an industrial workshop. The factories located in it include manufacture of textiles, garments, a large variety of machine tools, various consumer goods, consumer durables, and pharmaceutical drugs. The discovery of crude oil off its coast has led to establishment of petroleum refineries and factories manufacturing petrochemicals, synthetic yarn and various goods made of plastics. The area benefited from return of Gujarati traders from the East African countries—Uganda, Tanzania and Kenya—in the 1960s and the 1970s. They started manufacturing a variety of machine tools and other goods. The development of dairying to supply liquid milk to Mumbai and manufacture of dairy products (butter, cheese and baby food) has led to emergence of a sizeable class of well to do farmers among which there is a sizeable market for consumer durables.

The other parts of Gujarat, Saurashtra and Kutch are relatively poor and backward. Most of the cropland is unirrigated and production of the principal crops-sorghum and millets for food and groundnuts and cotton as cash crops—varies greatly with the adequacy and timeliness of rain from the summer monsoon. However, completion of the Sardar Sarovar dam on the Narmada river in Madhya Pradesh will lead to a major increase in the irrigated area and in agricultural output in Saurashtra. The recent completion of India's largest petroleum refinery and petrochemical plant located at Jam Nagar on the coast of Saurashtra could lead to growth of industries processing petrochemicals and goods made of plastics including textiles and garments. Industrial development in the duty-free export zone located at Kandla port on the coast of Saurashtra would also receive a major stimulus with the completion of the refinery.

Maharashtra

Maharashtra is the most industrialised state in India. Most of the industries in it are located in the environs of Mumbai (including New Mumbai and Thane), in Pune and in towns located along the rail-cum-road strip of 175 kilometres between the two cities and Nasik. Textile mills established since the 1870s are still important. A number of them are closed; others have diversified to manufacture cloth using mixtures of cotton or wool with polyester fibre. The proprietors of several mills which have closed have established power loom clusters in New Mumbai and Thane. Cost of production in them is much lower than in integrated spinning and weaving mills because of lower costs of land and labour.

Western Maharashtra is a major producer of sugarcane with high sucrose content and high yield per hectare of land producing the cane. Production is concentrated in valleys of several small streams that flow from the western Ghats to the sea. The establishment of sugar mills in the towns located in these valleys has led to establishment of enterprises for manufacture or repair of sugar mill machinery.

The industries located in Mumbai and its environs include besides textiles, machine tools, garments, cosmetics, consumer durables including passenger cars, light commercial vehicles and trucks and office and hospital furniture. The factory for manufacturing passenger cars was established in the late 1950s; that for manufacturing light commercial vehicles and trucks was established in the 1960s. Mumbai is the largest producer of films and television serials in India. Although employment and value added in the industry is difficult to estimate, there is little doubt about the large size of both.

There is a high propensity to emigrate to the Gulf countries in Goa and to Britain, the U.S.A. and Canada among the people of Gujarat. Mumbai is and is expected to remain the biggest financial centre in India. It has the best and busiest port in India. The building of another harbour at Uran on the mainland and improvement of the port of Marmagoa located in Goa have added to the freight handling capacity along the west coast.

Table 9.3: Per capita net state Domestic product at factor Cost at Current prices in 1996-97

States and Regions	*Rs. (00)*
I. Southern Region	
Andhra Pradesh	99
Karnataka	103
Kerala	91
Tamil Nadu	112
II. Western Region	
Goa	197
Gujarat	139
Maharashtra	173
III. North Western Region	
Punjab	182
Haryana	162
Delhi	198
IV. North Central and Eastern Region	
Bihar	38
Orissa	64
Uttar Pradesh	67
West Bengal	94
V. Hilly Forested and Desert	
Madhya Pradesh	74
Rajasthan	85
VI. Not Classified	
Assam	66
Himachal Pradesh	99
Jammu & Kashmir	74
Al India	109

Source: *Economic and Political Weekly*, Research Foundation; National Accounts Statistics of India, 1950-51, 1996-97, Mumbai, 1998, p. 84.

Goa is not an industrial centre at present. But with development of the port of Marmagoa and construction of the Konkan railway which provides it access to Konkan, western Maharashtra and eastern Karnataka, it has the potential for industrial development in the foreseeable future.

Pune is the second largest city and industrial centre in Maharashtra. The industries located in it include manufacture of machine tools, motor vehicles, defence related industries and manufacture by the Kirloskars of pumps for lifting water from wells and compressors for air conditioners and refrigerators, and manufacture of passenger cars and trucks. A large number of Mumbai-based industrialists have established their factories in New Mumbai, Thane and in towns located along the 170 kilometres rail-cum-road strip between Mumbai and Pune to avail of lower costs of land and labour than in either of the two cities.

Development of horticulture – grapes, mosambi oranges, onions and other vegetables in several districts of western Maharashtra has added a sizeable class of prosperous farmers who produce sugar cane or fruit and vegetables. The latter are sent all over India and also to the Gulf countries. Thus, western Maharashtra which was once a poverty stricken, famine prone area in which relief works had to be undertaken from time to time to avert starvation until the 1960s has been transformed during the last 3 decades into a prosperous agro-industrial region.

The other parts of Maharashtra—Vidharbha and Marathwada have little industrial development. Cotton, millets and oil seeds are the principal crops. There is little development of irrigation so that most of the farmers are poor subsistence farmers. The stated policy of the state government is to decentralise location of industries away from the Mumbai-Pune region to Vidharbha and Marathwada. However, the policy has not been implemented effectively so that these regions remain industrially under-developed.

The region around Nagpur is the principal centre for growing loose jacket oranges (tangerines) which are sent all over India. Fruit processing is a well established industry in the city. It could become a centre for producing a variety of consumer goods and consumer durables for regional market. It has suffered in recent years by poor rail or air communications with the other large cities and neglect of industrial development by the state government.

The values of indicators of social development are not so high in Gujarat and Maharashtra but are rising. Most of the villages are electrified. Adult and female literacy rates are rising. Rates of population growth are high and there is no indication of their decline. Further, the proportion of cropland irrigated is low.

Goa

Values of indicators of social development are high in Goa. Overall literacy and female literacy rates are the second highest among Indian states. The rate of population growth is only marginally higher than in Kerala. Almost all villages are within 2 kilometres of a motorable road, are electrified and have access to safe and adequate water supply. Goa has also a large tourism industry. Both Indian and foreign tourists flock to its sunny beaches in the winter. The music and dances of its population, influenced greatly by the Portuguese, are a major attraction for foreign and domestic tourists.

Table 9.4: Proportion of population below the poverty line – 1993-94

State and Region	*Population below poverty line*
I. Southern Region	
Andhra Pradesh	22.2
Karnataka	33.2
Kerala	25.4
Tamil Nadu	35.0
II. Western Region	
Goa	14.9
Gujarat	24.2
Maharashtra	36.9
III. North Central and Eastern Region	
Bihar	55.0
Orissa	48.6
Uttar Pradesh	40.9
West Bengal	35.7
IV. Hilly Forested and Desert	
Madhya Pradesh	42.5
Rajasthan	27.4
V. Not Classified	
Assam	40.9
Himachal Pradesh	28.4
Jammu & Kashmir	n.a.
Al India	36.0

Source: Tata Consultancy Services: Statistical Outline of India 1998-99, Mumbai, 1998, p. 213.

III. North Western India

The region includes the states of Punjab and Haryana, the National Capital Territory of Delhi and tract 100-150 kilometres in breadth extending from Dehra Doon in the north to Bulandshahr in the south in western Uttar Pradesh.

The region has high levels of agricultural production because of extensive development of irrigation from canals, tube wells and shallow wells fitted with electric or diesel pumps. Wheat, rice and fodder crops in Punjab and Haryana and, in addition to these, sugarcane and oil seeds in western Uttar Pradesh are the principal crops. Completion of the Bhakra-Nangal irrigation-cum-power project greatly increased the irrigated area in Haryana and to a lesser extent in Punjab.

Agricultural output in the entire region has increased rapidly from the late 1960s due to use of very high yielding varieties of dwarf seed of wheat and rice along with chemical fertilizers, pesticides, improved ploughs and power driven implements including mechanical threshers and tractors. The region has the best milch animals in India which are fed on nutritious fodder crops grown in the summer. It is a large producer of milk and dairy products which are consumed however within the region itself.

Industrial development received a big boost in Punjab in the late 1950s when large supplies of electricity began to be available with completion of the Nangal part of the Bhakra-Nangal project. The government of the state actively assisted local entrepreneurs and those returning home with capital accumulated through stay in Thailand and Malaysia to establish small, medium and large sized industrial units in different cities of the state. Ludhiana, which has an enormous number of factories manufacturing or repairing farm implements, machine tools and consumer durables, motor bicycles, etc.—is the largest industrial city in the state. Production in its woollen hosiery industry, established since 1920s, has increased rapidly to meet increasing domestic and foreign demand. Exports from the late 1950s to the late 1980s were mainly to the Soviet Union.

Amritsar, which has a large mill manufacturing carpets and woollen textiles is another large industrial centre. Kapurthala has a factory manufacturing precision machine tools and watches which has been established in the environs of Chandigarh, the capital of both Punjab and Haryana.

A large proportion of the industrial units in Haryana are located in two satellite cities of Delhi, Gurgaon and Faridabad. Elsewhere in the state the industrial units are concerned primarily with processing of agricultural produce, wheat and rice mills and cotton gins. Production of the traditional handicrafts—manufacture of brass utensils in some cities and manufacture of furnishings for home and office on powerlooms at Panipat has also increased steadily to meet both domestic and export demands.

Table 9.5: Net Irrigated area as per cent of net cultivated Area

	State and Region	*Net irrigated area/Net cultivated area (per cent)*	
		1993-94	*1996-97*
I.	**Southern Region**		
	Andhra Pradesh	37.5	40.6
	Karnataka	21.6	21.9
	Kerala	14.5	15.7
	Tamil Nadu	47.4	52.7
II.	**Western Region**		
	Gujarat	27.0	n.a.
	Maharashtra	14.9	14.4
III.	**North Western Region**		
	Punjab	93.2	93.0
	Haryana	75.8	n.a.
IV.	**North Central and Eastern Region**		
	Bihar	47.5	49.4
	Orissa	33.2	35.0
	Uttar Pradesh	65.6	68.7
	West Bengal	35.0	35.0
V.	**Hilly Forested and Desert**		
	Madhya Pradesh	27.1	32.3
	Rajasthan	28.3	33.3
VI.	**Not Classified**		
	Assam	21.1	20.9
	Himachal Pradesh	17.5	18.8
	Jammu & Kashmir	42.4	42.7
	All India	36.0	38.6

Source: Tata Consultancy Services: Statistical of India, Mumbai 1998-99 p. 15 and 2000-2001 p. 132.

Punjab and Haryana have the highest levels of per capita income. All the villages are electrified and except in parts of Haryana are within two kilometres of a motorable road and have access to adequate and safe drinking water.

However, the values of indicators of social development—adult literacy rate, female literacy rate, infant mortality rate and rate of growth of population although rising slowly are not high. They are low particularly in Haryana.

In the strip of 100—150 kilometres in western U.P. that extends from Dehra Doon to Bulandshahr, wheat, sugarcane and oilseeds are the principal crops. Most of the crop land is irrigated by canals and tube wells owned by the state or shallow wells fitted with electric motors or diesel driven pumps owned by the farmers. As in Punjab and Haryana, production of wheat increased spectacularly in this area with introduction from the late 1960s of dwarf, high yielding varieties of wheat. Yields of sugarcane and oil seeds have also been increasing steadily but not spectacularly, with improved farm management by the hard working farmers.

As in Punjab and Haryana, production of fodder crops to feed milch animals is an important part of the crop rotation system so that the area has high quality milch animals and is a large producer of milk all of which is consumed locally.

There is a large number of sugar and a few cooking oil mills in the area. Sale of wheat and of sugarcane and oilseed to the mills is the principal source of cash for the farmers.

The area includes the multi-industry complex at Modi Nagar. Besides, a large number of medium sized and large industrial units are located in the two satellite cities of Delhi—Ghaziabad and Gautam Buddh Nagar. Meerut, with a population of almost 1 million also has a number of industrial units. Per capital income and level of living of the farmers and residents of urban areas are not as high as those in Punjab and Haryana. However, they are far higher than those in other parts of Uttar Pradesh.

Furthermore, although most villages have adequate water from wells, they are not kept clean so that water borne diseases of the respiratory tract are endemic. Lack of any significant effort by the government to promote industrial development is a major factor impeding development of industries. Altogether it is an area in which industrial development is much below potential.

Domestic and foreign tourism is a source of income for the population of several cities in the region. Agra, one of the largest cities in the region, is visited by millions of foreign and domestic tourists every year because of location in it of Taj Mahal. Millions of domestic tourists visit the region due to location in it of the birth place of Lord Krishna and several places of pilgrimage along the Ganga at the foothills of the western Himalayas. There is, however, an acute shortage of tourist infrastructure—hotels for tourists of high or middle income groups, bus services, taxis and guides for the tourists.

It is not possible to comment on the values of indicators of social development because the region forms part of Uttar Pradesh and separate data are not available for it.

Table 9.6: Proportion of Villages Electrified

	States and Regions	*As on 31 March, 1996*
I.	**Southern Region**	
	Andhra Pradesh	100.0
	Karnataka	98.0
	Kerala	100.0
	Tamil Nadu	100.0
II.	**Western Region**	
	Goa	n.a
	Gujarat	98.8
	Maharashtra	99.4
III.	**North Western Region**	
	Punjab	100.0
	Haryana	100.0
	Delhi	–
IV.	**North Central and Eastern Region**	
	Bihar	70.8
	Orissa	73.6
	Uttar Pradesh	77.0
	West Bengal	76.9
V.	**Hilly Forested and Desert**	
	Madhya Pradesh	95.1
	Rajasthan	88.0
VI.	**Not Classified**	
	Assam	99.5
	Himachal Pradesh	100.0
	Jammu & Kashmir	96.9
	All India	86.8

Source: Tata Consultancy Services: Statistical Outline of India, Mumbai, 1988, p. 76.

IV. North Central and Eastern India

The region includes West Bengal, north and south Bihar, coastal Orissa and Uttar Pradesh, except the strip mentioned in III above.

The region is densely populated and despite the fact that it is endowed with well watered plains the great majority of the farmers are poor subsistence or below subsistence farmers. The Kolkata Metropolitan District (CMD) which includes the cities of Kolkata and Howrah and a number of jute mill towns located along the river Hooghly and the Durgapur-Asansol multi-industry complex are the principal industrial areas in West Bengal. In Bihar, the principal industrial centres—Jamshedpur and Bokaro both of which have large integrated steel plants and several industries processing steel and chemical and Ranchi which has a factory manufacturing heavy machines are all located in the Chhotanagpur region. There are few industrial units in north or south Bihar.

There was large flight of capital from the CMD in the late 1960s on account of militancy of trade unions and insecurity of life for managers and owners of many industrial units. A large number of non-Bengali industrial entrepreneurs closed their works in the CMD to reopen them in Chennai, Mumbai, Pune or in coastal Gujarat. A number of industrial units fabricating large steel structures such as bridges, owned by the Government of India were closed on account of militancy of trade unions. There has been significant reversal of these conditions thanks to the efforts of the present government led by the Communist party which had been in office for more than 25 years. The government has eliminated shortages of water and power which had been endemic in the 1970s and the 1980s and greatly reduced militancy of trade unions. The jute mills and tea packaging units have experienced expansion on account of increase in output of both crops and many of the steel fabricating units have reopened.

There are literally thousands of industrial units in the CMD manufacturing or repairing machinery for mines or making spare parts or components for such variety of consumer goods—garments, hosiery, pharmaceutical drugs and toiletries. A new harbour with a petro-chemical complex has come up at Haldia located about 60 kilometres south of Calcutta. There is a large factory manufacturing passenger cars in the environs of CMD.

Land reforms and extension of irrigation through installation of large numbers of electric pumps on irrigation wells has increased agricultural production and has created a class of well-to-do farmers in West Bengal. The frequency and intensity of floods has also been reduced to an extent by construction of flood control works on the Damodar and Teesta rivers. There is good potential for development of the information technology industries. Due to location of the Institute of Technology at Kharagpur, the Institute of Management and the Indian Statistical Institute at Barrackpur, in the CMD and two reputed universities—Calcutta and Jadavpur—in the city itself, there is a large number of graduates in the sciences who could provide the manpower for establishment of the industries. The state government should create the infrastructures for establishment of the industries. The industries would cater initially to the demand of banks and other financial institutions, business houses and manufacturing units, located in the CMD but could develop progressively an export market.

Irrigated area has increased also in parts of Orissa as a result of construction of the Hirakud dam on the Mahanadi river at Sambalpur. There is a large integrated steel mill at Rourkela, with its associated metallurgical and chemical industries. However, there has been little development of industries or improvement in agriculture in the rest of the state.

On the other hand, due to insecurity of life and property in large parts of Bihar, and parts of U.P. where dacoity, kidnapping and murder of wealthy merchants and entrepreneurs is not uncommon, there has been little industrial investment.

The poor, below subsistence farmers of Eastern U.P. and Bihar have a propensity to migrate to large metropolitan cities, particularly Kolkata, Mumbai and Delhi to work there as unskilled industrial workers or doing a variety of odd jobs such as of rickshaw-pullers, doormen in banks and other commercial establishments. They have also been migrating in large numbers since the 1970s to Punjab and Haryana to work as casual agricultural labourers in the farms in the busy agricultural season when there is a shortage of local labour.

During the last century, they migrated in large numbers to work on tea plantations in Assam or as indentured labourers to work on sugar plantations in various British possessions from Trinidad and Tobago in the Caribbean to Natal in South Africa to Fiji in the South Pacific. They settled there and in some countries such as Mauritius and Fiji their leaders are now heads of governments. However, migration to metropolitan cities in India has only kept hunger at bay and has not led to significant improvement in level of living of the families of the migrants.

Table 9.7: Proportion of children in primary schools

	States and Regions	*Proportion of Children in Primary Schools*+	
		1996-97	*1997-98*
I.	**Southern Region**		
	Andhra Pradesh	82	90
	Karnataka	106	105
	Kerala	91	90
	Tamil Nadu	106	109
II.	**Western Region**		
	Gujarat	115	n.a.
	Maharashtra	111	113
III.	**North Western Region**		
	Punjab	81	82
	Haryana	80	n.a.
IV.	**North Central and Eastern Region**		
	Bihar	71	76
	Orissa	89	99
	Uttar Pradesh	73	62
	West Bengal	104	92
V.	**Hilly Forested and Desert**		
	Madhya Pradesh	97	102
	Rajasthan	94	97
VI.	**Not Classified**		
	Assam	109	109
	Himachal Pradesh	95	90
	Jammu & Kashmir	68	67
	All India	91.0	90

Source: Tata Consultancy Service: Statistical Outline of India, 1998-99, Mumbai, 1998, p. 15.

\+ Enrolment as percentage of total children in 6-11 age group.

The values of indicators of economic and social development—growth rate of population, overall and female literacy rates, infant mortality rate, per capita income, proportion of population below the poverty line, proportion of villages electrified are close to the national averages in west Bengal. However, per capita income is one third of the national average and the proportion of population below the poverty line is 50 per cent higher than the national average in Bihar. The indicators in the other two states are significantly higher than in Bihar, but are still quite low.

A part of the backwardness of the region is due to the legacy of the *Zamindari* system of land tenure. Although the system was abolished in the 1950s, its psychological impact in terms of lack of initiative among farmers to improve productivity of their small land holdings through more intensive cultivation still persists. A second factor is the class struggle in Bihar between the high castes who were the former non-cultivating owners of land but now have to cultivate the land left to them for self-cultivation with the use of hired labour and the low castes who have now become peasant proprietors. A third and more important reason is that U.P. with a 1991 population of 138 million and Bihar with a population of 86 million in 1991 are so large that division of the states into smaller states, proposed from time to time, though difficult in the present political environment cannot be postponed indefinitely.

Flood control in north Bihar, where large areas of fertile lands get covered every year with coarse sand and gravel brought down by the floods of Kosi, Gandak and other rivers, and in parts of northern U.P., and curing alkalinity of soil by suitable reclamation measures in central U.P. would contribute greatly to increase in agricultural production. However, a beginning in regional development has to be made with a massive effort to improve indicators of social development.

The state governments have shown little inclination to promote industrial development. There could be significant industrial development through improvement of quality and expansion of output to meet domestic and export demands of the traditional handicrafts of U.P. such as manufacture of decorative brassware in Moradabad, weaving of carpets in and around Mirzapur and of silk sarees in a suburb of Varanasi.

There is a potential for development of the information technology industries in U.P. also. There is an Institute of Technology at Kanpur and three universities in the state—Allahabad, Varanasi and Lucknow—were considered to be centres of excellence until the 1950s. Standards of teaching and research in them could be improved to provide the basis of training of graduates in the sciences who would provide the man-power for establishment of the industries. As in West

Bengal, they will cater initially to the domestic banks and financial institutions and manufacturing units.

Bihar and U.P. could develop religious tourism by providing the needed infrastructures in the places of birth, enlightenment and preaching of the first sermon by Lord Buddha which are located in Bihar, or the border of Nepal and Bihar and near Varanasi in U.P. and which are visited by millions of Buddhist pilgrims from South East and East Asia, from Thailand to Japan. The Japanese have indicated their willingness to provide financial and technical assistance for development of tourism infrastructure. However, the state governments have shown no inclination to accept the offer and provide the infrastructures for development of tourism—from well-maintained deluxe and low priced hotels, well maintained roads, improvement and expansion of the airports at Varanasi and Patna to bring them to international standards.

Varanasi and Allahabad in U.P. and Gaya in Bihar are visited by millions of Indian pilgrims. However, infrastructure, such as small, clean, low priced inns for their stay in comfort, are woefully lacking. Development of tourism besides providing employment to large numbers of people could generate the capital and foster growth of entrepreneurs for promoting industrial development and improving agriculture.

V. Hilly Forested and Desert India

The region includes Madhya Pradesh, Inland Orissa, Chhotanagpur region of Bihar, forested areas of Maharashtra and Gujarat and Rajasthan. The region has a large population of scheduled tribes who subsist on cultivation of their small plots of cultivable land and judicious use of forests to obtain fuel wood and thatch for building or repair of their huts, for food during some seasons of the year and for medicinal herbs. The region is rich in mineral resources and has a large potential for development of both thermal and hydro-power. There are in it four large integrated steel mills, a heavy machinery plant at Ranchi in Bihar, plants for making trucks, machines for generation, transmission and distribution of electricity, several cement mills, plants for manufacture of rolling stock (wagons) for the railways and a number of hydro-electric or thermal power based electricity generating stations that supply power to cities in northern India—from Kolkata to Delhi and to cities/towns and villages in the region itself.

However, exploitation of the rich mineral and power resources by these heavy industry units or of forests to obtain timber and plywood for construction of houses, commercial and office building in the cities in northern and western India has not benefited the tribals. On the contrary, they have been badly exploited by the mining and forest contractors. They work as unskilled workers in mines and industrial units at subsistence wages. The location of the industrial units and power plants etc. has displaced large numbers of them from their traditional village homes. Schemes for their resettlement in villages chosen by the state governments have been most unsatisfactory. They have not been provided with large enough plots of cultivable land and are also virtually denied access to neighboring forest lands. Even adequate and safe drinking water is not available in many resettlement villages.

During the last two decades a number of socially concerned citizens and organizations have protested so vehemently against exploitation of the tribals that the concerned state governments are being forced to pay attention to their grievances. Their protests have induced a change in the attitude of some state governments and it is hoped that greater attention will be paid in future to their welfare including rehabilitation in states in which their traditional lifestyle is not disturbed.

There is acute scarcity of food in parts of the region whenever the monsoon fails and starvation deaths are not uncommon in the backward districts of Orissa. In the desert region of western Rajasthan, large numbers of livestock perish in years of acute drought which is not uncommon. Famine relief works have to be undertaken and fodder has to be imported to save the livestock which are the principal wealth of the people.

Values of indicators of both economic and social development are low in both Madhya Pradesh and Rajasthan. Per capita income is lower than the national averages in both states. Rates of population growth are high and average and female literacy rates are low. The female literacy rate in Rajasthan is barely half the national average. Almost all the villages in Madhya Pradesh have electricity but the proportion is less than 90 per cent in Rajasthan.

VI. Not Classified

Assam and the 7 small hill states of the North East are included in this region.

These states have poor communications with the rest of India. Assam which comprises most of Brahmaputra valley has fertile plains which are subject, however, to floods during the monsoon. Rice in the plains and tea on the hill slopes are main crops. There is hardly any industry except for a small refinery which processes crude oil: the products are transported by a pipeline to Barauni in Bihar. The tea gardens, owned before independence by Scots are now owned mainly by non-Assamese businessmen. The tea is sent to Kolkata for packing for consumption within India and abroad. Although production has increased progressively to meet rapidly rising demand within India and to maintain a sizeable export, the benefit does not accrue to the Assamese because the labourers and the tea plantation owners are all non-Assamese. One large multi-national Anglo-Dutch company has a commanding position in packing and sale of tea for both the domestic and foreign markets.

The hill states, small in size have subsistence agriculture, with rice as the main crop and as the principal means of livelihood. Levels of social development are high in states such as Mizoram and Nagaland in which most of the population has been converted to Christianity. Nagaland was in the grip of insurgency for a long period, which has been contained through action by the Indian Army. In occasional periods of scarcity when the rice crop fails, food has to be dropped by air and road in order to avert starvation because of lack of rail and poor road communications with the rest of India.

Himachal Pradesh

Himachal Pradesh was formed in 1948 through merger of a large number of tiny hill states located to the north of Punjab and Haryana and two districts of Punjab. Simla, the capital, which was the summer capital of British India for more than a century and was a beautiful hill station is now an overgrown medium sized city which suffers from serious problems of pollution of air and shortage of water during the summer which is also the busy tourist season. Besides, subsistence agriculture, catering to tourists and growing apples for consumption in the plains are the principal means of livelihood in some parts of the state. Industrial development is limited to packaging of fruit, processing it to make fruit juice, jams, honey etc. and making woollen shawls on handlooms. Parts of the state remain snowbound for 4-5 months in the year. Since it is located on the border with Tibet, there is a large presence of the army. Repair of border roads and catering to the needs of the army provide employment to thousands of men.

Jammu & Kashmir

The state has three distinct regions:

(i) *Jammu*: an area of plains and hills which borders Punjab and has a mixed Hindu and Muslim population.
(ii) *The Kashmir valley*: A densely populated extremely fertile valley with a Muslim population which is located between lesser and greater Himalayas. Rice is the main food crop.
(iii) *Ladakh*: a thinly populated dry mountainous area located on the border between India and China. The capital, Leh is located at an altitude of about 13,000 feet. The population is mixed—Buddhist and Muslim.

There are large orchards of temperate fruits—apples, pears, peaches, apricots and cherries. Growing the fruits and packaging it for sale in the plains is the major source of income for large numbers of people.

Production of rice is not sufficient to meet the needs of the population and large quantities have to be imported. All other foods—sugar, tea and cooking oil have also to be imported.

Before the insurgency which gripped the state during a part of the 1990s, catering to the needs of hundreds of thousands of tourists and export of its superb handicrafts—delicately embroidered fine woollen shawls, woollen and silk carpets, silk cloth, wood work papier mache, etc., were and continue to be a major sources of income for the population. These activities have now resumed with control over insurgency.

There is a very large presence of the armed forces because of strategic location of the state on the border with Pakistan and Tibet. Catering to the needs of the army provides employment to large number of people.

The available data on values of indicators of social development indicate that they are close to the national average.

CONCLUSION

This broad ranging survey of levels of economic and/or social development among different states and within different regions of some large states indicates that there are large inter-state and intra-state differences in these levels. These differences would increase unless determined efforts are made by the national and state governments to reduce them.

Two examples can be cited here. First the Green Revolution as a result of which large increases in output and yields per hectare of the two main cereal crops—wheat and rice—have occurred with use of new dwarf high yielding varieties of these crops under conditions of adequate and assured water supply along with use of chemical fertilizers and/or organic manure, pesticides and improved implements is confined to certain limited areas in which these favourable conditions are met. Similarly, high yields of cotton and sugarcane, important cash crops are obtained in areas having adequate and assured moisture provided by assured rainfall and/or irrigation. However, there has not been similar increase in yields of these cereals or of sorghum and millets which are the principal food crop, or of cotton or oil seeds which are the principal cash crops of farmers in the nearly 70 per cent of the cropland which is totally dependent on rainfall. As a result, large differences have appeared in income and levels of consumption among the farmers and the rural population in different states and regions.

Second, factory industries are concentrated in the environs of some large metropolitan cities or in some regions of some states. Thus, there are differences in levels of industrial development between these states and regions and the rest of the country. These have led in turn to large differences in income, consumption and levels of social development in these areas and of those in the rest of the country.

While some regions such as the desert and semi desert areas of Rajasthan and the hilly or mountainous regions of some states, might remain backward because of agro-climatic or physiographic reasons, there is no reason why large areas in well watered plains, which are endowed with physiography and climate to be highly productive should remain economically and/or socially depressed.

The determined efforts of the present government of West Bengal have raised the productivity of farmlands and income of farmers as also halted and to an extent reversed the industrial decline in the

Kolkata Metropolitan District. Governments of other backward states—Uttar Pradesh, Bihar, Madhya Pradesh and Orissa—should make similar efforts to raise levels of social and economic development of their people. A beginning should be made with raising levels of social development because a literate and healthy population will itself make a determined effort to raise income and consumption levels. In U.P. and Bihar it is necessary also to improve the law and order situation so that there is security of life and property for the citizen and entrepreneurs can invest in industrial development. In Madhya Pradesh and Orissa, exploitation of the large tribal population by mining and forest contractors should be minimized and schemes for rehabilitation of those who are displaced as a result of construction of dams, power stations or large industrial units are so designed that they can resume their traditional economic activities and social life.

NOTE

1. *National Geographical Journal of India*, Vol. 44, pp. 1-4, March-December 1998.

10

Progress of Rural Development Programmes—Regional Differences[1]

INTRODUCTION

The experience with agricultural and rural development programmes of more than a decade has shown that progress of these programmes is significantly better in some States than in others. Even within the State progress has been markedly uneven.

A study of these differences is important because in all these programmes success depends in large part upon the response of the local people – their understanding of the objects and methods of the programmes, their capacity to avail of the assistance offered, etc.

Further, the success or failure of these programmes affects the economy and social life of large numbers of people.

This Chapter points to the emergence of regional differences in the progress of rural development programmes and emphasizes the need for detailed and systematic studies to identify these differences and to locate their causes. Such studies are essential for remedial action to remove these disparities and to enable areas of low progress to overcome their handicaps and achieve a more satisfactory rate of progress. Some data on inter-State differences in progress have been given for two fields: cooperative credit and technological change in agriculture. The data are primarily illustrative; they are not intended for comparisons of progress among different States. In the case of technological change in agriculture, data have been given for only two indicators: use of chemical fertilizers and installation of mechanical pumps (electrically and oil engine operated) for irrigation. These data would need to be supplemented by other indicators of technological change (e.g. use of improved seed) as well as by statistics of increase of agricultural production for a comparative picture of agricultural progress in different States. However, the indicators selected are useful as pointers to progress in the particular fields and, therefore, adequate for the limited purpose of this paper.

The other iimitation of the data is that they are for States as a whole. It is known that in case of many programmes, areas of good as well as poor progress – differences between which are as large, or even larger than those between States – are found within the same State. Thus Maharashtra and Andhra which make a good showing in cooperative credit including areas (*e.g.* most districts of Marathwada in Maharashtra and Telengana, which formed part of the former Hyderabad State, in Andhra, in which the cooperative movement is much less developed than in States like Punjab which make only a medium showing). The progress indicated by data for the whole State is in these cases due primarily to spectacular progress in some districts, e.g. several of the districts of the former Bombay State part of Maharashtra. Thus the credit advanced by cooperatives in the Jalgon district of the old Bombay State alone is of the order of Rs. 8 crores in 1960-61, which is equal to the total credit advanced in the four eastern States of Bihar, West Bengal, Orissa and Assam.

Such areas of spectacular progress as well as areas of particularly poor progress should be identified through detailed studies. Thereafter, analysis of the factors responsible for these disparities can be undertaken. The value of such case studies of sharply contrasting developmental experiences in identifying factors which contribute to or retard progress of development programmes hardly needs any emphasis.

COOPERATIVE CREDIT

Data on agricultural credit advanced by primary (agricultural credit and multi-purpose) societies in the three years 1951-52, 1956-57 and 1959-60 are given in Table 10.1. The States have been arranged in four regional groups to bring out regional differences more clearly. The period covered is one of rapid expansion in cooperative credit, primarily due to the availability of large funds from the Reserve Bank of India from the early fifties. The increase for the country as a whole is seven times during this period. Several of the States show comparable or higher rates of increase; but in certain others, progress

Table 10.1: Co-operative Credit Loans Advanced by Primary Agricultural Credit and Multi-Purpose Societies

States	*Loans Advanced (Rs. Lakhs)*			*Percentage increase in 1959-60 over 1951-52*	*State Total As Per Cent of All-India Total*	*Gross Cropped Area in 1958-59*	*Co-operative Loans per Acre of Cropped Area Rs.*	*Overdues as Per Cent of Outstanding Loans in 1959-60*	*Number of Members in 1959-60 (in thousands)*
	1951-52	*1956-57*	*1959-60*						
1	*2*	*3*	*4*	*5*	*6*	*7*	*8*	*9*	*10*
Southern Region									
Andhra	292	865	1750	499.3	10.39	29872	5.86	14	1262
Madras	318	722	1737	446.2	10.31	17097	10.16	11	1584
Mysore	NA	539	1203	NA	7.14	26031	4.62	33	1054
Kerala	52	153	409	686.5	2.43	5537	7.39	20	756
Western Region									
Maharashtra	640	1207	2937	358.9	17.44	45836	6.41	27	1531
Gujarat	188	899	2126	1030.9	12.62	23570	9.02	25	750
Northern and Central Region									
Uttar Pradesh	257	656	2922	1037.0	17.35	53794	5.43	6	2883
Punjab	176	566	1129	541.5	6.70	24527	4.60	26	1126
Rajasthan	16	104	539	3268.8	3.20	33921	1.59	19	513
Madhya Pradesh	128	505	1301	916.4	7.73	43813	2.97	21	789
Eastern Region									
Assam	1.2	75.7	66.9	5475.0	0.40	6003	1.11	55	204
West Bengal	69	116	227	229.0	1.35	15055	1.51	43	571
Bihar	4	69	129	3125.0	0.77	27378	0.47	55	620
Orissa	41	170	235	473.2	1.40	14958	1.57	20	369
Total: All India	2421	6733	16840	695.6	100.00	367392	4.58	21	14468

Sources: "Co-operative Movement in India: Trend of Progress in the States, 1950-51 to 1959-60", Government of India, Ministry of Community Development and Co-operation, 1961. Statements 1.6 and 1.7 to 16.6 and 16.7.

has been much below the national average. Andhra, Madras, Gujarat, Maharashtra and UP are the big five in cooperative credit; followed by Mysore, Punjab and Madhya Pradesh. The differences in the volume of cooperative credit are due in part to differences in the size and cropped area of the States. The high figure for UP is due partly to its large size. The influence of this factor has been eliminated in column 8 in which cooperative credit per 1,000 acres of cropped area has been given. The regional differences which emerge are discussed below.

Southern Region

All the States in this region show rapid and constant progress. Andhra (in the former Madras area only) and Madras starting with well-developed cooperative movements, have maintained steady progress. In 1959-60 Madras achieved the figure of Rs. 10.31 of co-operative credit per acre of cropped area, which is the highest in the country. In Kerala, progress has been from small beginnings, but has been rapid, so that by 1959-60 the State had the third highest figure of cooperative credit per acre of cropped area. The percentage of overdues to outstanding loans is medium to low in all three States and the cooperative movement can be considered to be progressing satisfactorily. In Mysore, on the other hand, progress is slower and the percentage of overdues is also higher.

Western Region

Both Gujarat and Maharashtra show steady progress in co-operative credit. Together they account for about 30 per cent of the total cooperative credit in the country. The movement was already well developed in the former Bombay State areas of these States, but not so in other areas like Marathwada in Maharashtra, where it is even now less advanced than in the other areas.

Northern and Central Region

The four States grouped together in this region all show rapid advance during this period. In Punjab and parts of UP and MP the movement was already well developed; but in the other areas, advance has been from small beginnings. In Rajasthan, for instance, the movement was very small until the early fiftes, because a large number of the princely States, from which the new State was formed, did not have any cooperative movement worth the name. Only in a few of the larger princely States had a beginning been made with organization of co-operatives. But even in these, the movement was relatively less developed as it was started comparatively late, in the 30s or the 40s. In Madhya Pradesh, while in certain parts there were well-developed co-operatives, in others, like the areas of the former Vindhya Pradesh, conditions were similar to those in Rajasthan. The rapid progress recorded by both Rajasthan and Madhya Pradesh during this period has enabled them to overcome the disadvantage of a late start to a considerable extent. But this rate of progress will have to continue from some years more before these States can come up to the levels of Punjab and UP.

The Eastern Region

All the four Eastern States show poor progress. The total cooperative credit advanced in these States in 1959-60 is only Rs. 6.6 crores or about 4 per cent of the total for the country. The number of cooperative societies and their membership is not too small (13 per cent of the total for the country), but the credit advanced by them is very small, mainly because a large proportion of the societies are not working satisfactorily. This is brought out by the high percentage of overdues in Col. 9 of Table 10.1. Orissa is a little better off than the other three. In spite of a late start in a large part of the State, it can claim better progress and a better overdues position. But in the other three States the movement is clearly not making progress. These States have had experience of cooperation for as long as the rest of the country. So there is no question of their being handicapped by a late start or lack of administrative experience. Their's is clearly a case of poor response, which needs to be investigated in detail.

TECHNOLOGICAL CHANGE IN AGRICULTURE

In use of fertilizer also the Southern and Western States are much ahead of the rest of the country. Together, they account for nearly 60 per cent of the total fertilizer used (Table 10.2). In contrast, use of fertilizer is limited in most of the Eastern and all the Northern and Western States except Uttar Pradesh. The large figure for Uttar Pradesh is due to its size.

Table 10.2: Technological Change in Agriculture—use of Chemical Fertilizers and number of Mechanical Pumps Used

States	Use of Chemical Fertilizers, 1959[1] NF_2O_5, K_2O		Figure for State as Per Cent of All India Total	No of oil Engines and Electric Pumps Used for Irrigation[2]						
	Total (tons)	Per Acre of Agricultural Land (lbs)		1951	1956	1961	Increase in 1961 over 1951	Figure for State as per cent of All India Total for 1961	Area Irrigated by Wells in 1958-59 ('000 acres)	No of Pumps per 1000 Acres of Well-Irrigated Area
1	2	3	4	5	6	7	8	9	10	11
Southern										
Andhra	36911	2.64	13.16	9526	19991	50964	435.0	13.66	728	70.0
Madras	40232	5.38	14.34	28684	53729	135313	371.7	36.28	1346	100.5
Mysore	11847	1.03	4.22	7461	11109	22520	201.8	6.04	304	74.1
Kerala	11322	4.65	4.04	2788	3227	5937	113.0	1.59	35	169.6
Western										
Maharashtra } Gujarat }	42664	1.36	15.21	31588	48848	121484	284.6	32.57	2484	48.9
Northern and Central										
Uttar Pradesh	44170	1.87	15.75	3394	6319	11377	235.2	3.05	5754	2.0
Punjab	7124	0.67	2.54	1973	11896	NA	NA	NA	2322	NA
Rajasthan	3158	0.21	1.13	1644	1659	2941	78.9	0.79	1944	1.5
Madhya Pradesh	9913	0.51	3.53	2389	5730	11909	398.5	3.19	741	16.1
Eastern										
Assam	1644	0.62	0.59	74	376	127	71.6	0.03	—	—
West Bengal	12283	1.83	4.38	1173	1476	3893	231.9	1.04	39	99.8
Bihar	15129	1.35	5.39	886	3653	5117	477.5	1.37	681	7.5
Orissa	5172	0.77	1.84	129	936	1322	924.8	0.35	94	14.1
Total: All India	280467	—	—	91709	168949	373000	306.7	—	—	—

Source: 1. *Fertilizer Statistics* 1960, Fertilizer Association of India, New Delhi, 1961.
2. *Indian Livestock Census* 1956. The Directorate of Economics
3. Ministry of Food and Agriculture, New Delhi.
4. *The Economic Weekly*, Annual Number, February 1963, pp. 175-177.

The influence of this factor is eliminated in col. 3 of the table in which figures of use of fertilizer per acre of cropped area have been given. These figures range from 0.2 lbs per acre in Rajasthan to 4.65 lbs in Kerala and 5.38 lbs in Madras. Differences in use of fertilizers are due in part to differences in climate and cropping pattern. In this country use of fertilizer has so far been successful only in areas of assured rainfall and or irrigation facilities. The principal fertilizers used are nitrogenous and are used largely for irrigated paddy. In contrast, the millet growing areas of low and uncertain rainfalls use very little fertilizer. The low figure for Rajasthan is due mainly to this.

But, this factor does not explain the marked differences between Madras and Andhra on the one hand and the Eastern States of West Bengal and Assam on the other. The per acre figure for Bengal is one-third and for Assam one-ninth of that for Madras. The differences would have been even greater if paddy lands alone were considered since the average for Madras is depressed by the inclusion of large areas under millets and other dry zone crops. The much higher use of fertilizers in Madras (and Andhra and Kerala) appears to be due mainly to better acceptance by the cultivators. The reason for this as also for the poor acceptance in Bengal and Assam where the climatic conditions are equally favourable and fertilizer equally needed would be a fruitful subject for study.

A similar picture emerges from figures of installation of pumping sets driven by oil engines or electric motors. Madras, Andhra, Maharashtra and Gujarat are prominent with more than 80 per cent of the total pump sets in the country. The six States of the Southern and Western regions together account for 90 per cent of the total. In contrast, the number of sets in the Northern and Eastern States in very small. Here again, we should draw attention to the figures in Column 11 of Table 10.2 which show the number of pump sets per 1,000 acres of area irrigated by wells, because these eliminate the influence of the size of area under well irrigation in different States. These figures show striking contrasts between the Southern States on the one hand and the Northern States like Uttar Pradesh and Rajasthan on the other. The latter have large numbers of wells but very few pumping sets.

These differences again are not due to any differences in natural conditions: mechanical pumping will benefit the farmer just as much in UP and Rajasthan as in Madras and Andhra Pradesh. The differences are due partly to greater rural electrification in the Southern states, which facilitates installation of electric motors and partly to better response to mechanical pumping by cultivators.

INTRA-STATE DIFFERENCES

The very limited data presented here points to striking differences in progress in different States. Similar analysis should be carried out for the entire range of rural development activities, and for areas smaller than States (districts or groups of districts) so that differences in progress between different areas are more clearly and accurately identified. The value of such analysis need hardly be emphasized. Identification of regional differences and demarcation of areas of outstanding and poor progress is essential so that programmes and policies can be modified to suit particular regional conditions and the example of areas of outstanding progress can be followed by others and the causes which hamper progress in the latter can be removed.

NOTE

1. *The Economic Weekly,* Annual Number February 1963, pp. 175-177.

11

Regional Dimensions of Rural Poverty in India[1]

INTRODUCTION

The object of planning and policy-making in India was to attain a high rate of economic growth without increasing poverty and inequality. It became more and more apparent that development and growth were not the same thing. As the planning process unfolded in India, two things became clear. Firstly, the growth in the gross national product (GNP) was sluggish, barely keeping pace with the growth in population. Secondly, the benefits of such growth as there was seemed to go more to the better-off than to the worse-off sections of society; that growth and distribution do not always improve together. A decrease in poverty is not always accompanied by a decrease in inequality; it may in fact be accompanied by an increase in it.

The data on economic growth and development in the 1960s and 1970s, indicate that while there might have been some economic growth during the first three Five-Year Plans, it could hardly be described as development since both poverty and inequality had increased. A turnaround appears to have occurred between the late 1980s and the early 1990s. Most economists now seem to agree that by the criteria adopted in the 1960s, poverty in India is in decline and there has been a decline not only in the proportion of the poor but also in their total number, despite the increase in population. The turnaround in magnitude of poverty in the 1990s has been some of the most significant developments in India since its independence.

It is in a way ironical that signs of the decline of poverty began to appear clearly only after disenchantment had set in with development planning, one of whose principal objectives was the reduction of poverty. While poverty is on the decline, and there is increase in the growth of the middle class in rural and urban areas there are large regional variations in the decline of poverty and in concentration of pockets of poverty.

In order to understand, the dynamics of economic change of rural and urban India during the last five decades, we have to get rid of stereotypes inherited from texts in economics and surveys undertaken two or three decades ago. Instead we have to pay attention to more recent and current data that are available. To support the basic contention of this chapter that the size of the population above the poverty line is much larger than is commonly assumed, we give in Appendix Table 11.1*a* figures on levels of consumption of food, cloth, and type of housing as derived from official sources. Poverty, however, if defined as meaning human deprivation (*i.e.* not having access to proper health care, education of children or housing with safe and adequate drinking water) the numbers would be larger. The figures given in Appendix Tables 11.1*a* and 11.1*b* show an unmistakable improvement in level of living of the population. The geographical distribution of regions of rural poverty shows that more than natural resource deficiency, the policies of the State Governments are responsible for persistence of poverty. The example of the land reforms instituted by the West Bengal Government indicates that the neglect can be eliminated and productivity and levels of living of most of the rural population can be raised in two or three decades.

Rural poverty is the most serious problem in India's economic development. No government in India can survive without indicating its commitment to eradicating poverty among the people. There are large inter-state and intra-state sub-regional variations in rural poverty due to environmental and/or man-made reasons. The percentage of population below the poverty line is estimated to have declined steadily from about 55 per cent in 1973-74 to a projected 18.00 per cent during 2001-2002. There has been sharp decline in 1990s; the rate was 36.0 per cent in 1993-94 and is estimated at 26 per cent in 1999-2000. The decline is being attributed to the trickle down effect of the rapid growth of gross domestic product achieved during the 1990s.

In this chapter two most widely accepted definitions of poverty are discussed. The areas in which large proportions of the rural population suffer from poverty are indicated. It is argued that further progress in reducing poverty will be difficult until productivity and income of the farmers and agricultural labourers in the poverty stricken areas is increased. The nature of the programmes to achieve this objective is indicated. It is argued that the programmes will not be effective until they include food for work programmes in which nutritious and balanced food is distributed to workers as part of the wages for work on the programmes. The programmes should include enhancement of rural infrastructure as well as improving the natural environment. In this way the programmes will achieve the twin objectives of reducing incidence of poverty and reducing the environmental damage that leads to a large proportion of the rural population to subsist in poverty.

Definitions of Rural Poverty

There are two definitions of poverty which are in use at present.

(i) Those who do not get enough calories from cereals, cooking oil, sugar and other foods to maintain themselves in health. This definition, given first by Dandekar and Rath (Dandekar and Rath, 1971) in 1971 has been accepted by the Government of India; and

(ii) In addition, those who do not have access to clean drinking water, easy access to facilities for curative and preventive health care and suffer, therefore, from various epidemic and endemic diseases. Furthermore, they are ignorant and illiterate for lack of access to or unwillingness to use facilities for education of their children and literacy for adults.

The second definition is used often by the World Bank and other agencies of the UN system.

The narrower definition (i) is used here due to lack of easy access to the broader definition. The regions which are not in need of alleviation of poverty programmes and those which are in need and described below have been determined on *a priori* basis. It will hopefully be possible to define them more precisely when data of the decennial census of 2001, which will become available in a few months and are matched with those of the latest rounds of the National Sample Survey. However, it is the contention of this writer that decline in rural poverty according to the narrower definition, is accompanied also by a decline in the number of poor using the broader definition.

Programme for Alleviation of Poverty Pre- and Post-1950s

Food for work programmes have been undertaken by the British government since the 1880s. There were two widespread famines in the country in the last two decades of the 19th century. Millions died from starvation. In addition to organising food for work programmes in the famine affected areas the government launched a large programme of construction of canals. These programmes had the desired effect. The areas covered by the irrigation projects not only became self-sufficient in foodgrains but had also large surpluses which were sent to other states. Production of medium staple cotton, sugarcane and oil seeds is also concentrated in these areas. These areas included the followings:

(i) Undivided Punjab, Sindh, 2 districts of the then Bikaner state, and a large part of western Uttar Pradesh: Western Punjab and Sindh had an extensive system of canals. It went to Pakistan in 1947. River-daming works on Ganga are now in Bangladesh. The areas covered by the programmes in India include:

(a) Punjab, Haryana, almost 20 districts of western U.P. which are irrigated by canals on the Sutlej, Yamuna and Ganga and 3 districts of northern Rajasthan. The areas under irrigation in Haryana and Rajasthan have increased greatly after construction during the 1950s of Bhakra dam, a 700 ft. high concrete dam on Sutlej river in present Punjab. Furthermore, the governments of Punjab, Haryana and U.P. have encouraged farmers by giving medium term loans to install electricity or diesel oil driven pumps on their surface wells and by constructing deep tube wells. The latter programme initiated in U.P. in the 1930s and continued in the 1950s and 1960s covers a large area in western Uttar Pradesh and Haryana and a small area also in Punjab.

(b) The several major irrigation-cum-power generation projects constructed during the period of the first and second five year plans of independent India 1951-61 and the programmes to increase irrigated area through repair of tanks and giving loans to farmers to install electricity or diesel oil operated pumps on their wells have further increased the area provided by adequate and dependable irrigation. As a result, the area irrigated by canals, tanks, surface wells, tube wells, etc. has increased from just over 17 per cent in 1951-52 to almost 39 per cent in 1996-97. The irrigated areas produce a large percentage of the cereals, cotton, sugarcane and oil seeds, jute and tea produced in the country. Some of these areas were drought prone earlier and were in need of programmes for alleviation of poverty.

(ii) Construction of canals in coastal Andhra Pradesh especially in the deltas of Krishna and Godavari rivers.

(iii) Construction or improvement of old canals in the delta of the Kaveri river in former Madras presidency (present Tamil Nadu).

In both the later areas the canals were constructed or improved during the British period. The area under irrigation has been increased and irrigation made more intensive in the last 5 decades by improvement of canals and by use of electricity or diesel oil operated pumps on surface wells by the farmers.

(iv) Construction in the 1930s of a canal on Pykara river to irrigate a large area of land around Coimbatore in Tamil Nadu in which medium staple cotton is the principal crop.

(v) *Renovation or repair of tanks in large areas of peninsular India*: A number of princely states notably Mysore, Hyderabad, Travancore and Cochin in the south and Baroda in the west joined in this effort. The irrigated area in the former Mysore state (present Karnataka) was increased by renovation and repair of tanks and more important by construction of a dam and a canal on the Kaveri river to irrigate a large area located between Bangalore and Mysore city. The irrigated area has been increased further by giving loans to farmers to install electric pumps on their surface wells. In Hyderabad, the area under irrigation was increased by constructing dams on numerous small streams. The communities located below the dams depend on them for irrigation of their croplands and for drinking water.

(vi) *Western Maharashtra*: A large area is irrigated by construction of dams on a number of small streams that flow west from the Western Ghats to the Arabian sea. This is a development primarily of the period after independence. This area was drought prone earlier and food for work programmes were undertaken in it from time to time. Now, however, it produces large crops of rice and sugar cane, both of which have high yields. There is a number of rice, flower and sugar mills and other industrial units which manufacture machine tools. Mumbai, Pune, the rail-cum-road strip between the two cities and the highway from Mumbai and Delhi have the largest concentration of factories in India.

(vii) *Coastal Gujarat between Mumbai and Ahmedabad*: The area receives adequate rainfall in most years to produce large crops of cotton, coarse grains (sorghum or millets) and oilseeds. After establishment of Amul dairy at Anand in central Gujarat and its branches in two other towns, production of milk for sale as liquid milk to Mumbai, Ahmedabad and other cities in Gujarat and for manufacture of dairy products—butter, cheese and baby food for distribution throughout northern and western India has become important. A large variety of machine tools are produced as well as clothing and pharmaceutical drugs.

(viii) *A large area in eastern and south eastern Rajasthan*: which receives dependable rainfall in the monsoon season and in which large areas are irrigated by tanks or by wells fitted with electricity or diesel oil operated pumps. Wheat, coarse grains (sorghum or millets), oilseeds and cotton are the principal crops. After discovery of oil in offshore and on-shore Gujarat, refining of petroleum and petro-chemical industries including manufacturing of various plastic goods for households have become important industries. They have increased significantly in the area.

Altogether these areas together with those in the Gangetic plain in U.P., Bihar and West Bengal comprise 36 per cent of the total cropped area leaving 65 per cent of the cropland without irrigation facilities.

The areas in need of alleviation of poverty programmes and those in which there is no need for these need to be separated in order to make the programmes more target oriented and hence more effective.

DISTRIBUTION OF HUNGER AND OF RURAL POOR

There are large regional differences in the incidence of hunger. It is least in the 30 per cent of the area in which there is security of production as a result of adequate and dependable rainfall or irrigation. There is little hunger in states such as Punjab, Haryana, a part of western U.P., coastal Andhra Pradesh, most of Tamil Nadu, which have benefited from the Green Revolution which raised yield of the principal food crops—wheat and rice—with use of high breed seeds, fertilizers and pesticides.

Similarly, in areas such as coastal Gujarat and western Maharashtra which are industrialized and farmers have the means to buy food in case of need, hunger is confined to (i) hilly and forested areas of Peninsular India—parts of Andhra Pradesh and Karnataka, Marathwada and Vidarbha regions of Maharashtra, a large part of western Rajasthan, Sourashtra in Gujarat in which most of the cropland is unirrigated and production depends upon vagaries of the monsoon rainfall and (ii) Inland Orissa, Chhotanagpur region of Bihar, most of the Madhya Pradesh and parts of Maharashtra, Gujarat and South East Rajasthan which are forested and inhabited by tribals. Hunger in these parts is due partly to low production and partly to difficulties of commercialization.

Large parts of U.P. and Bihar which are densely populated and do not produce enough food despite having fertile plains; hunger is the legacy of the *Zamindari* system and social backwardness of the people.

However, in other areas where agricultural development accompanied by increase in area under irrigation and improved varieties of seeds, fertilizers and technological advances, has led to improvement in levels of living and social change. Ten thousands of new schools were opened. Every village above a certain population had a primary school, which served also for a group of villages. Ten thousands of new drinking water wells were constructed. People of lower castes who were not allowed to draw water from the wells of high castes, were encouraged to construct their own wells. Tens of thousands of primary health care centres were opened. Thousands of mini-hospitals (with 6 beds), 1-2 doctors and paramedical personnel were opened. These provided curative and preventive health care.

Thousands of miles of new approach roads and motorable roads were constructed so that every village had a bus within a kilometre of walking distance. There were problems of un-willingness of urban based teachers and doctors and para-medical personnel to man the schools and health care centres located in rural areas. Yet at the end of 5 decades of community development effort, 91 per cent of the children are in the primary schools in 1999; several villages had coverage of 96 per cent of children. All the villages have electricity; the proportion is 100 per cent in several states.

Panchayati Raj institutions have been opened and they have been functioning with varying degrees of efficiency. Food production has increased by 3½ times since the mid 1950s somewhat in excess of the increase in population. There has been no famine in the last 50 years. Yet according to a report of the UNFPA, 1/3rd of the population—an estimated 325 million go hungry, *i.e.* they consume less than 80 per cent of the minimum energy requirements. The principal reason for it is different stages of production and storage and maldistribution of food.

Poverty is thus Concentrated in the Following Areas

A. *Jharkhand, Inland Orissa, Chhatisgarh, Central and Eastern Madhya Pradesh, Telengana region of Andhra Pradesh and small parts of southern Rajasthan.* The number of poor in hilly and forested area of peninsular India would be reduced greatly by the following measures:

(i) Construction of good motorable roads so that food, fodder and potable water, medicines and building materials can be rushed to these areas when fields and villages of the tribal people are destroyed by cyclone during or after the monsoon. This will greatly reduce the casualties from communicable diseases when the people are stranded. After the floods recede, they should be given grants to buy building materials, cement, CI sheets to re-build their huts and ploughs, seeds, fertilizers, etc., to reclaim their fields and plant rice and other crops.

(ii) The tribals in many of the areas have a serious complaint that when the areas in which they had been living for generations are acquired for location of industrial, power or irrigation projects, they are neither given adequate compensation in time nor provided alternative forest areas in which to build their villages and farms. This grievance should be removed so that they can resume their normal life as quickly as possible after they are moved from their old villages. Voluntary associations of the tribal should be encouraged to manage the forest on which they depend for fuel, fodder, building materials, some food and medicines. They will manage the forest better than the officials of the forest department and end their exploitation by timber or money contractors.

(iii) Tribal young men educated up to higher secondary school level can be employed as white collar workers in the offices of the state government or industrial units located in their areas. They can also be quickly trained to become skilled workers in these plants, teachers in schools and para-medico educated tribal young women will make cleaner homes and raise healthier children. Some of them can become teachers, nurses and educators in nutrition and health for tribal women.

(iv) Educated and skilled tribal young men will assist in economic advancement of their own community and join the mainstream as white collar and skilled workers in the cities. Government of Jharkhand and Chattisgarh will assist in their advancement because the tribal people now feel that their welfare is not dependent on decisions of legislators and implemented by officials located in Patna, who do not understand their problems but on those located in their villages in Ranchi or Raipur.

B. *Semi-desert areas of western Rajasthan*: These areas are in need of food-for-work programme in two out of three years. In such years, the local pastures are destroyed and the woodlands in the semi-desert areas become thinner because of over-grazing by cattle, sheep and goats. The people migrate from these areas to greener pastures in eastern Rajasthan and adjoining areas of Madhya Pradesh. In the early stages of the drought, before the monsoon rains, food, fodder and water are sent by the state government by road to feed the people and their livestock. However, if the rains fail, the pastoralists and their herds leave for several months and return only in the cool season.

C. *Himachal Pradesh and Uttaranchal, which lack communications*: These areas suffer from natural handicaps of small areas suitable for cropping besides flooding during the rainy season, illiteracy and poor health of the tribal people and lack of network of roads in some areas. Steps taken or needed to reduce the number of rural poor in the areas mentioned above are:

(i) Emigration of some farmers to cities with increase in size of families and some education of sons;

(ii) Education of tribal youth both boys and girls, to secondary school (or higher) levels so that boys can become white collar workers in offices of the State and local government, teachers, agricultural extension officers and para-medicos. Girls can make cleaner homes and become rural extension workers, teachers and nurses.

(iii) In cities where steel, industrial and power plants are located, boys should be encouraged to be trained in skills so that they can become skilled workers.

Mainly as a result of the development reviewed above and the measures taken by the Governments of Himachal Pradesh and Uttaranchal, remunerative employment and level of living of large numbers of people of both States has increased significantly in recent years. One indication of the change is provided by the fact that up to the 1960s, large numbers of young men came out to work as domestic servants in Delhi or cites in Punjab. No longer! The emigrant from these states are now mainly educated young men who seek employment as white collar workers in offices of the Central Government or public sector undertakings or as professional such as teachers.

As a result of the measures detailed above the areas in need for food for work programmes would be reduced progressively because large areas of formerly eroded land or covered with coarse sands and boulders would become productive. The nature of food for work programme in various areas has been described below.

D. *Other Areas of Concentration of poor where poverty can be eliminated*: The rural poor will be confined to (i) areas which have serious handicaps of deficient or variable rainfall and under-development of irrigation facilities. These areas of Rajasthan and of the Peninsular states of Maharashtra, Gujarat, Andhra Pradesh and Karnataka have been mentioned in various sections of this chapter. However, their number has been reduced progressively by development of irrigation in these areas and by migration of landless labourers and small farmers to metropolitan cities. The size of the poor will reduce in areas in which productivity of land is high and in which most of the rural population lives, because the increase in productivity will lead to increase in income and consumption of the small farmers and agricultural laborers. It has been explained that the number of rural poor in the western Himalayan region has been reduced greatly in recent decades by various development programmes of the last 5 decades.

Areas in Need of Food for Work Programmes can be Divided into Two Broad Macro-Regional Classes

I. ***Northern India***

Central and Eastern U.P. and North Bihar

(i) *The sub-mountain areas of U.P. and North Bihar*: Large areas of inherently fertile lands are covered every year by coarse sand, pebbles and boulders brought down by the monsoon floods of Kosi, Gandhak and other rivers in Bihar and several small areas in UP. Production in the rest of the states is not adequate to meet the needs of the population, especially in years of deficient or unseasonal rainfall. The areas can be reclaimed by a combination of afforestation in the hills and land reclamation by tractors or machine tools used by the farmers. Food for work programmes have to be undertaken for varying periods before and in many years even after the monsoon. Sikhs from Punjab, have already reclaimed large areas of such lands in northwest U.P. and established highly productive farms, which produce wheat, rice and sugarcane. In West Bengal, the government has assisted reclamation of large areas, which used to be destroyed every year by monsoon floods of Teesta river by construction of a dam on the river and reclamation of the lands below it by manual and mechanical means. The tribal population displaced by industrial units such as a steel mill and a thermal and hydro-power plant should be settled quickly in new areas and given grants to rebuild their homes and for cultivation of lands allotted to them and food-for-work programme should be undertaken for them until they are well settled in their new villages. The reclaimed lands should be given to the actual cultivators together with short and medium term loans for buying improved seeds, livestock and fertilizers as needed and pumps for irrigation. Ownership rights have already been conferred on actual cultivators, and those of the intermediary tenure holders such as *Zamindars* have been extinguished. As a result of these reforms, production of rice has increased steadily so much so that the deficit has been eliminated. Production of jute has also increased steadily.

The governments of U.P. and Bihar should do the same for increasing production of cereals through a combination of soil conservation measures in the hills and reclamation in the plains. The cultivators are hard-working and loans provided by the states to buy modern inputs, would be returned particularly if they were given by farmers' co-operatives. Medium term loans given to buy tractors and electricity or diesel operated pumps to the former *Zamindars* to cultivate the land left to them for self cultivation will mean better cultivation of the croplands and major increase in the irrigated area and consequent increase in production of cereals (wheat, rice, maize, gram, pulses and oilseeds). Production of mangoes which can be grown in many areas would add further to the value of agricultural output and income of many farmers.

(ii) *South Western U.P. and adjoining areas of Madhya Pradesh*: Large areas of otherwise fertile land have been rendered infertile because of erosion by wind and water. As a result, large cultivable areas are cut by ravines. There is need for reclamation of the land by construction of small check dams on the ravines so that the areas above the dams can be used as pastures for livestock and those below the dams become available for cultivation. The pastures with soil binding grasses and the foliage of the woodlands will strengthen the dams. Grazing in the pastures and cutting of trees for fuel-wood should be controlled carefully, preferably by the co-operatives of farmers. Exploitation of the farmers by money-lenders should be prevented because many small farmers become dacoits when they lose their lands while trying to repay loans taken from moneylenders.

(iii) *Western and Eastern Himalayan regions*: In Uttaranchal in the west and the 7 states populated by tribals in the north east Himachal Pradesh and Jammu & Kashmir which had large deficits earlier are now self-sufficient in most years due to increase in irrigation, although there might be deficits in some years. The states inhabited by tribals are deficient in foodgrains in most years. The deficit increases in years in which the local crop of rice is damaged by floods in the monsoon season. Rice and other foods have to be supplied to the people by road and in isolated areas dropped from the air because these states are not connected with the rest of the country by railway.

II. *Peninsular India*

(i) *Coastal Orissa*: Rice is the main crop. Coarse grains and pulses and oilseeds are planted along or after the rice has been harvested. Production in most of the years is adequate to meet the food needs of the people. However, the area is visited often by cyclones during September to December. As a result, large areas are flooded, the rice crop is washed away and tens of thousands are rendered homeless. The government of the state, because of red tape and inefficiency has not been able to organize relief quickly by supplying food, medicines, blankets and building materials so that the marooned people survive and do not fall victims to diseases of the respiratory or digestive tracts while they clear their flooded fields or rebuild their homes.

(ii) *Inland Orissa and Chhatisgarh*: These are among the most backward areas of the country. In inland Orissa, there are few roads which connect the area with the rest of the country. Semi-starvation is chronic because the tribals are very backward and their small fields are often washed away during the monsoon. Additional havoc is caused by the cyclones that visit the area from time to time between August and December. Despite financial assistance from the Central Government and special release of building materials to enable people to rebuild their huts and supply of food and blankets by the International Red Cross to the affected population, the government of the state is unable to organize relief for months together. As a result, tens of thousands die or are taken ill for lack of food or shelter and outbreak of easily avoidable diseases. The first priority in this area is to organize disaster relief by the government with financial and technical assistance from the Central Government using the supplies provided by it and international relief agencies. Along with the food for work programmes, campaigns have to be organised to prevent spread of diseases of the respiratory and digestive tracks. After a semblance of normalcy has been restored and before the advent of the next monsoon, improved high yielding seeds of rice, chemical fertilizers and pesticides, ploughs and other tools must be supplied to the cultivators so that they can harvest crops of rice or other grains.

The other areas in need of such programmes are:

(i) The Jharkhand region of Bihar inhabited mainly by tribals; a large part of Madhya Pradesh is also inhabited by tribals;
(ii) Parts of Telengana region of Andhra Pradesh and Northeast region of Karnataka;
(iii) Gujarat, Saurashtra, Kutch and the hilly areas inhabited mainly by tribals in the north eastern parts of the state;
(iv) Similar areas in south west Maharashtra: Most of the drought prone area of Telengana, North eastern Karnataka and south west Maharashtra were part of the dominion of Nizam of Hyderabad.

Food for work programme have to be undertaken for varying periods in years of deficient rainfall in order to avert starvation in all these areas. However, the need for these programmes would be reduced greatly if the programmes include re-afforestation in hills and reclamation of flood affected lands by various soil conservation measures in the plains. The forests, which provide fodder, fuel and some food to the tribals, should be given for management to the tribals instead of being destroyed by forest and mining contractors. The tribals who have been living in these forests for millennia would ensure that check dams which protect their rice fields are quickly restored after the rains. The tribals' population displaced by industrial units such as steel mills and thermal and hydro power plants should be settled quickly in new areas and given grants to rebuild their homes and for cultivation of the lands allotted to them. There is much dissatisfaction among the tribals who are displaced by construction of industrial units or power plants. The dissatisfaction is due to two reasons: (i) There are long delays in allocation of land and establishing new villages and farms; (ii) no loans or grants are given to them to rebuild their huts or to buy seeds, fertilizers, livestock and implements to cultivate the land allotted to them. Food for work programmes should be undertaken for them until they are well settled in their new villages. Tribal youth should be given training in industrial skills and educated so that they find jobs of skilled and white-collar workers in the numerous industrial units located both in Jharkhand and Madhya Pradesh.

Areas Not in Need of Such Programmes

(i) Punjab, Haryana, Western Uttar Pradesh and 3 districts of northern Rajasthan: These areas receive irrigation from canals, and from electricity or diesel operated pumps on irrigation wells and tube wells owned and operated by large farmers in U.P., Haryana and Punjab. High yield wheat and rice in Punjab; wheat, cotton and oilseeds in Haryana and wheat, oilseeds and sugarcane in western U.P. are the principal crops. The areas produce a large surplus of cereals for distribution through the public distribution system. Medium staple cotton is sent to mills to produce fine cloth. There are a number of wheat and rice flour mills in Punjab and wheat flour, cooking oil and sugar mills in U.P. Furthermore, there are several cotton gins and textile mills in Haryana.

(ii) Coastal Andhra Pradesh including especially the deltas of Godavari and Krishna rivers: Rice and sugarcane are the principal crops. There is a surplus of rice and a significant percentage of the country's sugar is produced in this area.

There are a number of sugar and rice mills which provide employment to marginal farmers and agricultural laborers.

(iii) Coastal Tamil Nadu including especially the delta of Kaveri river: The area produces enough rice which together with course grains (sorghum, millets) produced in the rest of the state are enough to meet the food needs of the state in most years.

(iv) South West Karnataka especially the area irrigated by a canal from Kaveri river located between Mysore city and Bangalore: High yield rice and sugarcane are the principal crops. Output of rice is adequate to meet most of the needs of the rest of the state.

The rice produced in Andhra Pradesh, Tamil Nadu and Karnataka areas mentioned above together with coarse grains (sorghum and millets) produced in unirrigated areas of the states is adequate to meet the consumption needs of the people of the unirrigated areas of these states also. However, there may be deficits in years of deficient rainfall in some unirrigated areas of both Karnataka and Andhra Pradesh especially those which had earlier formed part of dominion of the Nizam of Hyderabad.

(v) Kerala: The state receives rainfall from both the southwest and northeast monsoons. Variability of rainfall is low. Production of rice and tapioca, the principal foods of the population, is barely sufficient or insufficient in some years for the needs of the population. However, the deficiency can be overcome by purchase of rice from the surplus states because with millions of dollars received annually from the natives of Kerala working in the Gulf countries or in other cities of the country, the households which do not produce rice for their needs can afford to buy it through private traders. There is no need for distribution of food through the public distribution system.

(vi) Western Maharashtra: The valleys irrigated by canals on the small streams that flow west from the Western Ghats to the Arabian sea. High yield sugarcane and high yield dwarf rice and coarse grains are the principal crops. There is a large surplus of sugar which is sent to other states. Production of rice and coarse grains is adequate for local needs.

(vii) The area around Nasik which specializes in production of vegetables including onions, tomatoes and potatoes and fruit (mosambi, oranges and grapes). Fruit and vegetables are sent to cities in Maharashtra, Gujarat and much of north western India and also to the Gulf countries mainly to meet the demands of Indians working in these countries. In this area also irrigation by electricity or diesel-operated pumps on surface wells or deeper tube wells is well developed and enough grains (rice or sorghum) are produced to meet local needs.

(viii) The drought prone areas of Maharashtra are those located in the south west and south east which had formed earlier part of the dominions of the Nizam of Hyderabad or formed part of the former British province of Central Province and Berar: These areas might be insufficient in food to meet the demand of the population and for development and implementation of programmes for increase in production from their lands.

(ix) Coastal Gujarat: Local production of rice and coarse grains (sorghum and millets) is sufficient to meet the needs of the population. There is a surplus of cooking oil. Dairying is another source of income for small farmers, as mentioned earlier.

(x) The drought prone areas of Gujarat (Saurashtra and Kutch and the hilly areas inhabited mainly by tribals): Food for work programmes are needed mainly in years when the monsoon rains are deficient.

(xi) West Bengal and Assam: Production of rice is enough to meet the consumption needs of the population including that of the Kolkata Metropolitan District in most years. There could be small deficits in years of deficient rainfall or heavy floods during the monsoon season.

Similar changes have yet to become significant in the hilly and forested areas of peninsular India.

Food-For-Work Programme

One of the most common programmes is food-for-work programme in which balanced food (cereals, sugar, cooking oil and powdered milk) is distributed to the workers employed on works such as construction of approach roads to villages, construction and repair of tanks and digging of wells which would supply water for irrigation and for drinking as part of the wages for work. Concentration and repair of water wells increases water supply and often to improvement of quality of water. Balanced food is distributed to women with instructions to prepare liquid milk from powdered milk and to boil the milk before feeding the babies or children or drinking by themselves. Instructions about principles of nutrition, child care and keeping their houses and villages (or slums in metropolitan cities) clean should form an essential part of the programme.

The cost of food and kerosene distributed through the programme forms part of the wages given to the men working on them. Thus, the programme not only provides remunerative work to small farmers and landless agricultural laborers but also make them healthier. The completed works increase the productive areas by construction of approach roads and increasing sources of water supply for irrigation and for drinking.

Effect of Land Tenure

It is interesting to note that all the areas detailed above which are not in need of poverty alleviation programmes were, with the exception of the areas in Rajasthan, not under the intermediary tenure holders such as *Zamindars*, *Jagirdars*, etc. before independence. The farmers paid their land revenues and were provided services directly by the governments of the provinces and some progressive princely states. On the other hand, all the areas in need of poverty alleviation programmes are those in which the farmers were under intermediary tenure holders. Large areas inhabited by tribals in peninsular India formed part of kingdoms of princelings whose territories were too small to provide them with the revenues that would enable them to invest in economic development of the state. The intermediary tenure holders in the Indo-Gangetic plain states from West Bangal to central and south western U.P. were interested more in exploitation of the tenants than in increasing agriculture output. In most of these areas the rights of intermediary tenure holders have been extinguished on paper but not in fact.

The increase in agricultural output experienced in West Bengal has been due partly to abolition of rights of intermediary tenure holders in fact. The farmers, freed from the obligation to pay a proportion of their income from farming have had a strong incentive to increase agricultural output and their income. The state government has assisted them by providing the seed capital needed to increase agricultural output. Such reforms have been done on paper in Bihar and U.P. but not in most of the areas in fact. On the contrary, attempts to achieve the reforms in practice are resisted so strongly by the former landlords in Bihar that there is literally a class war between them and their tenants in parts of north Bihar. The state government while claiming to represent the former tenants is too weak to control the violence of the landlords. Furthermore, it has made little effort to provide through various cooperative institutions of farmers the seed capital for increasing agricultural output. In U.P. the rights of the intermediary tenure holders have been extinguished, in fact in, many areas, but not in others. Furthermore, the state government has not provided to the farmers the seed capital to increase agricultural output. Part of the reason for this is that both states are so large and populous that it is difficult for their governments to maintain law and order. In both states, the rights of intermediary tenure holders must be extinguished in fact and sub-regional structures must be created below the level of the state governments both for providing peace and security to the citizens as also for providing inputs of improved agriculture.

Increase in agricultural output is hampered in the Telengana area of Andhra Pradesh partly by the conflict between the former *Zamindars* and their tenants. Agricultural output would increase rapidly once the state government effectively enforces the rights of the actual cultivators on the areas cultivated by them. Short and medium term loans should be given to them to buy improved seed and fertilisers for current cultivation. The former landlords should also be given medium term loans to buy tractors and install diesel oil or electrically operated pumps on surface wells. The increase in agricultural output experienced in Rajasthan during the last 5 decades has been due in large part to the policy of the state government to give loans to both tenants for buying inputs of improved agriculture and installation of diesel oil or electric motors on their surface wells and to the former intermediary tenure holders for buying tractors and diesel or electric pumps to irrigate more effectively the lands left to them for self-cultivation. Such loans given initially by the state government are now being given through agricultural credit or nationalised banks. The managers of banks enforce repayment to reduce bad debts and the borrowers repay so that they can continue to get loans. The increased repayment of principal and interest has been minimized so that the draft on the state is minimised.

In the areas inhabited predominantly by tribals, short and medium term loans should be channeled as far as possible through their own associations. This will result both in appropriate utilisation of the loans and their repayment on time. In all areas inhabited by tribals, grants need to be given for building huts and clearing the lands for cultivation when they are visited by cyclones or excessive rains in the monsoon season.

Similar grants should be given to assist resettlement of the tribals displaced from their traditional homes for construction of industrial units and thermal or hydroelectric power projects. As mentioned earlier, there is much dissatisfaction among the tribals who are displaced.

In the foregoing sections are discussed measures through which the proportion of the poor has been greatly reduced and that of middle income groups increased in rural areas in which productivity of land is high. This will be a factor for economic and social stability as well as of strength in dealing with external aggression.

The Second World War was caused partly because the German middle class had been liquidated by the Bolshevik in the 1920s and the 1930s. It was won by the American middle class led by a President who had assisted them to get out of the great Depression of the 1930s. The long period of peace that the world has enjoyed after Second World War has been due to steady rise in income and level of living of the people of Europe, North America, Japan and South East Asia and Latin America. The principal area of conflict has been Africa where there is grinding poverty. The prospect of peace in the subcontinent would be greatly enhanced if there were a larger middle class in both India and Pakistan.

CONCLUSION

The foregoing sections have indicated that through appropriate soil conservation and reclamation measures, construction of approach roads, improvement of water supplies and providing advice and loans or grants to small farmers, the area which are in need of poverty alleviation programmes will be greatly reduced. The latest data available from the National Sample Survey indicates that the proportion of the population which is poor and is in need of such programmes has gone down significantly during the last decade from 36 per cent in 1993-94 to 26 per cent by 1999-2000. The decline is being attributed to the trickledown effect of rapid economic growth experienced during the 1990s. Another decade of such growth with welfare should result in further reduction in the proportion of such population.

The planners of the food for work programmes should appreciate that some of the most productive areas located both in north India and in peninsular India were in need of food for work programmes not so long ago. Hence, special emphasis should be given in these programmes to land reclamation, soil conservation and soil upgradation measures so that more and more people are employed in the areas as farmers and as agricultural labourers and the need for food for work programmes is progressively reduced.

The size of middle class would increase and that of poor reduced because the processes that have led to increase in income and consumption of the small farmers and agricultural laborers in areas in which productivity of land is high and in which most of the rural population lives, will continue.

The rural poor will be confined to areas which have serious handicaps of deficient or variable rainfall and under-development of irrigation facilities. These areas of Rajasthan and of the Peninsular states of Maharashtra, Gujarat, Andhra Pradesh and Karnataka have been mentioned in various sections of this chapter. Their number has been reduced progressively by development of irrigation in these areas and by migration of landless labourers and small farmers to metropolitan cities. It has been explained also that the number of rural poor in the western Himalayan region has been reduced greatly in recent decades by various developments of the last 5 decades.

The hard case of rural poverty today is among the tribal people of Jharkhand, Chhatisgarh, inland Orissa, Central and eastern Madhya Pradesh, Telengana region of Andhra Pradesh and the hilly and forested areas of Maharashtra, Gujarat and Rajasthan. These areas suffer from natural handicaps of small areas suitable for cropping, flooding during the rainy season, illiteracy and poor health of the tribal people and lack of network of roads in some areas. A programme for education of tribals can go a long way in reducing poverty in these areas.

Tribal young men educated up to higher secondary school level can be employed as white collar workers in the offices of the state government or industrial units located in their areas. They can also be quickly trained to become skilled workers in these plants. Teachers in schools and para-medico educated tribal young women will make cleaner homes and raise healthier children. Some of them can become teachers, nurses and educators in nutrition and health for tribal women.

Educated and skilled tribal young men will assist in economic advancement of their own community and join the mainstream as white collar and skilled workers in the cities. Creation of Jharkhand and Chhatisgarh will assist in their advancement because the tribal people now feel that their welfare is not dependent on decisions of legislators for programmes of development and their implementation by officials located in Patna, who do not understand their problems but on those located near their villages in Ranchi or Raipur.

APPENDIX-I

Table 11.1 *a*: Per Capita Availability of Selected Articles of Consumption

Sl. No.		*1998-99*	*1980-81*	*Increase 1998-99/1980-81*
		(gms. per day)		
1.	Food grains (gram per day)	450.71	410.4	Marginal increase
2.	Edible oil (kg. p.a.)	9.5	3.8	Nearly thrice
3.	Sugar (kg. p.a.)	14.9	7.3	Nearly twice
4.	Tea (gms. p.a.)	676	511	Some increase
5.	Fabrics (m. p.a.)	28.2	17.3	Nearly double
6.	Electricity consumption (kWh. p.a.)	1997–98 64.3	13.5	Five times
7.	People below poverty line	1996-97 29.2	1973–74 54.9	

Source: Tata Consultancy Services: Statistical Outline of India 2000-2001 Mumbai- 400001, Table 248, p. 213.

Agriculture	*Million Hectares (1996-97)*
Net area irrigated	55.1
Total area cropped	189.5
Irrigated area/ cropped area (%)	38.7 per cent

Table 11.1 *b*: Output of Foodgrains

(*In million tons*)

Sl. No.	*Items*	*1996-97*	*1980-81*
1.	Food grains	199.3	129.6
2.	Rice	81.3	53.6
3.	Wheat	69.3	36.3
4.	Pulses	14.5	10.6
5.	Oilseeds	25.0	9.4
6.	Tea	0.57	0.6
7.	Sugar cane + Jaggery	277.3	154.2
8.	*Cotton	14.2	7.0

Source: Tata Consultancy Services (TCS): Statistical Outline of India 2000-2001 Mumbai-400001, Table 53, p. 50.
* TCS Table, 2000-2001. Table 35, p. 39.

NOTES

1. An edited version of the Chapter in, "*Reinventing Regional Development*" in Honour of Prof. Gopal Krishan. Eds. Suryakant *et al.*, Rawat Publication, 2004.
2. The per capita income at constant 1983-84 prices has increased 3 times since 1950-51 and 1998-99. The proportion of people below poverty line has fallen from 54.3 per cent in 1973-74 to 29.2 per cent in 1996-97 and an estimated 18.0 per cent in 2001- 2002. Even if the latter figure is discounted the fall in poverty level is undeniable.

REFERENCES

Bhalla, Surjit S., (2003): "Crying wolf on Poverty", *Economic and Political Weekly*, Vol. XXXVIII, No. 27.

Dandekar, V.M. and Rath, N., (1971): *Poverty in India*, Institute of Political and Social Studies, Pune.

Krishna, Anirudh, (2003): "Falling in Poverty", *Economic and Political Weekly*, Vol. XXXVIII, No. 6.

Rowntree's book: *Poverty: A Study of Town Life.*

12

The Growth of Indian Agriculture: A Regional Analysis[1]

INTRODUCTION

Since agriculture is the largest single sector in the Indian economy, providing about 50 per cent of the gross national product and nearly 70 per cent of the employment, an adequate agricultural growth rate is essential for sustained economic progress. The growth rate of agricultural output has a considerable influence on the overall growth rate of the economy and on the productivity of a large part of the workforce. Moreover, a rapid increase in agricultural output is essential to meet the increasing demand for food and other agricultural products, which results from the rapid population growth (currently estimated at 2.5 per cent per year) and from the rise in per capita consumption. This is particularly important, since India had a food-supply deficit, even at extremely low levels of per capita consumption, at the beginning of the economic development process.

The importance of adequate agricultural growth to the success of India's efforts at planned economic development was demonstrated dramatically, if painfully, during the years 1965-67, when the country experienced widespread drought and a steep drop in agricultural output. Foodgrain production, for instance, declined from 89 million metric tons in 1964-65 to 72 million tonnes in 1965-66 and rose only slightly, to 78 million tonnes, in 1966-67. The fall in production led to scarcity and local famines, and large imports of 9 to 10 million tonnes of foodgrains annually were necessary. But agricultural production in 1967-68 and 1968-69 has been high again, with foodgrain production in both years estimated at around 95 million tonnes, mainly as a result of more favourable monsoons. But the drought experience has led to a reappraisal of development objectives and to the initiation in 1966 of an agricultural development programme that concentrates on new high-yielding seed varieties, chemical fertilizers, pesticides, and efficient water management in selected areas to increase output rapidly (Saran and Chawla, 1967, pp. 461-483).

India's three Five Year Plans included large outlays for increasing agricultural production: expenditures amounted to 36,330 million rupees, or 23.9 per cent of the total spent. But it is noteworthy that, whereas in the First Plan, which had been drawn up against the background of an acute food shortage, agricultural expenditure formed 36.9 per cent of the total, the proportion declined to 22.3 per cent in the Second Plan and to 21.8 per cent in the Third Plan (Saran and Chawla, 1967, p. 480). The reduced emphasis on agriculture followed improvement in the food-supply position during the First Plan. The reappraisal of development objectives and priorities, which took place after the drought years, will probably result in agriculture receiving a greater proportion of the total investment in the Fourth Plan (which begins this year) than it received in the earlier plans.

The study presented in this chapter describes the principal features of agricultural growth in the period 1952-53 to 1964-65, which covers thirteen of the fifteen years of the first three Five Year Plans (Ministry of Food and Agriculture, 1966, p. 3).[2] It brings out regional differences in growth rates and examines their relationship with the availability of moisture, with such variables as population growth, with levels of productivity per hectare and per worker, and with some indicators of modern technology. In this chapter the entire analysis is by states because data on agricultural growth rates and other economic variables are available only by states.[3] But the state is a rather large unit for analyses of this type: several of the states include within their borders areas with very different physical conditions, cropping patterns, and levels of economic development. It is recognized that contrasts within states can be as great as the interstate differences. The district is, therefore, a more suitable unit for such analysis, and it is hoped that data on agricultural growth rates and the relevant physical and economic variables will become available by districts before long. Then a more precise delineation of patterns of agricultural growth and their correlation with the relevant variables will be possible[4] (Directorate of Economics and Statistics, 1965).

GROWTH-RATE COMPARISONS

The growth rate of agricultural production in India during the period 1952-53 to 1964-65 (3.42% per year) was higher than the growth rate of total population (2.15%) and male agricultural workers (2.64%) (Table 12.1, lines 10-11)[5]. This constituted a reversal of a trend; for several decades before independence, agricultural growth had been much slower than population increase. In the forty-five-year period 1900-1901 to 1944-45 the population of undivided India (present-day India and Pakistan) increased by 38 per cent, while agricultural production increased by only 12.6 per cent, and foodgrain production remained stagnant. As a result the index of foodgrain output relative to population declined by 27 points (Mukherjee and Sivasubramanian, 1958, pp. 1-43). This stagnation made India a net importer of food grains in the early 1920s, though the county had been a net exporter up to that time. It also meant a decline of about 25 per cent in per capita availability of foodgrains (Bhattacharjee and Roy, 1958, pp. 188-224).

When the rate of population increase in the period 1952-53 to 1964-65 is compared with the growth rate of foodgrains, the latter is found to be only slightly higher than the population growth rate. But in the populous states of Uttar Pradesh, West Bengal, Maharashtra, and Gujarat, which had deficits or marginal surpluses of foodgrains even in the early 1950s, population has been increasing more rapidly than foodgrain output. These four states accounted on the average for two-thirds of the total foodgrain deficit in India in the three years 1961-63[6]. Accordingly, the explanation for India's recent food difficulties lies (apart from the drought of 1965-67) in the relatively slow growth of foodgrain output in the country generally, and in a number of the large and populous states particularly.

EXPANSION OF CROPPED AREA AND INCREASES IN PRODUCTIVITY

The growth of total agricultural output results from some combination of the expansion of cropped area and the increase in productivity of cropland, but in the study period productivity increased considerably more than the cropped area (Table 12.1, lines 1-3). Analysis of the annual index numbers of agricultural production, cropped area, and productivity for all India indicates that the rate of expansion of cropped

Table 12.1: Growth Rates in Agriculture and Related Data for India and Fourteen States

	India	*Punjab*	*Gujarat*	*Madras*	*Mysore*	*Bihar*	*Maharashtra*	*Rajasthan*	*Andhra Pradesh*	*Madhya Pradesh*	*Orissa*	*Kerala*	*West Bengal*	*Uttar Pradesh*	*Assam*
(1)	*(2)*	*(3)*	*(4)*	*(5)*	*(6)*	*(7)*	*(8)*	*(9)*	*(10)*	*(11)*	*(12)*	*(13)*	*(14)*	*(15)*	*(16)*
I. Linear Growth Rates of Crops 1952-53 to 1964-65															*(per cent per year)*
All Crops															
1. Output	3.42	5.56	5.12	4.91	4.06	3.21	3.19	3.08	3.06	2.79	2.72	2.52	2.07	1.82	1.25
2. Area	1.28	2.06	0.46	1.13	0.83	0.71	0.44	3.23	0.27	1.35	0.84	1.38	0.60	0.74	1.32
3. Productivity	1.91	2.86	4.52	3.46	3.03	2.39	2.62	–0.08	2.72	1.30	1.78	1.00	1.41	1.01	–0.07
Foodgrains															
4. Output	2.75	4.30	2.09	4.89	3.71	3.28	2.29	2.68	3.65	2.58	2.60	4.37	1.16	0.91	0.80
5. Area	1.02	1.63	–2.19	0.75	0.91	0.64	0.33	3.03	0.84	1.28	0.79	0.51	0.26	0.40	1.36
6. Productivity	1.60	2.26	5.34	3.92	2.64	2.55	1.94	–0.23	2.63	1.16	1.75	3.74	0.90	0.49	–0.48
Non-foodgrain crops															
7. Output	4.79	9.46	8.03	4.96	4.91	2.61	5.15	4.89	1.83	4.50	3.40	1.83	4.23	4.28	1.62
8. Area	2.56	4.90	5.93	2.45	0.59	1.84	0.83	5.13	–1.59	1.67	1.65	2.06	4.29	2.19	1.21
9. Productivity	1.79	3.08	1.64	2.05	4.03	0.78	3.65	–0.09	3.93	2.44	1.54	–0.20	–0.09	1.72	0.35

(*Contd.*)

(*Contd.*)

(1)	(2)	(3)	(4)	(5)	(6)	(7)	(8)	(9)	(10)	(11)	(12)	(13)	(14)	(15)	(16)
II.10. Growth rate of population 1951-61 (%)	21.50	25.84	26.88	11.85	21.57	19.78	23.60	26.20	15.65	24.17	19.82	24.76	32.79	16.60	34.45
III.11. Growth rate of male agricultural workers 1951-61 (%)	26.38	12.00	28.56	41.34	42.11	19.89	28.56	29.04	31.90	20.68	31.86	–5.70	36.76	15.57	35.33
IV. Relative Growth Rates (% per year)															
12. Of agricultural production relative to population	1.05	2.36	1.92	3.33	1.57	1.03	0.67	0.36	1.29	0.30	0.61	0.03	–0.91	0.14	–1.63
13. Of foodgrain production relative to population	0.49	1.36	–0.47	3.31	1.28	1.09	–0.06	0.05	1.80	0.13	0.52	1.52	–1.60	–0.64	–1.97
14. Of agricultural production relative to number of male agricultural workers	0.62	3.89	1.76	0.55	0.99	1.02	0.25	0.14	–0.10	0.60	–0.35	3.28	–1.18	0.23	–1.69

(*Contd.*)

(*Contd.*)

(1)	(2)	(3)	(4)	(5)	(6)	(7)	(8)	(9)	(10)	(11)	(12)	(13)	(14)	(15)	(16)
V. *Linear Growth Rates 1952-53 to 1964-65 (% per year)*															
Foodgrain crops															
Rice															
15. Output	3.64	12.31	5.98	6.04	5.96	3.63	3.38	5.56	5.15	2.34	2.88	4.42	1.42	5.08	0.78
16. Area	1.57	9.21	1.13	3.19	1.97	0.23	1.75	6.48	3.19	1.28	1.14	0.53	0.13	1.97	1.32
17. Productivity	1.80	1.80	4.61	2.19	3.33	3.36	1.41	–0.50	1.56	0.93	1.60	3.70	1.29	2.61	–0.47
(per cent)	(100.0)	(1.5)		(11.0)	(4.1)	(12.8)	(3.8)		(11.5)	(8.5)	(11.5)	(3.1)	(14.4)	(9.0)	(4.9)
Wheat															
18. Output	3.80	6.79	3.59		4.88	2.35	4.17	2.24		3.61				1.65	
19. Area	2.57	3.92	0.15		0.98	0.98	2.10	3.36		4.50				0.78	
20. Productivity	1.00	2.09	3.22		3.46	1.18	1.85	–0.85		–0.53				0.80	
(per cent)	(100.0)	(27.2)	(3.3)		(0.9)	(4.1)	(3.7)	(9.3)		(18.5)				(30.2)	
Jowar															
21. Output	1.99	0.66	1.28	4.61	2.71		2.95	–0.59	1.62	2.81				–1.31	
22. Area	0.40	0.42	–1.59	0.10	1.78		0.87	0.59	0.18	–0.24				–0.78	
23. Productivity	1.57	0.15	3.21	4.46	0.91		1.91	–1.10	1.26	3.22				–0.58	
(per cent)	(100.0)	(0.5)	(4.5)	(6.2)	(14.6)		(34.4)	(3.8)	(13.9)	(16.0)				(5.9)	
Bajra															
24. Output	1.34	–2.32	–0.37	3.60			1.48	4.13	0.74					–1.12	
25. Area	–0.20	–2.59	–4.04	–2.24			–1.12	3.73	–0.89					–0.94	
26. Productivity	1.62	0.55	5.96	7.63			3.10	0.51	1.88					–0.27	
(per cent)	(100.0)	(8.0)	(16.1)	(7.7)			(12.3)	(25.2)	(8.0)					(15.2)	

(*Contd.*)

(*Contd.*)

(1)	(2)	(3)	(4)	(5)	(6)	(7)	(8)	(9)	(10)	(11)	(12)	(13)	(14)	(15)	(16)
Gram															
27. Output	0.85	1.35				–0.29		5.19		1.91				–0.04	
28. Area	1.16	2.01				–0.80		6.12		0.91				–0.08	
29. Productivity	–0.24	–0.66				0.57		–0.50		0.95				0.05	
(per cent)	(100.0)	(27.4)				(4.8)		(12.9)		(16.4)				(31.2)	
VI. Non-foodgrain crops															
Cotton															
30. Output	3.81	9.35	6.48	5.56	2.06		2.45	5.85	0.74	–0.98					
31. Area	1.27	5.78	2.65	1.11	0.66		0.63	2.70	–0.48	–0.87					
32. Productivity	2.25	2.89	3.08	3.87	1.23		1.70	2.74	1.29	–0.17					
(per cent)	(100.0)	(19.7)	(26.6)	(7.6)	(7.2)		(24.3)	(3.2)	(2.9)	(7.0)					
Groundnuts															
33. Output	5.64		11.04	5.49	0.72		6.06		–2.00	11.12					
34. Area	4.40		15.04	3.69	0.87		1.28		–3.16	8.15					
35. Productivity	0.84		–1.11	1.24	–0.10		4.18		1.58	1.84					
(per cent)	(100.0)		(24.0)	(20.0)	(10.9)		(14.1)		(14.3)	(5.4)					
Sugarcane															
36. Output	7.83	9.28	17.86	10.50	14.58	0.65	9.83	6.34	13.21	7.96			6.73	4.13	3.18
37. Area	4.93	5.71	16.83	10.56	7.60	2.20	7.97	7.76	8.56	9.91			7.32	3.72	1.23
38. Productivity	1.93	2.26	0.53	0.04	4.02	–1.21	1.02	–0.53	2.52	–1.03			–0.31	0.28	1.76
(per cent)	(100.0)	(8.9)	(1.4)	(6.1)	(5.7)	(5.2)	(10.4)	(0.6)	(9.5)	(1.4)			(1.5)	(46.0)	(0.9)

(*Contd.*)

(*Contd.*)

(1)	(2)	(3)	(4)	(5)	(6)	(7)	(8)	(9)	(10)	(11)	(12)	(13)	(14)	(15)	(16)
Jute															
39. Output	5.20					–1.83					4.05		7.21	12.13	0.10
40. Area	4.01					2.29					3.50		6.00	6.18	1.20
41. Productivity (per cent)	0.85 (100.0)					–2.82 (17.7)					0.50 (6.8)		0.92 (56.9)	3.29 (2.7)	–1.00 (14.7)
VII. Gross Cropped Area Distribution of annual rainfall(%)															
42. Abundant (more than 75")	4.32	2.58	–	–	4.05	–	3.14	–	–	2.77	–	100.00	12.78	0.19	67.95
43. Assured (45"–75")	26.80	3.19	–	24.85	9.30	81.43	9.73	–	–	68.23	100.00	–	87.22	16.70	32.05
44. Medium (30"–45")	33.49	25.73	32.63	54.25	18.55	18.57	39.56	4.50	73.43	28.24	–	–	–	69.34	–
45. Low (less than 30")	35.40	68.50	67.37	20.90	68.10	–	47.57	95.50	26.57	2.31	–	–	–	13.77	–
VIII.46. Gross irrigated area/gross cropped area (%)	18.88	42.22	7.79	45.21	9.24	19.89	6.74	12.53	29.48	5.63	16.42	20.96	21.53	26.62	23.33
47. Index of moisture availability	214.62	179.25	140.32	249.16	154.49	301.33	172.04	117.03	202.91	277.12	316.42	320.96	321.53	229.74	323.33

(*Contd.*)

(*Contd.*)

(1)	(2)	(3)	(4)	(5)	(6)	(7)	(8)	(9)	(10)	(11)	(12)	(13)	(14)	(15)	(16)
IX. Index of Productivity (based on averages of years 1956-57 to 1958-59; India =100.00)															
48. Per hectare	100.00	131.71	64.58	176.21	64.91	119.53	65.08	51.65	118.85	80.55	132.72	126.17	168.75	128.25	174.04
49. Per agricultural worker	100.00	215.99	105.90	111.24	88.71	62.83	88.94	88.24	103.68	94.35	132.72	110.06	144.15	101.11	111.49
X. Use of Modern Inputs															
50. Consumption of chemical fertilizers ($N + P_2O_5 + K_2O$), 1965–66 (kg. per hectare of gross cropped area)	5.30	5.22	4.70	14.49	4.63	3.31	4.60	0.82	9.74	1.64	2.99	14.49	7.61	4.52	3.02
51. Co-operative credit: loans advanced by agricultural cooperatives to members in 1963-64 (rupees per hectare of gross cropped area)	19.52	19.22	33.78	56.31	14.34	4.73	30.24	3.56	21.25	13.73	8.31	42.74	10.06	22.17	0.62
52. Use of mechanical power in agriculture in 1960–1961 (units per thousand hectares of gross cropped area)	2.58	3.36	5.65	18.86	2.31	0.73	3.88	0.66	4.61	0.88	0.28	2.76	0.72	1.18	0.40

(*Contd.*)

(*Contd.*)

(1)	*(2)*	*(3)*	*(4)*	*(5)*	*(6)*	*(7)*	*(8)*	*(9)*	*(10)*	*(11)*	*(12)*	*(13)*	*(14)*	*(15)*	*(16)*
53. Composite index of use of modern inputs in agriculture (India=100.00)	100.00	109.06	160.24	430.96	83.45	38.32	130.69	19.89	157.13	45.13	36.61	199.81	74.34	81.53	25.22
XI. Development of Services															
54. Rural literacy rate (%)	19.0	18.4	24.1	24.7	20.0	16.1	21.5	10.9	16.8	12.7	20.1	45.4	21.6	14.3	24.9
55. Number of doctors per million of population	227	382	230	192	209	157	316	133	196	134	127	215	481	127	257
56. Length of surfaced roads (in kilometres) per thousand square kilometres	76.91	93.62	70.22	259.40	194.40	64.04	83.38	44.89	99.17	54.91	52.44	207.20	155.00	75.03	31.20
57. Number of towns per million rural population	7.49	11.65	11.82	13.73	12.61	3.60	9.37	8.59	7.50	7.89	3.77	6.41	6.77	4.15	5.47

(*Contd.*)

(*Contd.*)

(1)	(2)	(3)	(4)	(5)	(6)	(7)	(8)	(9)	(10)	(11)	(12)	(13)	(14)	(15)	(16)
58. Composite index of development of services (India = 100.00)	100.00	135.60	119.32	183.80	154.61	71.29	121.47	72.26	100.96	75.65	69.94	172.16	155.04	71.05	89.47
XII. 59. Composite index of agricultural development (India = 100.00)	100.00	162.54	138.62	228.55	96.96	65.00	104.29	66.06	116.79	73.69	82.95	127.85	93.00	78.62	57.72

Note: Numbers in parentheses show percentages of all-India output produced in the state in the triennium ending 1964-65.

Sources: Lines 1-9 and 15-41: "Growth Rates in Agriculture" Ministry of Food and Agriculture1966;
Lines 10, 11, 54, and 57: Census of India 1961, Paper No. 1 of 1962, Final Population Totals (Delhi, 1962);
Lines 42-46: *Indian Agricultural Statistics 1962-63;*
Lines 48 and 49: J.G. Anand: Measurement of the Actually Realised Agricultural Productivities per Acre and per Worker; in the Different Crop Regions of India, *in Agricultural Situation in India: Annual Number 1964*, Directorate of Economics and Statistics, New Delhi, 1964, pp. 401-411;
Line 50: *Fertilizer Statistics 1965-66,* Fertilizer Association of India, New Delhi, 1967, p. 101;
Line 51: "Statistical Statements Relating to the Cooperative Movement in India 1963-64" (Reserve Bank of India);
Line 52: "Livestock Census of India, 1961" (Directorate of Economics and Statistics, New Delhi);
Line 55: "Stock of Health and Medical Manpower," *Institute of Applied Manpower Research Working Paper No. 6*, New Delhi, 1965 (mimeographed), pp. 17-18;
Line 56: *Statistical Abstract of the Indian Union 1965*, Central Statistical Organisation, Delhi, 1966, pp. 314-315.

area was relatively rapid at first and slowed down later, while the rate of increase of productivity, which was slow in the early years, picked up considerably. This is shown by the growth rates given below, which have been derived by dividing the study period into two parts of eight years each, 1952-53 to 1959-60 and 1957-58 to 1964-65 (Table 12.2).

Table 12.2: Linear Growth Rates in Agriculture

(*per cent per year*)

	First Period 1952-53 to 1959-60	*Second Period 1957-58 to 1964-65*
Output	3.55	4.30
Area	1.84	1.02
Productivity	1.38	2.55

Expansion of cropped area results from extension of cultivation to new lands (that is, increase in "net area sown") and from increased multiple cropping (that is, an increase in the proportion of "area sown more than once" to "net area sown"). The gross cropped area of India increased by 19 million hectares between 1952-53 and 1962-63 (Table 12.3), but only two-thirds of this total, 12.8 million hectares, represented an increase in the net area sown; the balance came from multiple cropping of the existing cropped area. The growth of multiple cropping is closely linked with the extension of irrigation facilities; irrigation is necessary in most parts of India to produce the second (post monsoon) crop. It will be seen from Table 12.3 that increase in the gross irrigated area has been nearly equal to the increase in the area sown more than once.

Greater productivity also results from two additional factors: improvement in per hectare crop yields and substitution of more productive crops for less productive ones; for example, sugarcane for wheat, or groundnuts for the millets—jowar and bajra. In several states substitution appears to be a major ingredient of increased productivity. Gujarat has experienced the highest rate of productivity increase (4.52%), but the high rate is attributable partly to extensive replacement of the less productive jowar and bajra by the more productive groundnuts and cotton. The rate of expansion of the area under groundnuts has averaged 15.4 per cent a year, which is truly phenomenal. It is noteworthy that productivity (average yield per hectare) of groundnuts has declined, while that of jowar and bajra has increased (Table 12.1, lines 33-35 and 21-26). This indicates that some of the substitution of groundnuts for jowar and bajra has taken place on marginal lands of low productivity and has had the effect of lowering the average yield of the expanding crops and of raising the average yields of the contracting crops.

Table 12.3: Expansion of Cropped and Irrigated Areas

(In thousands of hectares)

	1952-1953	*1962-1963*	*Increase*	
			Area	*Per cent*
Gross cropped area	137,675	156,736	19,061	13.84
Area sown more than once	14,233	20,492	6,259	43.97
Net sown area	123,442	136,244	12,802	10.37
Area sown more than once as percentage of net sown area	11.53	15.04		
Gross irrigated area	23,305	29,598	6,293	27.00
Area irrigated more than once	2,183	3,935	1,752	80.26
Net irrigated area	22,122	25,663	4,541	21.50
Gross irrigated area as percentage of gross cropped area	16.93	18.88		

Sources: *Statistical Abstract of the Indian Union 1965* [See Table 12.1, footnotes]; *Indian Agricultural Statistics 1962-63.*

INCREASE IN FOOD GRAIN AND NON-FOOD GRAIN CROPS

Nearly three-quarters of the cropped land in India is under foodgrains (Table 12.4), which include cereals—rice, wheat, bajra, jowar, and maize and pulses or beans. The Indian diet consists almost entirely of cereals and pulses. Rice, wheat, and jowar are the most important cereals, and together occupy 42.5 per cent of the gross cropped area; among the pulses, gram is the most important. The nonfood grain crops include fibres (especially cotton and jute), oilseeds (groundnuts, linseed, etc.), sugarcane, plantation crops (tea, coffee, and rubber), tobacco, chilies, fruits and vegetables, and a number of others. Obviously, not all the non-foodgrain crops are non-food crops. But since the Indian diet depends so heavily on foodgrains, calculations of supply and demand for food are generally made in those terms. Moreover, most non-foodgrain crops are grown for sale, while food grains are grown to meet the food needs of subsistence farmers.

Table 12.4: Distribution of Cropped Area among Selected Crops, 1962-63

(*in thousands of hectares*)

Crop	*Cropped area*		*Per cent of total area*	
Foodgrains				
Rice	34,934		22.29	
Wheat	13,657		8.71	
Jowar	18,021		11.50	
Bajra	10,800		6.89	
Gram	9,242		5.90	
All foodgrains		116,009		74.01
Non-foodgrain crops				
Cotton	7,845		5.00	
Jute	851		0.54	
Tea	334		0.21	
Sugarcane	2,280		1.45	
Groundnuts	6,804		4.34	
All oilseeds		14,796		9.44
All non-foodgrain crops		40,729		25.99
Total		156,736		100.00

Source: *Indian Agricultural Statistics 1962-63*.

The growth of non-foodgrain crops has been nearly twice as high as that of foodgrains in India as a whole—4.79 per cent as compared with 2.75 per cent (Table 12.1, lines 7 and 4)—and has been appreciably higher in ten of the fourteen states. In Madras, the growth rates are similar, and in only three states—Kerala, Andhra Pradesh, and Bihar—is the growth rate of foodgrains higher than that of the non-foodgrain crops. The higher growth rate of non-foodgrain crops can be explained almost entirely by the more rapid expansion of the area devoted to them. Productivity has increased at similar rates for both groups of crops; the figures for all India are 1.79 per cent for non-foodgrain crops and 1.60 per cent for food grains (Table 12.1, lines 6 and 9).

Within the foodgrain group, the growth rates of rice and wheat have been higher than those of the inferior grains. These two crops have similar growth rates for output—3.64 per cent for rice and 3.80 per cent for wheat—but the contributions of expansion of area and increase in productivity differ. The productivity of rice has increased more than the area, but the reverse is true of wheat. The relatively low growth rates of jowar and bajra reflect the small change in the area they occupy; on the other hand, the comparatively high rates of increase in productivity of these crops result mainly from withdrawal of the crops from marginal lands. The growth rates are highest in states in which contraction of area under these crops has been most pronounced: jowar and bajra in Gujarat, bajra in Madras and Maharashtra, and jowar in Madhya Pradesh.

Among the four selected non-foodgrain crops, sugarcane has the highest rate of growth of output, almost 8 per cent, and the growth rates for groundnuts and jute are also much higher than the rate for any foodgrain crop. These high rates of growth of output are due primarily to the rapid expansion of the area under the crop; the rates of increase of productivity are not high. On the other hand, cotton, which has had only a modest expansion of area, has the highest rate of productivity increase of any crop—2.25 per cent.

An adequate explanation of the differences in rates of increase of output, cropped area, and productivity of foodgrains and non-foodgrain crops, or of individual crops, would take us far beyond the scope of this study. It would require analysis of resource allocation among competing crops, and therefore, in turn, analysis of crop prices and of inputs at regional and farm levels. But two facts must be mentioned in order to place the observed trends in historical perspective and to relate them to the effects of overall economic growth. First, the faster growth of non-foodgrain crops than of food grains only means extension into the post-independence period of a trend that had existed for several decades. Second, the faster growth of non-foodgrain crops and, among the foodgrains, the faster growth of wheat and rice than of other cereals, is in accord with the observed elasticities of consumer demand. Preference for the superior cereals, rice and wheat, and high elasticities of demand for sugar, oil, tea, and other non-grainfoods are to be expected in the early stages of economic development: they show the first effects of even small increases in per capita income. This response is welcome because it reduces the unhealthy preponderance of grains in the Indian diet.

But faster growth of non-foodgrain crops than of foodgrains also represents a shift in resource allocation; it means that some resources, which would have been allocated to production of food-grains if the growth rates of output of the two groups were equal, are instead given over to production of non-foodgrain crops. The effect is marginal, however. It is roughly proportional to the difference in rates of areal expansion of the two groups of crops; their rates of productivity increase are similar, and there is no evidence of a marked shift of resources to secure higher rates of productivity increase for either group. But since non-foodgrain crops occupy only a quarter of the gross cropped area of India, a 3 per cent increase in the area under them means a loss of potential increase of only 1 per cent of the area under foodgrains. If the rates of increase of area for both groups of crops had been identical in this period, the area under foodgrains would have been higher than it actually was in 1964-65 by only about 5 per cent. Additional output of food grains would have been of the same order, since the rates of increase of productivity for both groups have been similar.

REGIONAL DIFFERENCES IN GROWTH RATES

The growth rate of agricultural output ranges from 5.56 per cent in Punjab[7] to 1.25 per cent in Assam. Only four states—Punjab, Gujarat, Madras and Mysore—have experienced growth rates higher than the all India average of 3.42 per cent (Table 12.1). If the states are ranked according to the rate of growth of agricultural output and are divided into two groups, "high" and "low", with seven states in each, it is seen that six of the seven states in the high group are in the west and south of India, and five of the seven states in the low group are in the east and north-central parts of the country. Fig. 12.1 shows a fairly clear west-east dichotomy in growth rates; most of the states with high rates form part of a belt that extends from Punjab in the extreme northwest to Madras in the south. The exceptions to this pattern are Kerala and Andhra Pradesh, southern states that are in the low-rate group, and Bihar an eastern state that is in the high rate group.

In five states—Rajasthan, Punjab, Kerala, Madhya Pradesh and Assam—the expansion rate of the cropped area has been higher than the all-India average (1.28 per cent), but no geographical implications can be found in the pattern. On the other hand, the rate of increase of productivity has been higher than the all-India average (1.91 per cent) in seven states (Fig. 14.2), and the west-east dichotomy noted in the case of agricultural output is repeated. Most of the states in the high productivity group also have a high growth rate for agricultural output. The only exceptions are Rajasthan, which has a high growth rate for agricultural output but a low rate of productivity, and Andhra Pradesh, which has a low growth rate for agricultural output but a high rate of productivity.

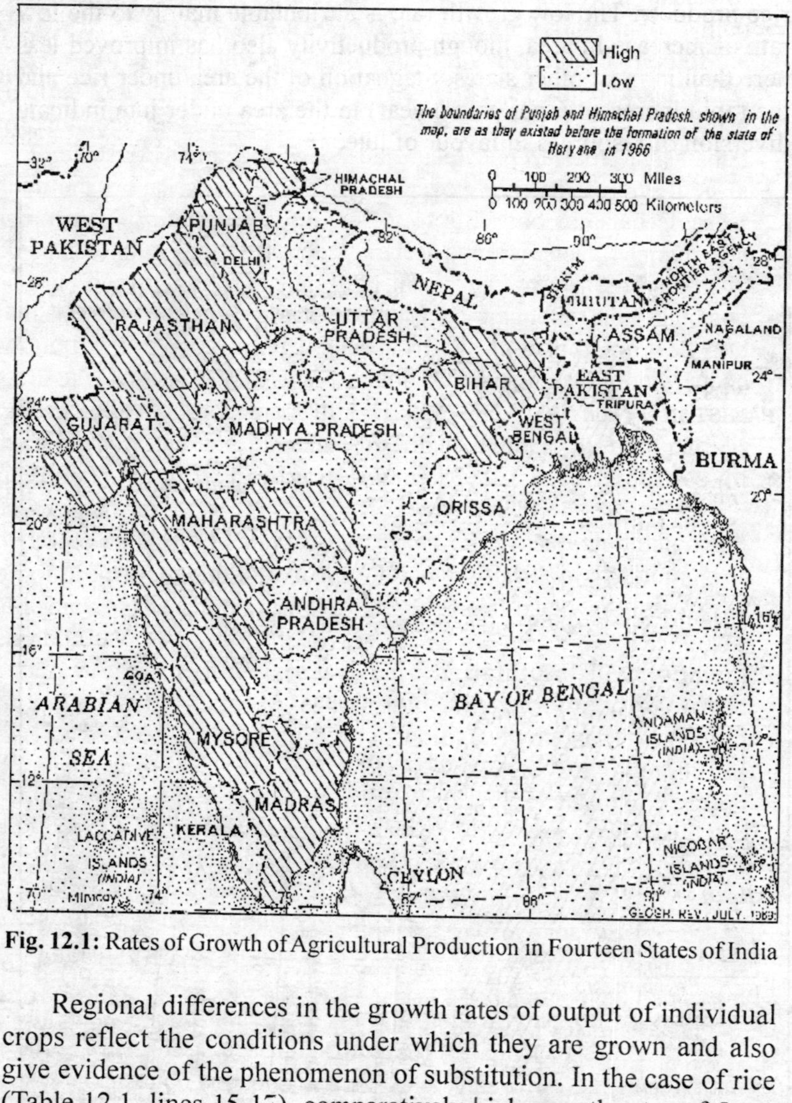

Fig. 12.1: Rates of Growth of Agricultural Production in Fourteen States of India

Regional differences in the growth rates of output of individual crops reflect the conditions under which they are grown and also give evidence of the phenomenon of substitution. In the case of rice (Table 12.1, lines 15-17), comparatively high growth rates of 5 per cent or more have been experienced in four major producing states—

Madras, Mysore, Andhra Pradesh, and Uttar Pradesh (Punjab and Gujarat are not major producers). The lowest growth rates have been experienced in Assam and West Bengal. The low rate in West Bengal is especially important because this state, with one-seventh of the all-India rice output in the triennium ending 1964-65, is the largest rice producer. The low growth rate is attributable mainly to the low rate of increase in area, though productivity also has improved less here than in most other states. Stagnation of the area under rice and the rapid increase (6 per cent a year) in the area under jute indicate diversion of resources in favour of jute.

Fig. 12.2: Rates of Increase of Agricultural Productivity in Fourteen States of India

In West Bengal and the other eastern and north-central states of India most rice is not irrigated, and yields are low in comparison with those in the southern states such as Madras, Mysore, and Andhra Pradesh, in which a large part of the crop is irrigated. It would appear that the growth rate of output, though not necessarily that of productivity increase, has been higher in the southern states. A similar phenomenon is noticeable, and in a more pronounced form, in the case of sugarcane. Yield differentials between the northern and southern states are even greater in this instance because the southern states have, in addition to irrigation, the climatic advantage of freedom from frost.

In the case of wheat, also, the major producing states show different rates of growth of output: Uttar Pradesh, the largest producer, has had slow growth, while Punjab, which comes next in production, has experienced rapid growth. In another important producing state, Madhya Pradesh, the total output of, and the area under, wheat have increased rapidly, but productivity has declined. Here areal expansion has been partly at the expense of jowar and on lands of lower productivity than those that were earlier under wheat.

Production of jowar, the third important cereal crop, is concentrated in the central and southern parts of the peninsula. Four states—Maharashtra, Madhya Pradesh, Mysore, and Andhra Pradesh—account for nearly 80 per cent of the total output. The output has grown at a lower rate than that of rice and wheat, principally because of the low rate of increase (or, in some states, a decrease) in the area under the crop.

Among the non-foodgrain crops, regional differences in the growth rate of jute and sugarcane have already been explained. The case of groundnuts is also interesting. Production of the crop is concentrated in the western and southern parts of the peninsula. It has experienced rapid growth of output in three of the five important producing states—Gujarat, Maharashtra, and Madras—with areal expansion the principal growth factor. But in Andhra Pradesh the groundnut area has contracted, and in Mysore it has expanded slowly, with corresponding effects on output. Cotton output, similarly, has increased rapidly in most producing states, but not in Maharashtra and Mysore; the differences in output are due primarily to different rates of expansion of cropped area. The reasons for such growth differentials, which are seen even in adjoining states, need more detailed analysis than is possible here.

AGRICULTURAL GROWTH RATES, AVAILABILITY OF MOISTURE, AND SELECTED ECONOMIC VARIABLES

The relationship of the agricultural growth rate to the availability of moisture and to certain economic variables has been examined through coefficients of correlation. The coefficients were calculated between the growth rates of agricultural output and of productivity and the variables and composite indices listed in Table 12.5. In addition, coefficients of correlation were calculated between certain of the variables (for example, the proportion of cropped area irrigated and the use of chemical fertilizers) in order to study the relationships among the variables.

Table 12.5: Coefficients of Correlation between Selected Variables and Agricultural Growth Rates

	Coefficient or Correlation
Growth rate of population and growth rate of agricultural output	–0.28
Growth rate of population and growth rate of foodgrain output	–0.51
Growth rate of male agricultural workers and growth rate of agricultural output	0.07
Average productivity per hectare and rate of increase of productivity	–0.18
Average productivity per agricultural worker and growth rate of agricultural output	0.33
Proportion of cropped area irrigated and rate of increase of productivity	0.09
Index of moisture availability and growth rate of agricultural output	–0.58
Index of moisture availability and rate of increase of productivity	–0.39
Proportion of cropped area irrigated and level of use of chemical fertilizers	0.58*
Proportion of cropped area irrigated and index of use of modern inputs	0.55
Level of use of chemical fertilizers and rate of increase of productivity	0.27
Index of use of modern inputs and rate of increase of productivity	0.52
Index of development of services and growth rate of agricultural output	0.48
Index of urbanization and growth rate of agricultural output	0.85*
Index of development of services and index of use of modern inputs	0.72*
Index of development of services and index of agricultural development	0.52
Index of urbanization and index of agricultural development	0.71*

* Significant at the 5 per cent level.

AVAILABILITY OF MOISTURE

The composite index of availability of moisture is based on annual rainfall and the proportion of irrigated land. All cropland was assigned to one of four rainfall zones (Table 12.1, lines 42-46), and the proportion of cultivated land in each zone was then multiplied by the weight assigned to the zone.[8] Finally the proportion of irrigated land was added to the total. Table 12.6 indicates that the states with high growth rates for agricultural output and productivity are drier than the states with low rates.

Table 12.6: Percentage of Gross Cropped Area in Each Rainfall Zone

State with	*Rainfall zone*				*Gross cropped area irrigated 1962-63*
	Abundant	*Assured*	*Medium*	*Low*	
High rate of growth of output	1.65	15.58	26.73	56.04	17.64
Low rate of growth of output	7.62	40.69	41.86	9.82	19.98
High rate of increase of productivity	1.69	15.96	38.42	43.93	20.45
Low rate of increase of productivity	7.42	39.52	27.69	25.37	16.83

In Gujarat, Karnataka, and Maharashtra, high growth rates for agricultural output and productivity have been achieved in spite of unfavourable moisture supply. In these states most of the cropped area is in the zone of low rainfall, and less than 10 per cent of it is irrigated. Only in Bihar and Tamil Nadu do favourable rainfall and high growth rates go hand in hand. On the other hand, several states with low growth rates for agricultural output and productivity—Orissa, Kerala, West Bengal, and Assam—have favourable moisture conditions. The entire cropped area of these states is in the zones of abundant or assured rainfall, and 16 to 23 per cent of it is irrigated. In Madhya Pradesh and Uttar Pradesh, two other states with low rates of agricultural growth, the moisture supply is only slightly less favourable. In Madhya Pradesh, the proportion of irrigated land is low, 5.63 per cent, but almost three-quarters of the state are in the zones of assured or abundant rainfall. Most of the cropped land in Uttar Pradesh is in the zone of medium rainfall, but 26.62 per cent of it is irrigated.

The coefficients of correlation of the index of moisture availability with the growth rate of agricultural output and with the rate of increase of productivity are both negative, –0.58 and –0.39 respectively (Table 12.5). The correlation between the proportion of cropped area irrigated and the rate of increase of productivity is extremely low, 0.09, and it is not significant. These coefficients confirm the lack of relationship that has already emerged between availability of moisture and agricultural growth rates.

The lack of relationship may come as a surprise to those who are concerned with agricultural development in India, since an assured moisture supply has always been regarded as the prime requisite of agricultural development. Development plans have emphasized expansion of irrigation and concentration of agricultural development efforts in areas with assured moisture supplies. More than 40 per cent of the total expenditure on agricultural development programs in the three Five Year-Plans was for irrigation (Saran and Chawla, p. 480).

Irrigated areas and areas with an assured moisture supply have been selected for intensive agricultural development programmes, on the ground that farmers will adopt modern, capital-intensive production techniques more readily because of greater security of return on investment. Districts with an assured moisture supply were chosen for the Intensive Agricultural District Programme (IADP), which started with seven districts in 1959 and now covers sixteen districts. Since India adopted the "New Agricultural Strategy" in 1966, development efforts have emphasized efficient water management, use of chemical fertilizers, high yielding seed varieties, and pest control on about 25 million hectares of land with adequate moisture. On about half the area quick-growing varieties of rice and other cereals are to be substituted for varieties that take longer to mature, so that a second crop can be obtained (Saran and Chawla, p. 475).

Long-term programmes of agricultural development also emphasize maximum expansion of irrigation facilities and the concentration of development resources, especially modern inputs, in the irrigated areas (Sivaraman, 1967, pp. 433-447). This strategy has been outlined in detail and occupies the central place in the programme of increasing agricultural output recommended in the report of India's population and food problems submitted recently by the (United States) President's Science Advisory Committee, Panel on the World Food Supply (William, pp. 673-711). The Panel recommended heavy concentration of resources in intensive-cultivation areas, which could be completely irrigated, holding other areas lightly. The Panel's projections anticipate that intensive-cultivation areas will increase from 2 million hectares in 1967 to 42 million hectares in 1986, when they will constitute about 33 per cent of the cropland under foodgrains, but will produce almost 60 per cent of the food grains, and will use more than 60 per cent of the chemical fertilizers applied to foodgrains. Average yields in intensive cultivation areas will be about three times the yields in the rest of the area under foodgrains (William, pp. 704-706). This strategy is backed by considerable experimental evidence which shows that per hectare yields of foodgrains increase with high yielding seed varieties and other inputs, under conditions of assured moisture.

The absence of a relationship between availability of moisture and agricultural growth rates should not be taken to mean that an adequate or assured moisture supply is not required for agricultural development, or that the policies of expansion of irrigation and resource concentration in areas with adequate and assured moisture supply are wrong. But although moisture supply may be a necessary condition for agricultural development, it is not the only requirement, and there is an urgent need to investigate the factors that prevent a number of Indian states with good rainfall and extensive irrigated areas from attaining high agricultural growth rates. Remedial measures aimed at removing the growth-inhibiting factors are just as important as the irrigation programmes that create a higher agricultural-production potential.

GROWTH OF POPULATION AND OF AGRICULTURAL WORKERS

Population growth influences agricultural output in two ways: it increases the demand for agricultural products, and it increases the supply of labour. However, the relationship between agricultural output and labour supply is most easily studied by considering the growth rate of agricultural workers (Table 12.1, lines 10-14). The coefficient of correlation between the population growth rate and the growth rates of agricultural output and of food grain output are both negative (Table 12.5); the latter has a value of –0.51, which underlines the difficulties arising in several states in which population has grown rapidly but foodgrain output has not. The low coefficient of correlation between the growth rates of male agricultural workers and of agricultural output (0.07) indicates that factors other than labour supply have had the major influence on agricultural output in this period. The finding is not unexpected, considering the widespread underemployment in Indian agriculture.

PRODUCTIVITY PER HECTARE AND PER AGRICULTURAL WORKER

The indices of productivity per hectare and per agricultural worker (Table 12.1, lines 48-49) are based on indices of intensity of land use, cropping pattern, and yield per hectare in the period 1956-59. The influence of the cropping pattern on the index of productivity per hectare is clear from the fact that all states in which rice is an important crop have significantly higher index values than do states in which the area under rice is small. The range of interstate variation of the index is of the order of 3:1; the highest values are for Tamil Nadu, Assam, and West Bengal, and the lowest are for Rajasthan, Gujarat, Mysore, and Maharashtra.

Interstate differences in productivity per agricultural worker are somewhat larger than those in productivity per hectare; the figure for Punjab is three and a half times that for Bihar. Differences of this order, which might appear surprising at first, indicate that large differences in productivity (and income) per worker can exist even in a situation of overall high population pressure. Moreover, the existence of pronounced differences between adjoining states (for example, West Bengal and Bihar, or Punjab and Rajasthan) indicates higher geographical immobility of labour. The coefficient of correlation between productivity per hectare and the rate of productivity is negative, –0.18, indicating a lack of distributional relationship between the two.

If a high positive correlation had been found between the level of productivity per agricultural worker and the rate of growth of agricultural output, it would have indicated that the capacity to achieve increases in output per worker is greater at higher levels of per capita income. This could have been interpreted as the result of higher levels of savings and investment, or of greater output per worker (which itself is the result of better nutrition and health), or of a number of other reasons. On the other hand, a high negative correlation would have suggested that tensions arise from farmers in poorer states attempting to catch up with their more prosperous neighbours (though one would expect the tension effect to be weak in a situation of pronounced immobility of labour). But, in fact, the actual coefficient of correlation is low (0.33), which indicates that the existing level of productivity per worker has little influence on the growth rate of agricultural output.

USE OF MODERN INPUTS

Three indicators—use of chemical fertilizers, use of mechanical power, and use of cooperative credit—have been selected as indicators of the adoption of modern technology in agriculture (Table 12.1, lines 50-53)[9]. The choice of the first two indicators is obvious, but inclusion of cooperative credit deserves comment. It was selected primarily as a measure of institutional advance: it indicates the successful adoption of cooperative institutions, which have played an important role in the development and modernization of agriculture elsewhere and which are being encouraged by the Indian government. But the amount of cooperative credit per hectare of cropland is not a good measure of agricultural investment, for several reasons. First, investment in agriculture is different from loans to farmers, since some of the loans are for consumption purposes, while some of the investment is financed from personal savings of the farmers. Second, loans from cooperative societies are only part of the total borrowings of farmers; other sources include the government, moneylenders, relatives, and friends. A survey of rural debt and investment conducted by the Reserve Bank of India in 1961-62 revealed that loans from cooperatives formed only 18.7 per cent of the total borrowings of farmers (Jakhade, 1967, pp. 540-549). Finally, the figures in Table 12.1 relate only to short-term and medium-term loans, which are used primarily to finance current agricultural operations or short-term investments such as buying a pair of bullocks; they do not include loans for long-term investments such as irrigation wells.

Data on the use of chemical fertilizers relate to nitrogen, phosphate, and potassium fertilizers and are given in terms of kilograms of plant nutrient ($N + P_2O_5 + K_2O$) per hectare of gross cropped area. Data on use of mechanical power in agriculture are derived from the number of tractors and electric or oil-driven pumps in use on farms, as reported in the Livestock Census of 1961. Each tractor has been considered equivalent to two units, and each pump as equivalent to one unit, in converting the figures into units of mechanical power. Data on cooperative credit, as indicated, relate to short-term and medium-term loans. The composite index of use of modern inputs has been calculated by converting the figures for each indicator into an index (with the all-India average as 100) and then averaging the values. In this way, each indicator has been given equal weight in the composite index.

The figures for individual indicators and for the composite index show large interstate variations. The range is in the order of 18:1 for chemical fertilizers, and it is even larger for the other two indicators and for the composite index. Madras has the highest figures for the three indicators and for the composite index; Rajasthan and Assam have the lowest. Most of the southern and western states have appreciably higher figures than the eastern and north-central states have. These differences reflect, to some extent, the influence of factors such as rainfall, cropping patterns and development of irrigation. But even more they indicate differences in the acceptance of modern technology. Use of chemical fertilizer, for instance, is higher in Tamil Nadu, where most of the cropped area is in the zone of medium rainfall and 45 per cent of it is irrigated, than in Rajasthan, where most of the land is in the zone of low rainfall and only about 12 per cent is irrigated. Similarly, use of mechanical power is higher in Tamil Nadu, where groundwater conditions facilitate development of lift irrigation, than in Madhya Pradesh, where conditions are less favourable. But such explanations do not adequately explain the large interstate differences that exist. Low indicator values in the eastern states—Assam, Bihar, West Bengal, and Orissa—and in Uttar Pradesh indicate, primarily, a lag in adopting modern techniques. Also, large interstate differences in the value of cooperative credit per hectare indicate differences in the willingness and the capacity of farmers to use cooperative credit for agricultural purposes.

The coefficient of correlation between the level of use of chemical fertilizers and the rate of increase of productivity, 0.27, is low; but that between the index of use of modern inputs and the rate of increase of productivity is higher, 0.52. However, even this last is not significant at the 5 per cent level. The correlations between irrigated land and the use of chemical fertilizers, and between irrigated land and the index of use of modern inputs, are both above 0.5, but again are not significant at the 5 per cent level. However, the index of use of modern inputs has a significant correlation, 0.72, with the index of development of services, which indicates that use of modern inputs is influenced by factors such as the level of literacy of farmers, the existence of good communications, and the number of towns.

INDEX OF DEVELOPMENT OF SERVICES

The index of development of services (Table 12.1, line 58) is a composite based on four indicators: the rural literacy rate (education), the number of doctors per million of population (medical care), the network of roads in kilometres of roads per thousand square kilometres (communications), and the number of towns per million rural inhabitants (urbanization). It was constructed by first calculating index values for the individual indicators and then averaging the values, in the same way as in the index of use of modern inputs.

The number of towns was selected as an indicator of urbanization in preference to the proportion of urban population to total population; it was felt that not only the size of the urban population but the pattern of its distribution may have an influence on the development of agriculture. An urban population concentrated in one or two cities is likely to have different effects on rural areas than the same population distributed among a number of small or medium-sized towns; the greater number of points for rural-urban interaction may have an influence on diffusion of new ideas and techniques among farmers. It was interesting to test this hypothesis, since the view has recently been expressed that the number of towns in India is unusually small in relation to the size of the rural population and that India should undertake a programme of building 10,000 to 12,000 new market towns with facilities for such activities as marketing and processing of agricultural products, distribution of consumer goods, maintenance of farm implements, agricultural extension services, and the like, which are needed for agricultural development and for the modernization of rural life (National Council of Applied Economic Research, Chapter 1, 1965).

Interstate variations in the value of the index of development of services are much smaller than was the case in the index of modern inputs; the range is in the order of 3.5:1. The southern states and all the western states except Rajasthan have much higher index values than most of the eastern and north-central states do. The important exception is West Bengal, an eastern state, which has one of the highest values in this index.

The coefficient of correlation between the index of the development of services and the rate of growth of agricultural output is less than 0.5 and is not significant at the 5 per cent level. But the correlation between the index of urbanization and the growth rate of agricultural output is high, 0.85, and is significant at the 5 per cent level. The index of urbanization also has a high and significant correlation, 0.71, with the composite index of agricultural development. These coefficients suggest the possible existence of a relationship between the number of towns in a state and its rate of agricultural progress.

INDEX OF AGRICULTURAL DEVELOPMENT

A composite index of agricultural development (Table 12.1, line 59) based on three factors—the growth rate of agricultural output, the use of modern inputs in agriculture, and the productivity per hectare—has been constructed to give an overall indication of comparative levels of agricultural development in different states. As in the other composite indices, the three constituents are given equal weight. The values of the index show an interstate variation from 228.55 in Tamil Nadu to 57.72 in Assam. The states have been ranked by values of the index and have also been divided into two groups, "high" and "low," with seven states in each (Fig. 12.3). It is noteworthy that the west-east dichotomy, to which reference has been made in discussion of growth rates, is even clearer here.

The coefficient of correlation of the index of agricultural development with the index of development of services is more than 0.5, but it is not significant at the 5 per cent level. However, the correlation of the index of agricultural development with the index of urbanization, 0.71, is significant. The relationship of the index of agricultural development with relevant socio-economic and physical variables needs further study in order to understand the causes of differential progress between states and, in particular, of the slow progress in some.

The causes of slow progress will, of course, differ from state to state, but it is worth mentioning that all the states with low values in the index of agricultural development are formed from areas that were formerly in the British provinces that had the *zamindari*[10] system of land tenure (for example, West Bengal, Bihar, and Uttar Pradesh) or in the small, backward princely states (for example, Rajasthan

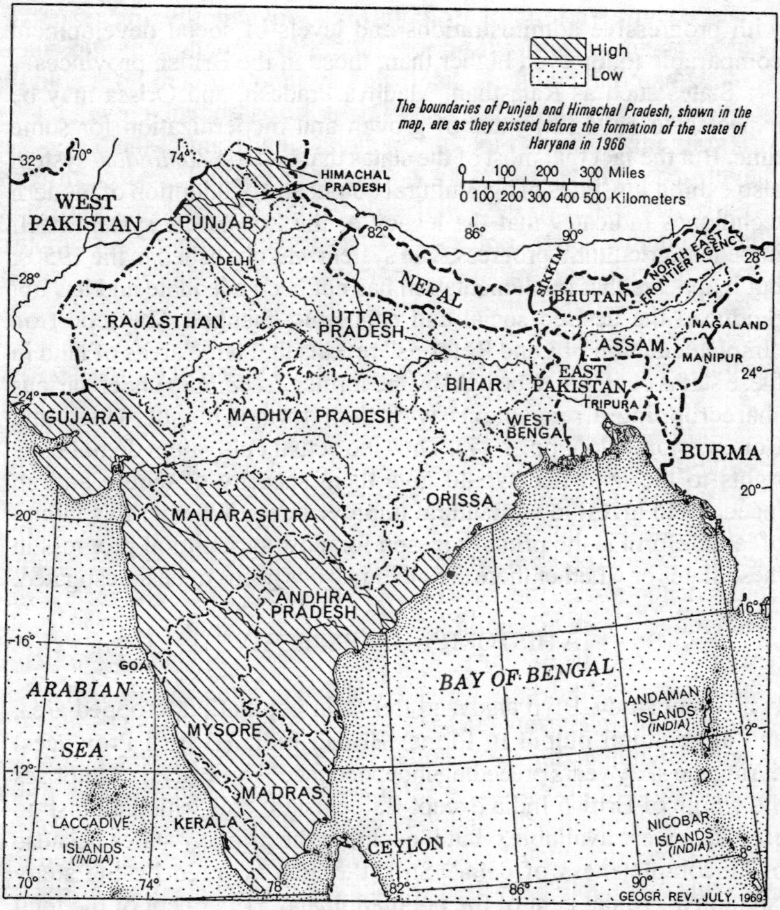

Fig. 12.3: Indices of Agricultural Development for Fourteen States of India

and Madhya Pradesh). In the case of Orissa, the coastal area was included in a British province having the *Zamindari* system, and the inland areas were within a number of small princely states. Moreover, Orissa and Madhya Pradesh have large tribal populations, which are at low socio-economic levels.

On the other hand, all states that have high values in the index of agricultural development are mainly formed either from British provinces with land-tenure systems approximating peasant proprietorship (now Tamil Nadu, Maharashtra, and Punjab) or from princely states (for instance, Mysore and Travancore now Kerala), with progressive administrations and levels of social development comparable to, or even higher than, those in the British provinces.

States such as Rajasthan, Madhya Pradesh, and Orissa may be expected to have low rates of growth and modernization for some time. But the fact that most of the states that had the *Zamindari* system also exhibit low rates of agricultural output and of adoption of modern techniques indicates that the legacy of the *Zamindari* system itself impedes agricultural progress. The system was abolished in the 1950s, but it appears that implementation has not been adequate and has not produced the desired social and economic changes. The report on "Implementation of Land Reforms" reveals that large areas of land in these states continue to be held by the former *Zamindars* under various sharecropping arrangements with their former tenants (Planning Commission, 1966, pp. 1-17). Thus the actual cultivators do not have rights to the land that would give them security of tenure and an incentive to invest in agricultural improvements. Whether this failure of land reform is the primary reason for slow agricultural progress in these states or whether there are other reasons needs to be investigated.

A HISTORICAL PERSPECTIVE

In a recent study, Blyn analyzed trends in population, cropped area, and agricultural output in former British India (British Provinces) during the sixty years preceding independence. The analysis comprises the whole of British India except Baluchistan, "for which almost no crop data were available," but it excludes the princely states because of "incompleteness of data." Still, the area covered by the study contained "76 per cent of the population and 51 per cent of the total area of all India in 1941" (Blyn, 1966, p. 33). A comparison of Blyn's data with the data in this study shows interesting differences and similarities between the trends in the two periods. The growth rates of both population and agricultural output have been appreciably higher in the recent period than before independence. But whereas in the recent period the growth rate of agricultural output has been well ahead of the growth rate of population; agricultural output in the earlier period had not kept pace with population growth. However, two trends noted in the present study—faster growth of output of non-foodgrain crops than of foodgrains, and faster growth of agricultural output in the south than in the east or in Uttar Pradesh (United Provinces in the pre-independence period)—had already appeared in the early years of this century. Of course, comparison of trends in the post-independence period with those in the period studied by Blyn must be confined to the most general terms because of the political changes that have occurred since 1947, including the formation of India and Pakistan, integration of the princely states, and reorganization of the Indian states.

The broad pattern of regional differences revealed by the present study will probably not change much as a result of the more detailed, district-level analysis that will soon be possible. The pattern has historical roots, which suggests the need to investigate the causes of differential progress and, in particular, the causes of slow progress in the eastern and north-central states. The investigation is essential for evolving remedial measures that will enable these states, which have a high potential for agricultural growth because of favourable moisture and soil conditions, to participate more effectively in agricultural progress.

NOTES

1. *The Geographical Review*, Vol. LIX, No. 3, 1969 pp. 348-372. New York.
2. A recent publication by the Economic and Statistical Adviser to the Ministry of Food and Agriculture, Government of India, gives linear and compound growth rates for two periods, 1949-50 to 1964-65 and 1952-53 to 1964-65, and also indicates the relative contributions of expanded cropland and of increased productivity to the growth of output. However, data by states are given only for the period 1952-53 to 1964-65 because "index numbers for the states are available on a uniform basis only from 1952-53".
3. The small Himalayan state of Himachal Pradesh has been omitted from this paper because data for most of the economic variables are not available. Its exclusion reduces the coverage, in terms of gross cropped area, from 99.1 to 98.8 per cent.
4. Data on area, production, and yields of individual crops by districts are found in *Indian Agricultural Statistics.* However, data on total agricultural output and growth rates are not available, and growth rates would have to be calculated especially because the boundaries of many districts have changed during the 1950s and 1960s.
5. Only male agricultural workers have been considered in this comparison, since data on the number of female agricultural workers are not comparable in the censuses of 1951 and 1961 because of changes in definition. Most female agricultural workers are women of cultivating households who help on the family farms; they are not wage earners. The change in definition of

"worker" adopted in 1961 resulted in a far larger number of women being returned as workers than had been the case in 1951. The number of female workers in all-India in 1961 was 52.2 per cent higher than in 1951, and the increases in some states were large (127.7 per cent in Andhra Pradesh and 188 per cent in Madras).

6. From unpublished data supplied in 1968 by the office of the Economic and Statistical Adviser, Ministry of Food and Agriculture.
7. Punjab refers to the State as it was before the creation of the new state of Haryana in 1966.
8. The rainfall zones with more than 45 inches were given a weight of 3; the zone with 30 to 45 inches, 2; and the zone with less than 30 inches, 1. An additional weight of 1 was given for irrigation in all rainfall zones.
9. Improved seed, important as it is as a factor in agricultural output, had to be excluded because of deficiencies of data.
10. *Zamindars* were revenue farmers who acted as intermediaries between the government and the cultivators. They acquired considerable social prestige and political power, and some were regarded as virtual rulers of their areas.

REFERENCES

Anand, J.G. (1964): "Measurements of the Actually Realized Agricultureal Productivities per acre and per worker in the different Crop Regions of India" in *Agricultural Statistics in India, Annual Number*, Directorate of Economics and Statistics.

Bhattacharjee, J.P. and Roy, S.M. (1958): "Trends of Consumption of Food and Foodgrains in India", in *Studies in Indian Agricultural Economics*.

Blyn, George (1966): *Agricultural Trends in India*, 1891-47, Philadelphia.

Central Statistical Organization (CSO): "*Statistical Abstract of the Indian Union*, 1965" Delhi 1966.

Census of India (1962): "Final Population Totals Paper No. 1 of 1962", Delhi.

Directorate of Economics and Statistics (1965): *Indian Agricultural Statistics*, 1962-63, Vol. 1, New Delhi.

Fertilizer Association of India (1967): "Fertilizer Statistics 1965-66" New Delhi.

Institute of Applied Manpower Research (1965): "Stock of Health and Medical Manpower". Working Paper No. 6. New Delhi (Mimeographed).

Jakhade, V.M. (1967): "Agricultural Production, Credit and Institutional Arrangements", *Indian Journal of Public Administration,* Vol. 13.

Ministry of Food and Agriculture (1966): *Growth Rates in Agriculture*, New Delhi [mimeographed].

Mukherjee, P.K. and Sivasubramanian, S. (1958): "Agricultural Output and National Income in India", in *Studies in Indian Agricultural Economics*, (ed. by Bhattacharjee, J.P.; Indian Society of Agricultural Economics, Bombay, 1958).

National Council for Applied Economic Research (1965): *Market Towns and Spatial Development in India*, New Delhi.

Planning Commission (1966): Government of India, *Implementation of Land Reforms*.

Reserve Bank of India (1963): "Statistical Statement Relating to the Cooperative Movement in India."

Saran, R. and Chawla, H.L. (1967): "Food Production Policies and Programmes since Independence-A Historical Review", *Indian Journal of Public Administration*, Vol. 13.

Sivaraman, B. (1967): "The Strategy of Food Production", *Indian Journal of Public Administration*, Vol. 13.

William Holst (1967): "Evaluation of Population and Food Production Problems of India", in the *World Food Problem: A Report of the President's Science Advisory Committee*, Vols. 2; Washington D.C.

13

The Geography of Production of Perishable Foods in India[1]

INTRODUCTION

The purpose of this chapter is to present the readily available facts about production, transport and storage of perishable foods for consumption in the cities and rural areas of agricultural prosperity in India. This is a subject on which so much is written in the print and electronic media in Europe and North America that even a grade school children knows where the milk, orange juice, eggs and bread for their breakfast, and vegetables and meat for their lunch and dinner come from. However, there is so little mention of the sources of supply of these foods in the print and electronic media in India that even college graduates do not know about the areas producing these foods.

The foods considered are: milk, vegetables, fruits, poultry (chicken and eggs) and fish. It is necessary to explain at the outset that adequate consumption of all or some of these foods is essential for health. They supply animal protein, vital minerals and fibre. Furthermore consumption of vegetables or fish in the form of curries makes a cereal-dominated meal palatable and enjoyable.

Production and consumption of all these foods have gone up rapidly during the last half a century. Although a large part of the consumption is in the cities, there is an increasing consumption also in rural areas of agricultural prosperity such as Punjab, Haryana and Western U.P. which benefited from the green revolution in wheat, and Andhra Pradesh and Tamil Nadu which benefited in rice. Sea fish has formed an essential part of the diet of most people (except Brahmins in some states) living along the east and west coasts of India for millennia.

The chapter discusses production, transport and distribution of milk, vegetables, fruits, poultry, fish and shrimp.

Milk

The traditional mode of supply of milk in cities is by milkmen who keep their buffaloes or milch cows within or on the outskirts of the cities. The increasing demand of the rapidly growing population of the cities, was met by milkmen in villages located within a radius of about 40 – 80 kilometres of the cities. Thus, before the establishment of the dairy cooperatives, Delhi obtained its milk from milkmen who kept their milch animals within the city or on its outskirts or from villages in the states of Haryana or U.P. A large number of households still obtains their milk from milkmen located within the city. However, since presence of cattle within the city creates insanitary conditions, they have been steadily removed to the outskirts.

Organisation of Large Milk Producers' Cooperatives

This development began in Gujarat in order to meet the demands of Mumbai and other cities of Gujarat – Surat, Vadodara, Ahmedabad and others. A dairy was established during the 1950s located in Anand, a medium-sized city in central Gujarat. Most of the producers of milk are rural women, who keep 1-3 buffaloes in order to supplement the income of the family from farming. The milk produced by them is collected at collection centres every morning and evening for transport in refrigerated vans to the processing plant in Anand. The volume and fat content of the milk is determined before the producer, and payment is made regularly at the end of the month.

The dairy was managed for almost 40 years by a very efficient administrator, Dr. V. Kurien. Within a few years of its establishment, it could meet the entire demand for liquid milk of Mumbai. Since, the milk is carried in refrigerated vans and is supplied to consumers from milk booths which have refrigerated containers for storage, there is little loss in transport and storage. Production increased so rapidly that there was a large surplus after meeting the demands of Mumbai and other cities. The surplus was converted into butter, cheese, powdered milk and baby food. The dairy, called AMUL, is the largest producer of these products in India.

With the profits of Amul Dairy, similar dairy cooperatives were established in other cities of Gujarat such as Mehsana. Thus the entire demand of Mumbai and cities of coastal Gujarat, and of milk products by the cities all over western, central and north western India is met by the cooperative which has a turnover of several hundred million rupees, and brings additional income to several thousand small farmers.

Supply of Milk to Other Large Cities

Impressed by the success of Amul Dairy, the Government of India established a National Dairy Development Board to prepare and oversee implementation of schemes for supplying milk to other large cities. Production and supply of milk to Delhi is described below as an example of schemes for supplying of milk in several other large cities. The Governments of Punjab and Andhra Pradesh formed their own milk producers' cooperatives. The cooperatives work along lines similar to Amul. They supply milk to several cities in the states and produce butter and/or cheese and ghee at their processing plants.

Supply of Milk to Delhi

Delhi is situated in the midst of an area in Haryana and western U.P., which has some of the best milch buffaloes in the country. They produce large quantities of milk with a high fat content. There are three sources of supply of milk to Delhi:

(i) The sweetmeat sellers (*halwais*) obtain their supplies from milkmen who bring it by train or buses from villages located within a radius of about 60–80 kilometres of Delhi.

(ii) In certain areas of the city and in its satellite towns where milch buffaloes are allowed to be kept, the residents obtain milk from them.

(iii) The principal source of supply is Mother Dairy organized along lines similar to Amul. Milk is brought by refrigerated tankers from villages located in Haryana, western U.P. and northern Rajasthan and sold in hundreds of booths in which it is kept in refrigerated containers in order to minimize losses in transport and storage. The system of collection of milk everyday, weighing it, and determining its fat content in the presence of the producer, and regular payments every month is similar to that of Amul Dairy. The size of the area from which milk is collected varies; in mid-summer and monsoon months of low supply, milk may be procured from distant villages but is processed in centres in Delhi and neighbouring districts of Uttar Pradesh and Haryana.

Furthermore, production of *khoya* (condensed unsweetened milk) used by the sweet-meat sellers is banned in this period so that the demand for liquid milk can be met. Schemes similar to that of Delhi have been established for other large cities, including Calcutta which is located in an area in which milk has to be brought from a long distance because the milk yield of the milch animals located in its vicinity is low.

Vegetables

The most widely used vegetables are potatoes, onions, tomatoes and brinjal. Potatoes and onions are consumed as an essential ingredient of curries all over India. Potato is a good source of calories and has minerals such as potassium. Onions are essential for preparation of curries throughout India. They have an astringent quality which helps digestion. Potatoes can be grown all over the plains of northern India. It is a winter crop which comes into the market between February and May. Since they keep well in cold storage for several months, in the lean season months of June to January, the principal source of supply are potatoes stored in cold storage and those grown in the Himalayan foothills where it is cool. The bulbs produced in the foothills have better keeping quality but their cultivation has caused severe soil erosion and the state governments should consider banning their cultivation in these foothill areas.

Potatoes are consumed in both rural and urban areas. The principal producing areas in peninsular India are widely dispersed. Thus supplies at prices which even the poor can afford are available throughout India.

In northern India, potatoes, onions and tomatoes are all produced as a cool season crop so that maximum supplies are available in the months of January to May. In other seasons onions are imported from Nasik and adjoining areas of Maharashtra which are the principal sources of supply for cities in Madhya Pradesh, Rajasthan, Punjab, Haryana, Uttar Pradesh, as well as Gujarat, and Maharashtra. Untimely or deficient rains in these districts cause a shortage of supply which leads to steep increase in prices. In such years, onions may be imported from Iran. In South India the producing areas are widely scattered in Karnataka, Andhra Pradesh and Tamil Nadu.

Tomatoes are not an essential ingredient of curries but their use in them has been increasing. Good quality tomatoes are also eaten un-cooked as an ingredient along with chopped onions, as a salad. It is again a winter crop with maximum local supplies in Western India, Madhya Pradesh, Eastern Rajasthan, Punjab, Haryana and U.P. in the spring months of March to May. In other months, the demand is met by production in districts neighbouring Nasik and certain areas in the Himalayan foothills.

Brinjal, a tropical vegetable is available throughout the year in all parts of India. It is an essential ingredient of south Indian curries; it is eaten fried or as a part of a curry in Bengal and other parts of India. It is popular because of its low price and because it has certain qualities which help prevention of some diseases.

Winter Vegetables: Carrots, peas, cauliflower and cabbage are grown mainly in northwestern India (Punjab, Haryana, around Delhi and Western U.P.) and in Maharashtra in western India to meet the demands of Mumbai, Pune and other cities in the state of Gujarat. In recent years, small production of temperate vegetables such as Brussels sprout and broccoli have been undertaken to tickle the taste buds of the affluent in Delhi and Mumbai.

The principal summer vegetables are different kinds of gourds. Supplies are available in season and at reasonable prices.

Fruits

The fruits discussed in this paper are bananas, mango, orange, grapes and apples. Other fruits are not considered because their production and consumption is small.

Banana

Banana is one of the most popular fruits over a large part of India. The medium sized sweet banana, derived from varieties grown in the Caribbean, is produced mainly in coastal Gujarat and Maharashtra and is popular in western and north western India. In eastern India and a large parts of south India small banana with a sweet and sour flavour is a table fruit. Its cousin the plantain, a fibrous variety rich in starch, is used extensively in eastern, western and southern India. It is eaten generally as fried chips.

Mango

Mango is the most popular fruit over large parts of India. Its various varieties are grown in Uttar Pradesh, Bihar, West Bengal, the coastal districts of Maharashtra and parts of Andhra Pradesh and Karnataka. Maximum production is in the monsoon months of June to August, although some varieties start arriving in the market from April. The most expensive mango is the Alphonso which is grown in coastal districts of Maharashtra, located south of Mumbai. It is prized for its delicate flavour and taste and because it does not spoil in storage for several weeks. Because of the latter quality, it was used to be exported to Britain for the royal table in pre-Independence years.

Since production of mangoes in the monsoon months is more than the demand and the processing industry is not well developed, there is much wastage. Housewives in both villages and cities make pickels and chutney at home. If the processing industry – canning the fruit, manufacture of squashes and chutneys – was developed in the producing areas, the wastage would be greatly reduced.

Orange

Oranges have two principal varieties:

(i) Tangerines (or loose jacket oranges) are grown around Nagpur in Maharashtra and in Assam. It is popular as a winter fruit all over northern India from Punjab to Assam and in central and western India. A large part of the production is processed into squashes and sweet chutneys.

(ii) The Mosambi variety is more fibrous and with much better keeping quality, and is grown again mainly in western Maharashtra and part of Andhra Pradesh. It is available from July to February.

Grapes

Production of grapes has increased very rapidly in the post-Independence period both for consumption as a table fruit and for production of wine. The principal areas of production are the irrigated valleys of western Maharashtra and parts of Andhra Pradesh and

Karnataka. The table varieties are somewhat fibrous but keep well in transport and storage.

Liquor

The principal wine producing areas are central Karnataka and the areas round Hyderabad. The quality of the wine has improved steadily in the last few decades to compare favourably with Italian wines.

Consumption of liquor – beer, wine and whisky – has increased rapidly during the last 50 years. Drinking has become a status symbol for the "noveau riche" and even the youth of the middle-income group. There is very little import because of high import duty. Furthermore, the quality of Indian liquor has improved steadily. It is interesting to note that prohibition, introduced in many states immediately after Independence, gave a stimulus to consumption of liquor.

The intoxicating drink for the poor all over India is palm wine, derived from fermentation of juice of Palmyra or coconut palm. In the hilly and forested areas of central India, which are inhabited mainly by tribal people, wine is made from rice or from some forest fruits.

Apples

The principal areas of production of apples in pre-Independence years were Kashmir and the Kullu valley in Himachal Pradesh. However in the post-Independence period, production has increased so rapidly in the Kotgarh area of Himachal Pradesh that it has become the principal source of supply for northern and western India. The area produces various varieties produced from stock imported from the U.S.A. The fruit is sweet and juicy and since it keeps well in cold storage, it is available through most of the year. The crop matures in the cool season months of October to December. Packaging it in wooden crates for transport to the markets provides employment to thousands in the state.

Other Temperate Fruits

Pears, peaches, apricots, cherries and plums are other important fruits. Kashmir Valley and Himachal Pradesh are known for these temperate fruits except apricot and cherries. Since there is increasing demand for peaches and plums, they have begun to be grown also in low altitudes in Himachal Pradesh and the western Himalayan foothills in U.P.

Trade in Vegetables and Fruits

Most of the trade in these is inland such as from producing areas in Maharashtra to Delhi and cities in Punjab to Bengal or from Kashmir and Himachal foothills to Delhi and cities in U.P., Rajasthan, Gujarat and Maharashtra. The vegetables and fruits coming from distant areas are brought mainly by trucks and stored in godowns of wholesalers in the vegetable markets who keep it in cold storage and release it to retailers to meet the demand. Often fruit is picked up in semi-ripe condition and allowed to ripen in these godowns. Cold storage has greatly reduced the loss in storage of fruits like apples, besides making them available for long periods during the year.

Foreign Trade

There is an increasing foreign trade in fruits and vegetables. Indian vegetables are exported in large quantities from Mumbai and Ernakulam in Kerala for consumption by people from Kerala, Goa and western coast of India working in the Gulf countries. Smaller quantities are exported to Sri Lanka. In recent years, there has developed a considerable trade in export of cut flowers such as roses, and chrysanthemum to U.K. and Europe. Similarly, Air India and Indian Airlines have flights from Mumbai and Ernakulam to Gulf countries for flying vegetables. There is little wastage since the quantities are large enough to justify the flights.

Canned vegetables and processed fruits like mango *chutnies* and pickles are exported to the U.K. the U.S.A., Canada and Australia for consumption of Indians settled in the cities of these countries. This trade is bound to grow as the number of Indians settled abroad increases. In recent years there has been a large increase in export of canned Indian vegetables to satisfy the demand of non-resident Indians.

The habit of using flowers for decorating oneself and for religious purposes is millennia old in India. The cave paintings of Ajanta, the rock sculptures in Ellora and the figures in the oldest Hindu temples are full of figures of gods and goddess having flowers as an important part of their attire. Buddha and his various incarnations (Bodhisatvas) are depicted as sitting on a lotus.

In recent years, use of flowers in offices of large companies such as banks, has increased enormously. The flowers used most often are roses and other winter flowers. The houses of the affluent have flowers as an interior decoration and bunches of flowers are taken as gifts for the host for inviting a person for lunch or dinner.

Poultry (Chicken and Eggs)

Consumption of poultry products too has increased enormously in the last half a century. Part of the reason for it is that even vegetarians have started eating eggs because of their high protein content. Most of the production is in the immediate hinterlands of large cities – western Maharashtra with the centre of production around Pune for Mumbai and Pune itself; Punjab and Haryana including the immediate outskirts of Delhi itself for Delhi. The same is true of other large cities. However, while frozen chicken is imported from the outskirts of the cities or over short distances, eggs travel over long distances. In Delhi, eggs may be imported from Maharashtra and Andhra Pradesh in winter when production in Punjab and Haryana is not sufficient to meet the demand. It is interesting to note that chicken is the cheapest meat available to those who have meat as a regular part of their diet.

Fish

Ocean fish is a staple of the diet of people living along the east and west coasts of India. In West Bengal there is a distinct preference for fish grown in ponds and rivers, and large quantities are imported from Bangladesh. Furthermore, large quantities of sea fish, caught by fishermen in the Bay are also eaten.

Most of the fish consumed in Mumbai is brought by fishermen fishing on the coast immediately south of the city. The coastal area of Saurashtra is the principal area from which sea fish is supplied to cities in north western, central and a small part of eastern India (Punjab, Haryana, Delhi and western U.P.). The catch is large but there is little local consumption because most of the population is vegetarian. The fish is frozen, put in wooden crates, transported by trucks, and put immediately in cold storage with the dealers so that there is little spoilage.

Prawns or Shrimp

In recent years there has been a rapid increase in production of prawns (or shrimp) for export from Kerala to Europe and the U.S.A. and cities in India. Prawn farms have been developed along the coast. The product is exported in tins or frozen in ships equipped with large cold storage facilities.

The Role of Producers' Cooperatives

Production and packaging of fruits, vegetables and eggs for consumption is highly labour intensive. Furthermore, employment is provided to landless labourers or small farmers who would otherwise be unemployed. Maintaining high levels of or increasing production requires also in most cases application of organic manure and/or chemical fertilizers. Use of pesticides is often required for protection, of fruit bearing trees or vegetables producing vines, against diseases.

The producers of milk and poultry must have also some knowledge of diseases of milch animals and birds. Producers' cooperatives are the best organization for disseminating knowledge about the need for application of chemical fertilizers, pesticides and medicines for milch animals, and vaccines for birds. They are best equipped for distribution of supplies of these among the producers as well as marketing in order to get remunerative prices for producers. The role of producers' cooperatives has been mentioned above in production and distribution of milk. They are also well developed in many areas of production of fruits and vegetables. However, there is a need for establishing or strengthening such cooperatives in the principal areas of production of mango in U.P., Bihar and West Bengal. Canning facilities for fruits and vegetables in the principal areas of production can be established by producers' cooperatives or by individuals; and this would provide off-season employment to men and/or women.

The governments of various states must appreciate the prospect of rapid increase in consumption of these foods in the future. They must strengthen producers' cooperatives in existing areas of production and encourage development of such cooperatives in areas of potential production.

NOTE

1. *The Indian Geographical Journal* 73 (2) December 1998. University of Madras, Chennai.

14

Industrial Location and Employment in India: 1950-2000 and Trends and Prospects for 2000-2020

PART I
INTRODUCTION

Part I makes a survey of growth and changes in spatial location of factory industries in the period of nearly half a century—1950-51 and 1997-98. The Indian economy has been transformed during this period from a primarily agricultural economy in which agriculture contributed more than half of the gross domestic product (GDP) to a diversified economy in which industry and service sectors contribute three-fourth of the GDP while agriculture contributes less than one-fourth. The transformation has been the result partly of policies and investments by the Government of India and governments of various states and partly to investments by private companies and initiatives of entrepreneurs.

Economic geographers have long debated the relative importance of different factors—advantage of an early start, proximity to mineral and non-mineral raw materials, availability of low cost unskilled and skilled labour, initiative of entrepreneurs, policies of governments and finally proximity to markets in explaining location of factory industries. This analysis shows, however, that proximity to raw materials is in some ways the least important and proximity to markets the most important factor in location of industries. Further, there is not likely to be a major change in the regional location of factory industries during the next decade. On the other hand states and regions, which are industrially advanced, could increase their lead over those that are industrially backward.

The three decades 1970's–1990's have seen rapid growth of knowledge based industries such as computer software and other information technology industries. Employment and value added in them has gone up exponentially during the past two decades and is expected to increase rapidly in the foreseeable future. Finally, the industries instead of being concentrated in one city—Bangalore as at present, would spread to several other metropolitan cities, as a result partly of efforts of some state governments which are creating the infrastructure for their development.

Changing Industrial Scenario 1950-1990s

This object of this section is to present the principal facts about distribution by states of employment and value added in factory industries in the mid-1990's and to relate them to the distribution of mineral and non-mineral resources, the level of economic development in different states and policies relating to industrial development, followed by the state governments. The present structure of the industrial sector and locational pattern of factories are discussed against the background of the transformation of the Indian economy from a primarily agricultural economy at the beginning of the 1950's to a diversified economy in which industry and service sectors contributed three fourth of the gross domestic product by the mid-1990's.

Agriculture contributed 56 per cent of the gross domestic product while the small industrial sector contributed only 15 per cent (Table 14.1). The sector comprised besides cottage industries and handicrafts, factories processing tea and jute for export and making a narrow range of consumer goods—textiles of cotton, wool and rayon, sugar, wheat and rice flour, cooking oil, shoes and other leather goods and cement, corrugated iron sheets, etc., for construction.

The traditional handicrafts—weaving of handlooms cloth of cotton, silk or rayon, making of brassware, etc., were also oriented towards meeting the needs for consumer goods. The basic industries—steel mills, plants manufacturing machinery for mining, generation, transmission and distribution of electricity, manufacture of locomotives, coaches and other equipment for the railways, light and heavy machine tools, vehicles for public, commercial and private transport (trucks, buses, passenger cars, motor bicycles, scooters, etc.) were virtually non-existent. By the mid-1990's, however these industries together with petroleum refining, manufacture of petrochemicals, other chemicals, pharmaceuticals and a wide range of consumer durables contributed the bulk of employment and value added in the factory sector. Furthermore, the knowledge-based industries such as computer software and other information technology based industries were well established and were experiencing very rapid growth. The contribution of the industrial sector to GDP is estimated to have increased to 30 per cent and of agriculture fell to 25 per cent by 1997-98 (Table 14.1).

Table 14.1: Distribution of GDP by Major Sectors 1950-51 and 1997-98

Contribution to GDP by Sectors	*1950-51*	*1997-98*
Agriculture	*55.8*	*25.3*
Industry	15.2	30.1
Services	29.0	44.6

Source: Government of India, *Survey of Industries*, New Delhi, p. 1.

Factories and Small Industries: Employment and Values Added

The industrial sector consists of two components:

(i) Factories: Industrial units employing 10 or more workers and using power or employing 20 or more workers if not using power, and
(ii) Small industries including cottage industries and handicrafts.

Table 14.1 (a): Factories and Small Industries: Employment and Value Added

	Employment (Millions)	*Percent*	*Value added (Rs. 000 crores)*	*Gross output (Rs. 000 crores)*	*Percent*
Factories	10.05	40	139.4	670.5	66
Small Industries	15.30	60	N.A.	356.4	34
Total	25.35	100	—	1026.9	100

Source: Government of India, *Survey of Industries*, New Delhi, pp. 89 and 91.

During 1995-96 the employment and value added figures for the two segments of the sector were the following:

Thus factories provided employment to about 40 per cent of the workers engaged in industries but contributed almost two thirds of the gross output, while small industries provided employment to 60 per cent of the workers but contributed only one third of the output.

Industrial Growth and Location of Industries

Rapid transformation of the economy began in the late 1950's and continued through the 1970's. Heavy investments were made during this period of about 20 years by the Government of India in establishing five large integrated steel mills, a factory for manufacturing heavy machinery, factories for manufacturing a variety of machine tools and equipment for generation, transmission and distribution of electricity, a factory for making telephone receivers and other telecommunication equipment and factories for manufacture of locomotives and coaches for the railways. Economic and/or technical assistance for establishing the factories was provided principally by the Russians, the British or by other European countries.

After the discovery of large deposits of crude oil off the coast of Mumbai and Gujarat in the late 1950's, large investments were made by the Government of India in exploration and exploitation of petroleum deposits, establishing petroleum refineries and establishing a network of dealers for distribution of motor spirit, diesel, kerosene and other petroleum products. Private companies including the multinational corporations that had been distributing petroleum products for decades were also allowed to establish petroleum refineries, some of which have involved foreign investment, have increased progressively. Indian private investors have made large investments in plants manufacturing a large variety of petrochemicals.

Private entrepreneurs made complementary investments also in steel rolling mills, manufacture of wagons for the railways, steel rods and corrugated iron sheets for construction and establishing pig iron plants for manufacture of castings. Their other major investments were in manufacture of telephone receivers and other telecommunication equipment, food processing and manufacture of drugs.

Manufacture of vehicles for public, commercial and private transport (trucks, buses, passenger cars, motor bicycles, scooters, etc.)

was also started by private entrepreneurs in the late 1950's or early 1960's with technical assistance provided by reputed foreign manufacturers. Production of all these as well as of a variety of consumer durables—refrigerators, air conditioners, radio and television receivers, office and hospital furniture, furnishing for home and office—has increased rapidly during the five decades, 1950's—1990's in response to rapid increase in domestic demand.

The computer software for export industry which began in Bangalore in the 1970's, has experienced very rapid growth during the subsequent two decades so that by the late 1990's, the turn-over of the industry is in billions of dollars and the shares of some of the leading software export companies are considered important enough to be listed on the New York Stock Exchange. According to one estimate, software exports amounted to $ 2.65 billion in 1998-99, 56 per cent higher than $ 1.75 billion in 1997-98 and are expected to reach $ 10 billion within 5 years (*Times of India*, July 1999).

The value of output of consumer, industrial and other electronic goods more than doubled during the four years 1993-94—1997-98 (Table 14.2). Such growth is a portent of trends of the foreseeable future; the information technology based industries are poised for very rapid growth during the next decade because of development of Internet. Furthermore, computerization in Indian industries, banking, finance, public administration and other services is just beginning.

Table 14.2: Electronics Production Profile Value of output

(*Rs. crore*)

	1993-94	*1997-98*
Consumer electronics	4150	7600
Industrial electronics	1170	3150
Computers	1820	2900
Communication and broad-casting equipment	3150	3250
Strategic Electronics	500	500
Components	2680	4400
Total	**14070**	**82100**
Computer Software for Export	1020	6500
Domestic software	695	3470
Grand Total	**15785**	**32070**

Source: Government of India, *Survey of Industries*, New Delhi, p. 79.

Another noteworthy development which will affect industrial growth in the next decade is entry during the last few years of Korean, American or other multinationals who have established factories manufacturing or assembling, from imported kits, passenger cars or trucks and a wide range of consumer durables. Their factories are located in the environs of Chennai, Delhi and Bangalore.

It may be mentioned that the environs of the large metropolitan cities especially Mumbai, Delhi, Bangalore, Hyderabad, Pune and Chennai have been the favoured locations for establishment of a number of public and private sector industrial units mentioned above. Excepting the steel mills and the heavy machinery plant, most of the other public sector industrial units have been located in the vicinity of the large cities. The three petroleum refineries established by the foreign companies in the 1950's were located in the environs of Mumbai. Many refineries established latter have also been located near cities along the west or the east coasts. The problem of pollution of air and water that their location creates for the residents of the cities were completely ignored while deciding on their location.

The green revolution in agriculture, which began in the late 1960's and continued during the next two decades and under which production of cereals—wheat and rice—increased rapidly with use of improved, very high yielding varieties of seed, chemical fertilizers, pesticides and improved manual or power driven implements including improved ploughs, tractors, mechanical threshers and electricity or diesel driven pumps on irrigation wells, has led to growth of large industries manufacturing fertilizers, pesticides, pumps for lifting water, tractors, etc. The agricultural equipment industry is also located in cities closest to the areas affected by the green revolution. Thus the Punjab-Haryana-Western U.P. region in which production of cereals has been increasing rapidly from the late 1960's is served by a factory manufacturing tractors located in a satellite town of Delhi, while Ludhiana, an industrial city in Punjab manufactures a wide range of power driven agricultural implements. Hyderabad, Chennai, Pune and Coimbatore are some of the other important cities manufacturing power driven implements for use in agricultural regions located within their hinterlands in which agricultural output has been increasing rapidly. However, the chemical fertilizer factories are located in Gujarat and near the petroleum refineries in various parts of the country.

Two other developments in the 1960's, which affected location of industries profoundly, were:

(i) Flight of capital from the Calcutta Metropolitan District (including both Calcutta and Howrah) due to militancy of trade unions. As a result, some large steel fabricating units, which manufactured bridges and other large steel structures for the railways, mining machinery, etc., and which the Government of India owned were closed. A number of private entrepreneurs also closed their factories in Calcutta or Howrah to re-open them in southern India especially Tamil Nadu or in the western Indian states of Maharashtra and Gujarat.

(ii) Industrial growth in these three states has been encouraged also by the influence that the industrialist based in them have had with the Ministers and Officers in the central government responsible for grant of licenses for establishing industrial units and providing them various incentives such as concessional credit from financial institutions, exemption from taxation of profits for the first few years of operation of the units and various facilities for export of products.

There has been no significant returning capital to the Calcutta Metropolitan District despite the fact that the present Communist party led government of West Bengal, which has been in power for almost 30 years, has kept militancy of trade unions in check. There is no shortage also of electricity or water in the Calcutta Metropolitan District. This shows that while flight of capital from a region can be triggered off by one or more causes, its return is difficult. A further reason for decline of West Bengal as an industrial state is that the elite in the state has always preferred becoming professionals—lawyers, physicians, teachers, and scientists, senior executives in large companies owned formerly by the Scots but by Indians after independence to becoming industrial entrepreneurs.

Distribution of Employment and Value Added by Factories by States

Data on distribution of employment and value added in factories in 1995-96 is given in Table 14.3. It may be noted that 25 per cent of the employment but as much as 36 per cent of the value added in factories was accounted for by factories located in the two states of Maharashtra and Gujarat. Maharashtra alone contributed 15 per cent of the employment and 24 per cent of the value added in factories. Tamil Nadu and Andhra Pradesh ranked next to Maharashtra and Gujarat as important industrial states. Together these four states accounted for almost half of both employment and value added in factories. On the other hand, Bihar and West Bengal, which have large deposits of coal, iron ore and other minerals and in which are located 3 integrated steel mills, the heavy machinery plant at Ranchi, the old multi-industry complex of Jamshedpur, the post 1960's complex of Durgapur—Assansol besides the industries located in Calcutta and Howrah contributed only 11.5 per cent of the employment and 8.5 per cent of the value added in factories.

Table 14.3: Shares of Selected States in Population and Employment and value added in Factories 1995-96

States	*Population (Millions)*	*Per cent of all India*	*Employment (000's)*	*Per cent of all India*	*Value added (Rs. Crores)*	*Per cent of all India*
Andhra Pradesh	68.5	8.1	1180	11.8	987	7.0
Bihar	86.4	10.2	336	3.3	5296	3.8
Gujarat	41.3	4.9	967	9.5	17621	12.6
Karnataka	45.0	5.3	512	5.1	6750	4.8
Madhya Pradesh	58.8	8.0	525	5.2	9522	6.8
Maharashtra	79.0	9.3	1518	15.1	32975	23.7
Punjab	20.3	2.4	473	4.7	4008	3.9
Rajasthan	44.0	5.2	—	—	—	—
Tamil Nadu	55.6	6.6	1237	12.3	14261	10.2
Uttar Pradesh	138.1	16.3	797	7.9	11675	8.4
West Bengal	68.0	8.0	825	8.2	6493	4.7
Others	—	—	1675	16.7	20979	15.0
Total	846.3	100.0	10,045	100.0	139397	100.0

Source: Government of India, *Survey of Industries*, New Delhi, p. 88.

These figures bring out that the old mineral resource based industries—steel mills, heavy machine building units, plants making machinery for mines, locomotive rails, passenger coaches and rolling stock (wagons for transport of goods) for the railways, cement mills etc. contribute relatively small shares of both employment and value added in industries and that much larger shares are contributed by industries manufacturing machines for generation and distribution of electricity, transport equipment, consumer goods and consumer durables.

The data of Table 14.4 give some indication of this. Food processing, beverage and textile industries contributed 40 per cent of the total employment but only 17 per cent of the value added in factories. On the other hand, machinery other than transport and transport equipment accounted for about 15 per cent of employment but more than 20 per cent of value added in factories. The importance in value added of chemicals is due primarily to the high value of pharmaceutical drugs. The basic metals group consists largely of steel mills. The heavy investment in them may be noted.

Table 14.4: Share of Major Industry Groups in Factory Sector, 1995-96

(*Per cent Share*)

Group	*Employment*	*Invested Capital*	*Value Added*
Food products	13.3	7.3	6.6
Beverages	6.5	1.0	1.9
Cotton Textiles	9.8	4.0	3.1
Wool and Silk Textiles	3.8	3.5	2.7
Jute Textiles	3.2	0.4	0.7
Textile Products	3.7	1.3	2.3
Paper	3.4	2.5	3.3
Rubber, Petroleum and Coal Products	3.2	5.3	6.6
Basic Chemicals and Products	6.7	14.5	17.0
Non-metallic Minerals	5.0	4.2	4.1
Basic Metals	7.3	16.1	10.0
Metal Products	2.7	1.7	2.3
Machinery other than transport	8.5	8.4	12.6
Transport Equipment	6.0	4.3	7.7
Electricity	9.8	23.3	14.7
Repair Services	0.6	0.2	0.3
Others	4.3	1.3	3.2
Total	100.0	100.0	100.0

Source: Government of India. *Survey of Industries*, New Delhi, p. 89.

Industrial Centers

Maharashtra

Most of the industrial units in Maharashtra are located in or around Mumbai (including New Mumbai and Thane) or Pune or along the rail-cum-road strip of about 175 kilometres between Mumbai and Pune. There are a wide variety of industries in this area. Textiles made of cotton, woolen or man-made fibers are still important. Located in the environs of Mumbai are the works of the biggest companies manufacturing office and hospital furniture and consumer durables such as refrigerators and air conditioners. The capacity of the three petroleum refineries started in the late 1950's has expanded steadily. Manufacture of cosmetics and pharmaceutical drugs are other important industries because the largest manufacturers of these have their head offices in Mumbai and factories in its vicinity or in Gujarat. References should be made also to production of films and television serials. Mumbai is the principal centre for producing them. Although it is difficult to estimate either employment or value added in the industry, there cannot be any doubt about the large size of both.

The biggest industrial units in Pune belong to the house of Kirloskar, which manufactures a variety of machine tools, pumps for lifting water from wells and compressors, etc., for refrigerators and air conditioners. The environs of Pune have also a number of defense related industries because of location near it of a factory making ammunition from the last century. The rapid growth of sugarcane production and establishment of sugar mills in several towns in western Maharashtra has provided the basis for growth of factories producing machinery and spare parts for sugar mills. Manufacture of passenger cars was started near Mumbai in the late 1950's; the late 1990's have seen location of a factory manufacturing passenger cars and trucks in Pune.

In contrast to concentration of industries in and around Mumbai and Pune or along the rail-cum-road strip between Mumbai and Pune, there is little industrial development in the other regions of the state, Marathwada and Vidarbha. Industrial growth has failed to take off in these regions despite the stated policy of the state government to promote industrial development in them. The principal reasons for it are low productivity of land, under-developed infrastructures and absence of a class of aggressive entrepreneurs.

Gujarat

Coastal Gujarat has often been called an industrial workshop. The discovery of crude oil off its coast has lead to establishment of petroleum refineries and petrochemical industries. Manufacture of a variety of machine tools was started by entrepreneurs who returned home from East Africa in the 1960's. Cotton textile mills, located in Ahmedabad and in a number of other cities in Gujarat since the last decades of the 19th century, have diversified in recent years to manufacture textiles made of man-made fibres. Anand, in central Gujarat, is the headquarter of Amul Dairy, which besides being the principal supplier of liquid milk to Mumbai is the largest manufacturer of dairy products—butter, cheese, baby food, etc., in India. Manufacture of pharmaceutical drugs is another important industry in Gujarat. Surat, which had an old established zari work industry, has become the center of cutting and polishing of diamonds for export; the industry has experienced rapid growth since the 1970's.

In contrast to concentration of industries in coastal Gujarat, Saurashtra and Kutch are industrially under-developed. The productivity of land is low, millets and groundnuts are the principal crops and there are no minerals. Groundnut oil mills are the most important industrial units. However, there is a potential for expansion of industries in the duty-free export zone in Kandla. The recent opening of India's largest petrochemical plant in Jam Nagar on the coast of Saurashtra could provide an incentive for location of industries using the output of the factory to make textiles and various consumer goods.

The principal reasons for development and continued expansion of industries in western Maharashtra and coastal Gujarat are the following:

(i) Advantage of an early start. The first textile mills owned by Gujarati or Parsee entrepreneurs were started in Mumbai and Ahmedabad in 1970's.

(ii) The growth of sugar production in Maharashtra and dairying in Gujarat has added a large class of farmers who have enough income to buy a range of manufactured consumer goods and consumer durables.

(iii) The availability of hard working labour among which militancy has never reached levels, which would jeopardize industrial growth.

(iv) Most of the villages are provided with electricity so that farmers use electric pumps on their irrigation wells and can use electrically operated kitchen gadgets and a large variety of consumer durables.

Karnataka

The importance of Karnataka as an industrial state is indicated by the fact that factories located in it accounted in 1995-96 for 5 per cent of both total employment and value added in factories. There are several reasons for this. First, a number of large public sector industrial units are located in the environs of its capital, Bangalore. Hindustan Aircraft, which is located about 30 kilometres from the city and was established during World War II for servicing and repair of aircraft, has diversified into manufacture of small trainer aircraft. Hindustan Machine Tools, which manufactures a variety of precision tools and watches and Indian Telephone Industries, which manufacture telephone receivers and other telecommunication equipment, were established in the 1960's. A number of private companies have also established factories making telephone receivers and telecommunication equipment, machine tools and watches. Production in both public and private sector units has increased rapidly in response to increasing demand.

A rapidly growing export oriented computer software industry was established in Bangalore in the 1970's. Location in the city of two institutes of science and presence of a large number of men and women science graduates were important factors in its establishment. The turnover of the industry now runs into billions as mentioned earlier. The industry should continue to experience rapid growth for a long time to meet both export and domestic demand. The rapid growth of this industry is an indication also of the prospect of rapid growth in the future of knowledge-based industries.

The phenomenal growth of this industry in Bangalore has led governments of several other states to build information technology parks in which all facilities—uninterrupted supplies of electricity, rapid telecommunication by satellite, etc. are provided to the computer software companies. One such state of the art technology park has been built by the Government of Andhra Pradesh on the outskirts of Hyderabad. It provides a basis for establishment of Hyderabad as a centre for the computer software and other information technology industries. The Government of Haryana has provided similar facilities in the environs of Gurgaon located about 30 kilometres from Delhi. The next few years should see emergence of a number of information technology parks in the environs of Pune, Mumbai, Ahmedabad, Chennai, Calcutta, Lucknow, Trivandrum and Chandigarh, i.e., wherever there are large numbers of graduates in the sciences and the state governments create the facilities for location of these industries.

The 175 kilometres strip between Bangalore and Mysore city receives dependable and adequate irrigation from a canal on the Cauvery River. The area produces large crops of rice and sugarcane, has two sugar mills, a number of rice mills and a sizeable class of prosperous farmers. These, along with the industrial and white-collar workers and professionals in Bangalore provide a large market for processed foods, high quality textiles and a variety of consumer durables including passenger cars, motor bicycles and mopeds. The South Kanara district in southwestern Karnataka receives large remittances from its residents working in the Gulf countries. Mangalore, the principal city has a petroleum refinery and a first rate multi-faculty university. Thus, there is a potential for growth of the information technology based industries and a market as in central Karnataka for a variety of consumer goods and consumer durables.

Thus, central and south-western Karnataka are likely to remain areas with a variety of industries and a large market among its white and blue collar workers, professionals and prosperous farmers for a variety of consumer goods and consumer durables. In contrast, the other parts of the state are underdeveloped. Most of the area is unirrigated; productivity of land which produces millets, cotton and oil seeds as the principal crops are low and there are few industries.

Calcutta Metropolitan District

The principal factor inhibiting revival of industrial growth in the Calcutta Metropolitan District is crisis of confidence. Despite the efforts of the present government to attract industrial entrepreneurs to Calcutta there has been no significant return so far. But this is bound to change in the not distant future. Calcutta has too many advantages as the only port and the largest city in Eastern India, wealth of mineral, agricultural and other resources in its hinterland and has a very large population to remain an industrial backwater. Its tea and jute processing industries were not affected by the exodus of entrepreneurs in the late 1960's and have continued to experience steady growth. There are hundreds of small and medium sized industrial units manufacturing components for mining machinery, railways and steel fabrication units. Furthermore, because of location of two Universities and a Statistics institute in the city, and an Institute of Management in Barrakpur, there are a large number of graduates in the sciences, which provide the basis for growth of the computer software and related information technology industries primarily for the domestic market. Agricultural output has been increasing steadily in West Bengal as a result of the land reforms introduced by the present government and installation of electric motors on a large number of irrigation wells. Thus, there is a potential for establishment of an agricultural equipment manufacturing industry as well as for consumer durable industries to meet the demands of the growing middle class of white collar and industrial workers in Calcutta and relatively prosperous farmers in the rest of the state.

Tamil Nadu

Chennai and Coimbatore are likely to remain the principal industrial centres in Tamil Nadu. Chennai has become over the last five decades a major centre for manufacturing motor vehicles—trucks and buses, passenger cars, motor bicycles and scooters. A factory for manufacturing trucks and buses and another for manufacturing motorcycles and scooters were established in its environs in the 1950's. Production in them has been increasing steadily. During the 1990's, a factory for manufacturing passenger cars has been added. Located in and around Chennai are large number of manufacturers making components (including tyres) for motor vehicles and a variety of consumer durables for the regional and national markets.

Coimbatore, located in the midst of an area that produces high quality cotton in fields irrigated by a canal from the Pykara River, has a large number of textile mills and sizeable industry manufacturing machinery for the mills.

The principal advantages of Chennai and Coimbatore are availability of labour—disciplined, untainted by militancy and able to learn industrial skills and an adequate number of entrepreneurs.

Chennai has become also a centre for the information technology industry. Some of the best computer software professionals working in the Silicon Valley in California are Tamils. Some of them could return home to establish the industry in their home state. Chennai is also very well located for Indian entrepreneurs in Singapore and other South East Asian countries wishing to establish a base in India. The delta of Cauvery River, which receives, assured irrigation from canals from the river, has a sizeable class of prosperous farmers who produce rice as the main crop. In the rest of the state also there are pockets of prosperous agriculture because most of the irrigation wells are fitted with electric or diesel pumps. Thus there is an adequate market for processed foods, garments and consumer durables among the growing class of prosperous farmers, white collar and skilled workers and professionals. There is also a market for agricultural equipment including pumps for irrigation.

Andhra Pradesh

The principal industrial centre in Andhra Pradesh is its capital, Hyderabad. The city has in its environs, a number of public sector industrial units including plants of Bharat Heavy Electrical, Hindustan Machine Tools, Indian Drugs and Pharmaceuticals and a number of defense related laboratories. As mentioned earlier, the infrastructure for establishing an information technology industry has been created and the industry is well established in it.

Large areas in coastal Andhra Pradesh receive dependable irrigation from canals from the Krishna and Godavari rivers. Rice, sugarcane and tobacco are the principal crops. There are a number of rice and sugar mills and a large class of prosperous farmers in this area. Thus, there is a sizeable market for industrial goods including consumer durables among the prosperous farmers and white-collar workers. Vijayawada the largest city in the area is not yet an important industrial center. The other industrial center in the state is Vijayanagaram (Visakhapatnum) a port city, which has a steel mill and a ship yard.

Punjab

Rapid industrial growth began in Punjab in the late 1950's, when with construction of the Nangal dam part of the Bhakra Nangal irrigation cum-power project, large supplies of electricity began to be available. Punjab was also the center of the green revolution of the late 1960's, which greatly increased agricultural output, and income of the farmers. Well-developed rail and road communications is another factor contributing to industrial development of the state. The government of the state actively promoted rural electrification and made a successful agricultural extension effort to increase agricultural output. Furthermore, it assisted industrial development by providing concessional loans and various other incentives to entrepreneurs. Most of them were those residing in the state; others were Ramgarhia Sikhs who returned home after becoming affluent in Thaïland and Malaysia to establish medium or large sized industries in Ludhiana. Although Ludhiana is the largest industrial centre in the state, several other cities have a number of industrial units. Amritsar has a large woolen mill and a factory making high quality carpets. Hindustan Machine Tools has established a unit for manufacturing machine tools and watches near Chandigarh. A factory manufacturing coaches for the railways has been established in Kapurthala. The industries located in Ludhiana include:

(i) Manufacture and/or repair of machine driven agricultural implements—electric or diesel pumps to lift water from irrigation wells, mechanical threshers, improved ploughs and tractors;
(ii) Consumer durables—fans, sewing machines, bicycles, motor bicycles, scooters, 3-wheeler tempos, stoves using liquefied natural gas for cooking. There is a large and growing demand in the towns and villages of the state for all these goods as well as for other consumer durables such as air coolers, television receivers and electrically operated kitchen gadgets;
(iii) The woolen/hosiery industry established in Ludhiana since the 1920's have experienced rapid growth to meet increasing domestic and export demands. Exports during the 1960's to the 1980's were mainly to the Soviet Union.

Prospects for the next decade

Several indications of the prospects have been given in the foregoing sections and are added to below:

1. There must be sustained growth in basic industries-manufacture of steel, cement, heavy, light and precision machine tools; equipment for generation, transmission and distribution of electricity; transport equipment for both

railways and roads; petroleum refining and manufacture of petrochemicals. These industries provide the infrastructure of industrial growth. But most of the employment and value added in industries will continue, as at present, to be in food processing, manufacture of textiles and apparel and other consumer goods and consumer durables.

2. Maharashtra, Gujarat, Tamil Nadu and Andhra Pradesh are likely to continue to be the states with larger shares of both employment and value added in factories than their shares of the population of the country. The states have besides the advantage of an early start, large and rapidly growing urban and rural middle classes.
3. Karnataka should continue to have similar shares of both employment and value added in industries as its share of the total population of the country. The information technology industry and the industries manufacturing machine tools and telecommunication equipment located in and around Bangalore should continue to experience rapid growth in the next decade. Use of computers in industries, trade and public services has scarcely begun in India and would increase rapidly in the foreseeable future. Growth of computer hardware industry *viz.* manufactures of small and medium sized computers initially by assembly of imported components in the environs of Bangalore are the prospect. Manufacture or assembly of heavy trucks and of passenger cars, which have started in the environs of the city in the 1990's, is expected to increase rapidly in the foreseeable future for two reasons. First, there is a large and expanding market for the vehicles in southern India. Second, the companies manufacturing the vehicles are reputed multinationals with access to the latest technology.
4. The principal advantages of Punjab are in innovative class of skilled workers and a large market for consumer goods, consumer durables and modern farm implements to meet the needs of its progressive and well-to-do farmers and middle income residents of the urban areas who have got accustomed to using manufactured consumer goods and consumer durables. Highly developed infrastructures—rail and road transport and near universal rural electrification—creates a large market for trucks, buses, passenger cars, motor bicycles, scooters, etc. Its share of employment and value added in

factory industries should continue to be larger than its share of the population of the country.

5. Steady growth of factory industries would continue to be experienced in the satellite cities of Delhi-Gurgaon and Faridabad in Haryana and Ghaziabad and Gautam Buddha Nagar (NOIDA) in U.P. A variety of consumer goods—processed foods, clothes for domestic consumption and export, consumer durables such as passenger cars, refrigerators, air conditioners, office furniture, furnishings for home and office, tractors and other farm equipment are already being manufactured in these cities.
6. There should be relatively rapid growth of industries in Rajasthan because of the policies adopted by the government to promote it. The government has built in various parts of the state a number of townships in which developed land with adequate and dependable supplies of electricity and water and good telecommunication facilities as well as good rail or road connections (for import of raw materials and export of products) are provided to the industries established in them. Furthermore, the entrepreneurs are given exemption from taxation of profits for the first few years. They are assisted also in getting concessional loans from financial institutions. One such township, Bhiwadi, located about 100 kilometres south of Delhi is fully occupied by factories owned by entrepreneurs based in Delhi or Jaipur. Another factor assisting industrial growth in the state will be growth of tourism. The traditional handicrafts of the state—manufacture of jewellery, tie and die cloth and decorated leatherwork should have a large market among foreign tourists.
7. Bihar, Orissa, Madhya Pradesh, U.P., and Assam would continue to have much smaller shares in both employment and value added in factories in comparison to their shares of the population.
8. Relatively small shares of U.P. and Bihar, which have 37 per cent of the population of the country but only 11 per cent of the workers in factories and contribute only 12 per cent of the value added in factories need to be explained. One reason is that except for a few district of western U.P. both states are poor and backward. Furthermore, the governments of the states have not made any noteworthy attempts to promote industrial

development. An additional factor impeding industrial growth in Bihar at present is lack of security of life and property. There is literally a class war in parts of Bihar between former non-cultivating owners of land and their labourers most of whom have become peasant proprietors.

9. Madhya Pradesh and Orissa remain industrially backward despite the fact that they have large mineral resources and established industrial centers in the steel mill cities that are located in them—Rourkela in Orissa and Bhilai in Madhya Pradesh. Madhya Pradesh has also the industrial city of Indore in which there could be considerable expansion of industries due to availability of an experienced industrial labour force.
10. Apart from packaging of tea and a small petroleum refinery located near Guwahati and its traditional handicrafts, there are few industries in Assam. One reason is the relative isolation of the state from the rest of India. However, a determined effort has to be made, initially by the Government of India to establish industries such as a petrochemical plant in the state. With improvements in quality, the products of the distinctive handicrafts of the state should also have a sizeable market in India and abroad.
11. Industrial growth could pick up in U.P. if the government actively promotes it. The productivity of the large area irrigated by canals, tube wells and wells fitted with electric or diesel pumps in western U.P could also be increased through vigorous agriculture extension efforts. There is a potential also for large increase in output and employment through modernization and improvement in techniques of some of the handicrafts of U.P., such as weaving of carpets around Mirzapur, weaving of silk saris in a suburb of Varanasi and manufacture of decorative brassware in Moradabad which have large domestic and export markets. The expansion could be more rapid especially for export, if some exploitative practices such as use of child labour in carpet weaving and payment of bare subsistence wages to weavers are ended. The industrial promotion efforts should concentrate on modernization of design and introduction of improved equipment—larger looms in weaving of saris and use of power in larger manufacturing units.

There is a prospect also for growth of computer software industry (principally to meet local demand) in Kanpur, which has an Institute of Technology and is an old industrial center. Lucknow, Allahabad and Varanasi which have universities which had high standards of teaching until recently could be other centers for growth of this industry.

12. Industrial growth should accelerate in Kerala. Kochi with its naval base, a shipyard and a petroleum refinery is already a large industrial city. There is a prospect of establishment of consumer durable industries for the local market. Kerala receives remittance of thousands of million dollars every year from its residents working in the Gulf countries. Thus there is a sizeable market for consumer durables among the large class of well-to-do residents of the rural and urban areas of the state. Trivandrum could become the centre of an information technology industry based on an adequate supply of educated manpower and the facility of export of products through its airport. Kerala is also well equipped for winter tourism because of its excellent beaches and a warm, largely storm-free winter. The distinctive handicrafts of the state - decorative brassware and products of coir—should also find an expanding market both within India and abroad.

It will be clear from the foregoing survey that there are likely to be only marginal changes in the spatial distribution of factory industries during the next decade. Furthermore, inter-state and intra-state disparities in industrial development are likely to increase instead of decreasing during this period.

Economic geographers have often discussed the relative importance of different factors—an early start, proximity to raw materials, access to a disciplined or skilled labour force, capital, entrepreneurs with vision and ability to take risks, professionals with innovative skills and proximity to a large market in explaining location of industries. The foregoing survey has shown that among these factors proximity to raw materials, mineral or nonmineral, is the least important. Industries processing raw materials—steel, heavy machinery, cement, paper, sugar, jute, wheat and oil mills, petroleum refineries, factories producing chemical fertilizers and other petrochemicals, although they involve heavy investment contribute relatively small shares of both employment and value added in factory industries. Much larger shares of both employment and value added in industries are contributed by factories, which make a variety of machine tools, equipment for generation, transmission and distribution of electricity, transport equipment including motor vehicles and a large variety of consumer goods and consumer durables. These industries are located typically in the metropolitan areas of large cities, which are close to the principal markets for them.

The militancy of trade unions induced in the late 1960s led to shift of industries from the Calcutta Metropolitan District to the south and West Indian states of Tamil Nadu, Maharashtra and Gujarat. Return of capital to CMD has not been significant despite the efforts of the present Government of West Bengal to secure the return.

The phenomenal growth of the computer software and other information technology based industries in and around Bangalore shows the influence of skilled professionals in the beginning and rapid growth of an industry. The next decade should witness establishment and progressive growth of this industry primarily to meet domestic demand in a number of other centres.

The successful efforts of the Punjab Government to promote industrial development in the state in the late 1950s and early 1960s aided by an abundance of skilled workers and venturesome entrepreneurs has led to establishment of a variety of industries ranging from manufacture of carpets and woolen textiles to agricultural machinery in different cities of the state.

On the other hand the indifference of the governments of U.P., Bihar, Orissa and Madhya Pradesh towards promoting industrial development in their states is partly responsible for the industrial backwardness of these states. Their shares in both employment and value added in factories are much smaller than their shares of the population of the country. However, government policies also have their limitations. The effort of the government of Maharashtra to promote industrial development in the backward regions of the state has had little success so far.

The environs of metropolitan cities including their satellite cities are the most favoured locations for factories. Even resource based industries such as petroleum refineries and factories making machine tools and motor vehicles, besides those making a variety of consumer goods and consumer durables locate in them. The developments of the last decade indicate that such spatial distribution is unlikely to change in the next decade. A detailed analysis of the reasons for such location in one metropolitan area would be a fascinating study.

PART II

Trends in location of factory industries in India during the half century 1950-2000 and prospects of growth of industries and modern service activities during 2000-2020 are discussed in this chapter. The Indian economy has been transformed in this period from a dominantly agricultural economy in which agriculture contributed more than half of the gross domestic product in the mid-1950 to a diversified economy dominated by manufacturing industries and modern services. The latter contributed 75 per cent of the GDP while agriculture contributed only 25 per cent by the late 1990s.

The transformation began in the late 1950s. In the first phase, extending from the late 1950s to the early 1970s, the Government of India made large investments in establishing five large integrated steel mills, two mills for making aluminium and aluminium metal from bauxite, plants for making heavy and light machine tools; plants for manufacturing machines for generation, transmission and distribution of electricity, telephone receivers and telecommunication equipment, basic drugs and even photographic films. Large investments were made also in building thermal and hydroelectric power plants. After the discovery of large deposits of crude oil off the coast of Mumbai and offshore and on-shore of Gujarat, large investments were made in exploration and development of the oil fields, production of petroleum products and establishing a country-wide network of distribution of products—motor spirit, diesel, lubricants, kerosene and cooking gas. Economic and technical assistance for these projects was given by the Soviet Union, Germany and Britain and of a much smaller amount also by Canada. Switzerland and the U.S.A.

Private entrepreneurs with one exception confined their attention to processing steel for construction and manufacture of consumer goods. The Tatas, with loans given or guaranteed by the Government of India, modernised and expanded capacity of their existing steel mill and also added a thermal power station to augment electric supply to Mumbai.

By the early 1970s, the government's policy was reversed. It has been concentrated since on reducing losses of the loss making enterprises by improving management and ending deficiencies of infrastructure. The government plans also to disassociate itself from industries and modern services such as generation and distribution of electricity and operation of airlines by finding strategic partners for them. However, because of strong opposition to it in parliament and by trade unions of workers of loss making enterprises, there have been little disinvestments so far.

Meanwhile, private entrepreneurs have established large manufacturing units for various consumer goods and consumer durables including chasses for buses and trucks, passenger cars and 2-3 wheeler motor bicycles and scooters. They have also established petroleum refineries and plants for manufacture of petrochemicals and steel mills. Vibrant information technology (IT) industry and manufacture of pharmaceutical drugs and heavy and light chemicals have also been established by private entrepreneurs.

The prospects for the next two decades are for:

(i) Continued expansion of the IT industries with increasing participation by non-resident Indian and foreign (mainly American) companies;
(ii) Entry of foreign companies in management of airlines, hotels and tourist agencies, banking, finance, and insurance in which quick profits are assured. There could be foreign investment also in some infrastructures such as 4 and 6 lane highways and construction or repair of ports;
(iii) Withdrawal of government from industries and services and encouraging Indian private and foreign direct investment in them.

The government will concentrate on programmes for expansion of agricultural output and expand greatly facilities for health and education and eradication of poverty.

Information Technology Industries

The Information Technical (IT) industries are expected to maintain their exponential growth rate for another decade or more. This expectation is based on the following premises:

(i) The largest IT companies have continued to experience rapid growth and make rapidly increasing profits. The fastest growing area in these industries is Internet. After seeing the growth potential of the IT industries, some of the largest industrial houses in the country have opened their own IT industry wings. These wings will service all the companies managed by the industrial houses and will also sell IT services, in order to make them independent profit centres.

(ii) The use of computers in various sectors of the Indian economy—manufacturing and services (marketing, banking, finance, insurance, travel, broadcasting, entertainment, transport and communications) has just begun and is expected to increase rapidly in the foreseeable future.

(iii) There is not likely to be any major change in the location of the industry. The primacy of Bangalore will continue during this decade. It has the advantage of an early start and the largest concentration of IT industry companies. Chennai and Hyderabad in the South, Mumbai, Ahmedabad and Pune in the west, Kolkata in the east and NOIDA-Gurgaon, the two satellite cities of Delhi in the north are expected to remain the principal centres of the industry. Chandigarh, Pune and Ahmedabad could also emerge as increasingly important centres.

Chandigarh

The principal advantages of Chandigarh are: potential access to venture capital and expertise of a large number of Punjabi IT specialists who are settled in the Silicon valley, California at present but who would like to locate their Indian operations in their home state. The government of the state would provide them all the needed facilities. The city has a salubrious climate and relative freedom from pollution of air and water. Furthermore, due to location in it of the university, a regional engineering college and a first rate teaching hospital there is an ample supply of graduates in science, engineering and medicine.

Pune

The principal advantage of Pune is its proximity to Mumbai which give the companies located in it access to the large commercial, financial (banking and insurance) and entertainment (television serial and film) sectors of Mumbai. Furthermore, it has a large number of scientists and engineers.

Ahmedabad

The principal advantage of the industry in Ahmedabad is access to the large market of the industrial units located in coastal Gujarat. Besides it has a number of very dynamic IT companies.

The latest forecast of the growth potential of the industry and its contribution to India's total export, based on the report of an internationally reputed consultant[1] is that, "by 2008, the sector will attract foreign investment of $4.5 billion; that the overall revenue from the IT sector would be $90 billion, and the exports would be $50 billion per year. The value of the export would form 35 per cent of the total exports."

COMPUTER HARDWARE AND OFFICE EQUIPMENT INDUSTRIES (PERSONAL COMPUTERS, ELECTRONIC COPIERS, DESKTOP PRINTERS, ETC.)

The office equipment industry is confined at present to some multinationals (American and Japanese) assembling products like high-speed copiers from imported components. Manufacture of personal computers is limited simply to assembling the computers from imported components. However, having in view the prospect of rapid increase in demand within India and neighbouring countries and relatively low cost of skilled labour in India, some leading manufacturers of some components are establishing facilities for their manufacture in India. These facilities are designed to meet the demands both within India and the neighbouring countries. Increasing availability of components that meet internationally acceptable standards will provide a strong incentive to the major producers of personal computers to expand their output. The industries would be located in cities like Bangalore, Mumbai, Pune and Chennai in which there is a large demand for their products.

Biochemical Industries (Pharmaceutical Drugs)

Development of pharmaceutical drugs, based on original research, promises to be another rapid growth industry during the current and the next decades. The present centres of the industry are Delhi and Hyderabad because the two companies that have developed drugs based on original research, which have rapidly expanding markets in

India and abroad, are located in the two cities. Probable other centres are expected to be:

(i) Vadodara or another city in coastal Gujarat. Vadodara has two highly successful companies manufacturing Ayurvedic drugs. Furthermore, located in its vicinity are large companies manufacturing antibiotics and other modern drugs from formulations provided by foreign drug companies. There is increasing appreciation in India and in the western countries of efficacy of some Ayurvedic drugs in prevention and treatment of some diseases of the aged. One of the Ayurvedic drug companies could develop a drug which would prove efficacious in treatment of such a disease.

(ii) Other possible centres of the industry would be Chennai/Thiruvananthapuram, because Ayurvedic drugs are used far more in southern India than in northern India.

(iii) Lucknow could be another centre if the Central Drug Research Institute, located in it, develops some drugs which prove efficacious in treatment of diseases of the aged.

(iv) Chandigarh could be another centre. A company located in Delhi has chosen a satellite town of Chandigarh for expansion of its operations.

Emphasis in this section has been on diseases of the aged because the aged, whose number is increasing rapidly, in the developed countries are the largest users of drugs. But drugs that are effective in treatment of common diseases of children or of women would also have similar large and rapidly increasing markets both within India and in the developed countries.

Consumer Goods Industries

These industries include textiles (cloth made of cotton, silk, man-made fibres and wool), garments, shoes and leather goods, furnishings for homes and office, soap and toiletries, food products (wheat and rice, flour, sugar, cooking oil) packaging of tea and cigarettes.

These industries will experience fairly rapid growth due to increase in population and per capita consumption of foodgrains (cereals, rice, sugar, tea, coffee and tobacco products), cloth, shoes and other leather goods.

There is unlikely to be any major changes in the location of the industries. Location of food and beverage industries is oriented towards availability of raw materials—thus rice and flourmills, sugar and cooking oil mills are located in areas producing rice, wheat sugarcane and oil seed. Packaging of tea for domestic consumption and export is concentrated in Kolkata and is expected to remain so, because of proximity to the tea gardens and presence of a large number of companies which have been established in the city for a long period.

Factories for manufacture of cigarettes and other western style tobacco products are located in Hyderabad in the south, Mongher (Bihar) in the east and Saharanpur in U.P. in the north because the Indian Tobacco Company which has a commanding position in this field has established its factories in these cities.

In view of the prospect of rapid increase in demand for ready-made garments, several new centres for manufacturing them could emerge; these cannot be specified at present. Furthermore, reputed foreign manufacturers of brand name garments are planning to establish factories in India to meet the demands of the fashion conscious buyers in metropolitan cities and for export to neighbouring countries. These would be located in metropolitan cities such as Mumbai, Delhi and Chennai.

In textiles, the policy of the Government of India has, since the 1950s, encouraged weaving of cloth by handloom and power looms, at the expense of that made in mills. This policy is unlikely to change in the foreseeable future. While weaving of handloom cloth is concentrated in traditional centres, power loom clusters are located mainly near the principal centres of mills such as Mumbai in Maharashtra, Ahmedabad and other textile mill cities in Gujarat and Coimbatore in Tamil Nadu. They have come up also in several of the older handloom centres in order to avail of the facility of being near skilled craftsmen.

In several food and beverage industries, the entry of multinationals has driven the older Indian manufacturers out of business. Entry of Pepsi and Coke in bottling of soft drinks has driven out the older bottlers of soft drinks out of business. Similarly, entry of American restaurants selling fast foods has led to closure of Indian restaurants, which served similar foods earlier.

Manufacture of leather garments, shoes and other leather products: location of the industries is market oriented. The industries are primarily located in metropolitan cities, Mumbai, Delhi, and Chennai or in their satellite cities (New Mumbai, and Ghaziabad). The three cities also contribute most of the garments, shoes and other leather goods for export. Kanpur in U.P. was and continues to be one of the main centre for tenneries and production of leather and leather goods. Available in the cities are the entrepreneurs and skilled workers needed for these industries.

Consumer Durable Industries

Manufacture of motor vehicles (scooters, motor bicycles, mopeds, passenger cars, light commercial vehicles, buses and trucks), radio and TV receivers, fans, refrigerators, air conditioners and electrically operated kitchen gadgets are some consumer durable goods.

The demand for these goods has increased very rapidly during the last nearly two decades. The value of purchases of these products increased from Rs. 1,507 crores (15.07 billion) in 1980-81 to Rs. 19,789 crores (197.89 billion) in 1996-97 or more than 13 times (Tata Consultancy, 1999). Even after allowing for increase in prices of these goods, the thirteen-fold increase in value of purchases represents a quantum jump in use of these goods by the rapidly increasing urban and rural middle classes.

Keeping in view the large existing demand and the prospects of its rapid growth in the current and the next decades, Korean, American or continental European manufacturers of these products have established facilities for manufacture (initially by assembling from imported kits but progressively from domestically produced components) of these products. The Indian manufacturers have also expanded their manufacturing capacity and output. The principal centres of manufacture of these goods are:

(i) Mumbai-Pune: Motor vehicles (passenger cars, scooters and motor cycles, light commercial vehicles, chasses for buses and trucks), refrigerators, air conditioners and kitchen appliances. Mumbai is the largest centre of the industries and is expected to retain its primacy; some of the industrial units could be located in New Mumbai and Thane, the satellite cities of Mumbai in order to avail of lower costs of land and labour.

(ii) Chennai: Motor vehicles, chasses for buses and trucks, scooters, motor bicycles and mopeds. Tyres for motor vehicles.

(iii) Bangalore and its environs.

(iv) The satellite cities of Delhi: Gurgaon and NOIDA. Motor vehicles (passenger cars), refrigerators, air conditioners and kitchen appliances.

(v) Dharu-Heda (Haryana) and Ludhiana (Punjab) motor bicycles, scooters and mopeds, kitchen appliances, fans, etc.

(vi) Kolkata: It has already a motor vehicle manufacturing unit and another manufacturing tyres.

(vii) Kanpur: Scooters and tyres.

Location of these industries is primarily market oriented and they will concentrate in peri-urban areas of metropolitan cities or large megapolis. Mumbai and Pune are the biggest centres of the industries. They have the advantages of an early start and access to very large markets especially in western, central and northern India and a very well developed network of distributors of the products. The reasons for location of the industries in the other centres mentioned above have been explained in some detail below.

Location of Industries of the Old Economy

Steel, cement, heavy machine tools, transport equipment (rails, rolling stock, passenger coaches and locomotives for the railways), buses and trucks; machinery for generation, transmission and distribution of electricity; heavy chemicals, petroleum refining and manufacture of petrochemicals etc.

There must be steady growth in these industries because they are the industries, which manufacture the raw materials and machines for manufacture of consumer goods, commercial durables and some classes of producer goods. The industries will continue to be located near (i) sources of raw materials, *e.g.* in the coal steel belt of West Bengal and Chhotanagpur plateau of Bihar and (ii) where the Government of India or big industrial houses like Tatas and Reliance or petroleum refining companies have established their plants.

There is not likely to be any major changes in the location of the industries except that petroleum refineries and associated petrochemical plants will be located on the harbours of east and west coasts of India. Thus Jamnagar where Reliance has its big refinery and petrochemical plant, Haldia and Paradeep in West Bengal and Orissa respectively will emerge as major centres.

The increase in demand for machines for generation, transmission and distribution of electricity is expected to be met primarily by expansion of existing facilities of Bharat Heavy Electricals, located in various cities.

Changes in the Relative Importance of Major Industrial Centres

The Mumbai-Pune rail-cum-road strip; coastal Gujarat especially the area between Ahmedabad and Surat; Bangalore and Chennai would continue to be the four most important centres of factory industries. The areas have large concentrations of manufacturing units for products of most of which there is a potential for rapid expansion of output and increase in demand. Furthermore, the governments of the states in which they are located have both the resources and the will to expand infrastructures—roads, power and water supplies and telecommunications—needed for expansion of industries. The governments of Tamil Nadu (for Chennai) and Karnataka (for Bangalore) have been aggressively wooing industrial entrepreneurs for location of industries in these cities. Hyderabad has become a major centre of the IT and drug manufacturing industries and also of several others (including defence related industries), partly because of the aggressive policy of the state government to promote location of these industries. The government of Haryana has aggressively promoted location and development of industries in Gurgaon and Faridabad by expansion of infrastructures—roads, electricity, water and telecommunications with Delhi. However, its resources, which are far smaller than those of the western and southern states set a limit to its capacity to promote industrial expansion.

The Kolkata metropolitan district should continue to be an important industrial centre with emphasis on its traditional export-oriented jute processing and tea packaging; fabrication of steel structures, manufacture of mining machinery and of components of machines for mining and railways, etc. as the principal industries. The determined effort of the present government to check militancy of trade unions have reversed industrial decline and fostered resumption of growth of industries in the district.

On the other hand, NOIDA-Gurgaon, Faridabad and Ghaziabad, the four satellite cities of Delhi, are unlikely to experience rapid growth of industries (consumer goods, consumer durables, or IT) because the U.P. government is not promoting location of industries in NOIDA or Ghaziabad. Besides, there are serious problems of pollution of air and water and of law and order in both cities.

The Government of Punjab, which had aggressively promoted industrial development in the 1950s and 1960s, is promoting it again. The Government of Rajasthan is promoting development of tourism in its two most visited cities—the pink city of Jaipur and Udaipur. At the other end, the policies of the Governments of Uttar Pradesh, Bihar and Madhya Pradesh have been marked by indifference towards promotion of either industries or tourism. These policies must be reversed before these three large states can attain their potential for development of either industries or tourism.

Handicraft Industries

This is mainly manufacture of decorative brassware, jewellery, cutting and polishing of diamonds for domestic consumption and export, weaving of carpets, weaving of sarees for everyday use and for festive occasions, making of garments, shoes and other leather goods for domestic consumption and export.

All these industries have experienced rapid expansion during the last 5 decades, due partly to the policies of the national and state governments to promote the expansion. Their expansion has provided employment and subsistence wages to millions of poor craftsman (6.7 million are classified in 1991 to be working in household industry alone, figures for their numbers in the factory industry producing handicraft is not separately known). There is potential for rapid increase in output in them, in the current and the next decade, if:

(i) use of child labour in industries such as carpet weaving, and other handicrafts is stopped so that the products are acceptable in countries such as the U.S.A. which prohibit import of carpets in which child labour is used;

(ii) in making of jewellery, the producers maintain internationally acceptable standards of quality of the precious metal that they use and modernise designs; and

(iii) in cutting and polishing of diamonds, value added would increase considerably, if the producers added cutting and polishing of larger diamonds instead of concentrating on that of very small, low value diamonds. The master craftsman could be sent for brief periods for observation and training to established centres of the industries such as Tel Aviv in Israel, Antwerp in Europe and New York in the U.S.A.; most of the diamonds used in the U.S.A., Europe and other developed countries are cut and polished in these cities.

The industries will continue to be located in their existing production centres: Moradabad (U.P.) for brassware; Mirzapur (U.P.) and Sri Nagar (Jammu & Kashmir) for carpets; Varanasi (U.P.), Kanchipuram (Tamil Nadu) and Murshidabad (West Bengal) for weaving of sarees for festive use; Surat and Mumbai for cutting and polishing of diamonds and Agra, Kanpur, Mumbai and Chennai for production of shoes and other leather goods.

Stitching of garments for domestic use and export has experienced rapid expansion since the 1970s. The principal centres are Mumbai, Chennai and Delhi. The quality of the garments has improved considerably since the 1970s, because of use of high quality fabrics, use of power driven machines in production and continual improvement in designs.

There is considerable scope for improvement and further expansion, primarily for domestic use because the middle and high-income groups not merely in metropolitan cities but also in smaller towns and cities now use ready-made garments. The industry should experience rapid growth in the next 15 years also because reputed foreign manufacturers of brand name clothing are planning to establish factories in India to meet the demands of fashion conscious buyers in India and for export to neighbouring countries.

MODERN SERVICES AND TRAINING

Service Industries have much greater importance in the foreseeable future than at present. Training, tourism, health care, banking and insurance has been considered in this chapter.

Training

Facilities for training of professionals are adequate in India and in case of computer professionals there are opportunities for work abroad. Similarly, in other fields such as physicians, engineers, accountants and business managers the best-trained professionals can find opportunities for highly remunerative work abroad.

The demand for trained software professionals is increasing so rapidly that companies such as NIIT (National Institute of Information Technology) and APTECH which train these professionals and individuals in use of personal computers have opened training centres in all large cities in India and several training centres in metropolitan cities—Delhi, Mumbai, Chennai and others. They are opening training centres also in neighbouring countries of South and Southeast Asia. Several British, American and Australian universities are advertising in India to attract Indian students for training in business management, hotel management, fashion technology and other professional degrees for holders of which there is a large demand in India. The fees from foreign students make a handsome contribution to the cost of running these courses.

Indian universities such as Delhi and Jawaharlal Nehru University in Delhi and Chennai which have internationally acceptable standards of teaching in many subjects (economics, business management, sociology and others) could also attract foreign students for post-graduate studies in these subjects. They could be charged fees which would not only cover the cost of training them but also make some contribution to the cost of running these courses.

India has as part of its technical assistance programme to neighbouring countries of SAARC or Africa provided facilities from the 1960's for training of agricultural scientists at regional agricultural universities. The persons trained at these universities remember their stay at Indian universities as a rewarding experience. The technical assistance programme should be expanded to include training of software professionals and pharmacists for which there is a large demand in the developing countries of South and South East Asia and Africa.

In training there is a great imbalance between training of professionals and sub-professionals. The facilities for training of professionals, engineers, technologists, physicians and surgeons, accountants and others such as lawyers are adequate. Furthermore, standard in the best institutions are comparable to those in the better institutions in the developed countries. India's outstanding success in the IT industries is due to the high quality of the engineers and technologists who graduate from the institutions of technology.

However, facilities for training of sub-professionals are inadequate or virtually non-existent in many fields. Thus, in medicine, the dispensers in most privately run hospitals are inadequately trained and the chemists who sell medicines, including antibiotics prescribed by doctors have no clue to their adverse side effects. There have been cases of severe disability or even death of patients caused by adverse side effects of medicines dispensed wrongly by the pharmacists in many hospitals and nursing homes. Facilities for training of nurses are adequate only because of the initiative taken by the church authorities in Kerala to train them. But the facilities established by the state governments are grossly inadequate and need to be greatly increased to meet the needs of an increasing number of hospitals and nursing homes.

There are no facilities for training of accountants and clerks; they are trained by their seniors while on the job. Similarly, most of the repairmen of motor vehicles, electrical or electronic appliances have been trained while working under experienced motor mechanics, electricians, etc.

Considering the rapid increase in the number of motor vehicles, electrical appliances and electronic goods such as radio and T.V. receivers, there is an urgent need for establishing a large number of institutions for training of such repairmen. Availability of an adequate number of trained sub-professionals will assist industrial development greatly because there will be an adequate supply of trained industrial workers. Some of the trained craftsmen could establish small industries themselves, as is apparent from the initiative of skilled craftsmen in establishing small industries in Ludhiana in Punjab.

Training is, however, an area in which it is necessary for the government or another accreditation agency to grade various training institutes and grant recognition to only those which maintain the minimum acceptable standards of efficiency for training of software professionals. A number of unscrupulous individuals have opened training institutions which do not have the staff to provide training of acceptable standards. They should be closed by the Information Technology Department of the Central Government or the various State governments.

Tourism

Despite location of an immense number of places of tourist interest in its various regions, growth of tourism has been slow in India. Total net foreign exchange earnings from it were nearly $3.00 million or

0.69 per cent of the world total in 1996-97 and a fraction of the earnings by a city like Hong Kong (Tata Consultancy, 2002).

The principal factors inhibiting growth of tourism are: deficiency of infrastructures, attitude of people dealing with tourists and policies of the governments of states in which places of tourist interest are located regarding promotion of tourism.

Deficiency of Infrastructure

Shortage of hotel rooms for tourists of different income levels in several places of tourist interest, absence of good roads and dependable airline operations are some of the reasons retarding growth of the industry. Another and far more serious deficiency relates to attitude and behaviour of people dealing with the tourists. Most of the staff and officials of the hotels and airlines, operators of taxis and tourist buses and tourist guides see the tourists not as people whose gratitude is to be earned by efficient and courteous service but as people from whom quick money is to be made by exploiting their ignorance of local conditions.

The deficiency of infrastructure could be overcome by capital expenditure partly by the State governments and partly by domestic or foreign operators of hotels. However, changes in attitude and behaviour of people who deal with tourists, the passport clerks and custom officers at the airports, operators of buses and taxis, clerks and officials of tourist agencies, in officials of foreign Airlines and finally, that of the Indian Airlines are more difficult to change. But until the attitude and behaviour of these people change, growth of tourism will continue to be slow.

The existing major centres visited by domestic and foreign tourists will retain or increase their importance. The Delhi-Agra-Jaipur triangle in the north west; Chennai-Tirupathi (temple) and Mysore-Bangalore in the south; Mumbai in the west; Varanasi in U.P., the temple villages of Khajuraho in Madhya Pradesh and Konarak and Puri in Orissa and Kashmir are likely to remain the most visited centres by international and Indian tourists. Among the governments, that of Rajasthan has been most aggressive in promoting tourism, so that its two major centres, Jaipur and Udaipur, will continue to experience rapid growth of tourist arrivals. On the other hand, because of indifference of the governments of Bihar and U.P. towards promoting tourism, the immense growth potential of the centres for religious tourism (Varanasi, Allahabad, Hardwar,

Mathura and the Himalayan temples of Badrinath and Kedarnath in U.P.) for Hindu tourists and Varanasi, Patna, Gaya, Nalanda and the birth place of the Buddha in Nepal across the border from Bihar for Buddhist tourists from south east and east Asia (from Thailand to Japan) is unlikely to be realised.

HEALTH CARE FACILITIES IN TREATMENT OF PATIENTS FROM DEVELOPED COUNTRIES

Surgical Procedures for Patients from Britain

The British National Health Service is looking at Indian hospitals for sending patients for undergoing surgical procedures such as removal of cataract for which internationally acceptable standards exist in many Indian hospitals. This is because there are long waiting lists for patients needing these procedures in Britain. The British patients would travel for brief periods to hospitals accredited for such procedures in India.

The probable centres are expected to be Mumbai, Pune, Goa, Chennai, Thiruvananthapuram and possibly Chandigarh. The cities should have hospitals with competent surgeons and equipment of internationally acceptable standards. Furthermore, the standards of sanitation and nursing care in the selected hospitals should also meet international standards. Delhi, despite having some of the best equipped hospitals and competent surgeons would not qualify because the staff in many of the hospitals is prone to going on strikes for varying periods and standards of cleanliness in them, also do not meet internationally acceptable standards.

The potential of the industry in generation of foreign exchange would not be large initially but could increase rapidly. Appreciating its importance, the government of Singapore has successfully made the city a centre which attracts patients needing such and other surgical procedures from neighbouring countries (mainly Malaysia, Thailand and Indonesia) for treatment in hospitals in the city.

BANKING AND INSURANCE

Banking

The Government of India has under its liberalisation policies thrown open banking and insurance to foreign companies. Foreign banks have been operating in India since before independence. Their number and activities in consumer banking and finance of foreign trade have witnessed a major increase in recent years. Foreign banks offer stiff competition to the nationalised banks in consumer banking in the metropolitan cities. The best nationalised banks have steadily improved their efficiency in order to compete with foreign banks.

Insurance

There has not been any significant entry of foreign companies in insurance so far. Life insurance and certain classes of general insurance are well developed. Foreign companies entering these lucrative fields will offer stiff competition to established Indian, public sector enterprises and will hopefully contribute to improving efficiency of service in them. However, other areas such as health insurance, which is virtually undeveloped in India, foreign companies, will enter virgin territory and can make large profits until Indian companies can compete with them.

Telecommunications

Foreign multinationals (with or without Indian partners) have virtually captured the TV news and serials industries in which large profits are being made. They are entering telecommunications sector with increasing success and offering stiff competition to the publicly owned telecommunication companies.

A RELATED ISSUE: PUBLIC-PRIVATE AND DOMESTIC FOREIGN INVESTMENT

In the first phase of rapid industrialization which started in the late 1950s and ended in the mid-1970s, large investment was made by the Government of India in establishing four large integrated steel mills; a factory for manufacturing heavy machines; factories for manufacturing locomotives, coaches and wagons for the railways; factories for manufacturing machines for generation, transmission and distribution of electricity; light machine tools; basic pharmaceutical drugs such as penicillin, chemical fertilizers and even photographic films. After the discovery of petroleum off the coasts of Mumbai and Gujarat in the late 1950s, large investments were made also in exploration and development of the oil fields, constructing petroleum refineries and establishing a large network of distributors of petroleum products throughout India.

Economic and technical assistance was provided in establishing these factories mainly by the Soviet Union, Germany and the United Kingdom and to a much smaller extent by Canada. The U.S.A. and Switzerland provided technical assistance also.

Indian industrialists with the notable exception of the Tatas did not participate in establishing heavy industries. The Tatas expanded capacity and modernized their steel works at Jamshedpur with loans given or guaranteed by the Government of India. Furthermore, they established a thermal power plant in Mumbai to augment capacity of their existing hydroelectric power plants, in order to meet the increasing demand for electricity in the rapidly growing metropolis. They established also a factory at Jamshedpur for manufacturing chasses for buses and trucks with technical assistance provided by a reputed German company and a factory in Saurashtra for manufacturing heavy chemicals.

Other Indian industrialists confined themselves to manufacturing consumer goods—establishing mills for rice and wheat flour, sugar and cooking oil, cloth, garments, shoes and other leather goods. Some industrialists also took to processing steel to make corrugated iron sheets and rods for construction; tubes for drinking water supply and large concrete pipes for sewerage in large cities. Two foreign oil companies, which had been operating in India for some decades, were also allowed to establish oil refineries and expand their networks of distributors. Refining capacity has been increased progressively as the demand for petroleum products has increased by establishing new refineries. The Government of India has established some of them with a part of the investment by foreign partners. Large investments were made by the Government also in constructing pipelines for transport of petrol, diesel and natural gas from the oil fields to various cities.

The late 1970s and 1980s can be considered to be a period of consolidation. While some enterprises such as Hindustan Machine Tools (HMT) which had become profit making quickly and others like Bharat Heavy Electricals (BHEL) which became profit making somewhat later, most others notably the steel mills and the heavy machine tool factory, continued to incur losses due to deficiencies of infrastructure and expert managers. The efforts of the Government of India were concentrated on reducing the losses by eliminating deficiencies of infrastructure and management. However, another large integrated steel mill was established to meet the increasing demand for the metal. The steel works were modernized or their capacity was expanded and a fifth steel mill was established in Visakhapatnam in Andhra Pradesh in order to meet increasing demand for steel. Economic and technical assistance was provided by the same countries that had assisted establishment of the enterprises such as HMT and BHEL, which had become profit making and were allowed to expand their capacities in order to meet increasing demands. The expansion was financed partly out of their own resources and partly by loans from the Government of India. Petroleum refining and distribution had been profit making from the beginning. Capacity in this sector was increased progressively to meet increasing domestic demand.

Indian industrialists participated increasingly in manufacture of consumer durables (motor vehicles including chasses for buses and trucks, passenger cars, scooters, motor cycles and mopeds), T.V. receivers, refrigerators, air conditioners, electrically operated kitchen appliances and furniture for offices and hospitals. Most of the enterprises were established with technical assistance provided by reputed foreign manufacturers. They invested also in expanding capacities in manufacture of cement, C.I. sheets and other building materials. Although, production was directed primarily towards meeting domestic demand, increasing attention was given also to exports, particularly to developing countries of south and south east Asia and the Soviet Union. While traditional exports such as tea, jute goods and cotton textiles remained important in the exports, others such as garments (of cotton, wool or of mixtures of these with man-made fibers) woollen hosiery, shoes and other leather goods and some classes of machine tools assumed increasing importance in the exports.

The 1970s witnessed also the beginning of rapid increase in export of computer software, which was to assume much greater importance in the two subsequent decades.

The second phase of rapid industrial growth can be considered to have begun in the 1990s. With more rapid economic growth, the demand for consumer goods and consumer durables has increased rapidly and has been met primarily by Indian industrialists by increasing capacities of existing factories and establishing new ones. Increasing attention has been given also to increasing exports, principally by improving quality of Indian goods to meet demands of countries in South and South East Asia. Export of computer software has assumed increasing importance as mentioned earlier.

The policy of the Government of India now is to withdraw progressively from industrial development and leave it to private industrialists. However, because of strong opposition in Parliament and by unions of workers against sale of any public enterprise or closing down any loss making enterprise, there have been virtually no disinvestments.[2]

Foreign Investment

The stated policy of the Government of India is to encourage foreign investment in all areas of industries and services, except those relating to defence, atomic energy, space research etc. However, although a large number of proposals for foreign investment have been approved, actual investment has remained limited. It is confined to services such as banking, insurance, entertainment and telecommunications or in establishing facilities for manufacturing motor vehicles and consumer durables. Significant American investment is being made also in computer software including Internet, advertising and manufacture of components for personal computers.

Foreign investors have selected service areas in which large profits can be made rapidly. In banking (including export finance and consumer banking) and insurance, foreign establishments offer stiff competition to Indian enterprises (including nationalized banks and insurance companies). Consumer banking and export, finance and life and general insurance have been mentioned earlier. In case of consumer durables, factories have been established by multinationals in order to secure an assured place in the anticipated rapid increase in the domestic market. British, or American investment has been concentrated in the service sectors: banking (consumer or export finance), telecommunications and entertainment in which quick returns on investment are assured. American companies are participating also usually in partnership with Indian Companies in IT industries and manufacture of drugs, soft drinks, establishing tourist's hotels or chains of fast food restaurants, that cater to tastes of urban youth. With notable exceptions British or American companies have not participated in infrastructure sectors (construction of electric power or water supply, roads etc.). Korean or Japanese investment has been primarily in manufacture of consumer durables (motor vehicles, refrigerators, air-conditioners, TV. Receivers, electrically operated kitchen gadgets etc.). Foreign investors have avoided investment in steel or heavy engineering in which it would assist economic development of the country. Their participation in manufacture of modern drugs is confined to establishing fully owned subsidiaries. Altogether foreign private investment can be expected to assist economic development at a somewhat higher, later stage of development of the economy. Some of the production would be exported also to neighbouring countries. One American company has invested in augmenting power supplies for Maharashtra on guarantees of assurance of capital and large profits within a limited period.

Furthermore, considering the fact that the life and general insurance (such as insurance for motor vehicles) are adequately covered by the nationalised corporations, the entry of foreign companies would initially be in areas such as health insurance and marine insurance which have not been developed by Indian companies. As the demand for such insurance services increase, Indian companies may also be expected to begin to render such services.

CONCLUSION

The types of industries and service activities that are expected to experience rapid growth during the next decade and a half have been indicated in the foregoing sections. It has been explained that there is not likely to be any major change in the location of the industries which are expected to experience rapid growth. All of them are expected to continue to be located in the areas (particularly peri-urban areas of the metropolitan cities) in which they are located at present. The prospects of growth of four service industries have been reviewed. Their growth could be much faster than in the past decade or that can be expected at present. The conditions essential for their growth have been indicated. It should be added that rapid growth in selected industries and services will contribute to,

(i) raising the level of living of a large proportion of India's urban and rural populations; and

(ii) making a significant contribution to the growth of export earnings of the country.

Some companies, which have a commanding position in sale of a product, have established several factories for serving regional markets. The outstanding examples at present are:

(i) Indian Tobacco Company, which has a commanding position in the market for cigarettes and other tobacco products. It has factories in Hyderabad, Mongher and Saharanpur to serve the markets of south, east and north India; and

(ii) Hindustan Lever, which has a similar commanding position in manufacture of soap and other toiletries, cooking oils and tea. It has similarly several factories to serve consumers in different markets. The principal reason for this is one well known to students of geography, *viz.* the cost of transporting raw materials is much less than that of transporting finished products. The trend could spread to manufacture of other products. One leading bicycle manufacturing company which has a main factory in Haryana but has established 8 other factories in other regions of India and in neighbouring countries.

The governments of Andhra Pradesh and Karnataka are aggressively promoting location of IT industries in cyber cities in Hyderabad and Bangalore. They are creating the infrastructures for location of these and other industries. The governments of Tamil Nadu, Maharashtra and Gujarat are also creating infrastructures and providing all facilities for location of IT and other industries within their states. The government of West Bengal has successfully arrested the decline in industries in the Kolkata Metropolitan District and is now developing successfully a petroleum refining and petrochemical complex at Haldia. In the north, the Government of Haryana has successfully promoted location of industries including IT industries and offices of commercial business in the two satellite cities of Delhi-Gurgaon and Faridabad.

It is concluded that:

1. Industries which process high weight but low value raw materials such as steel and aluminium mills, cement and fertilizers plants, plants for making heavy chemicals, locomotives, wagons and rails for the railways, machinery for mines, hydro and thermal power plants will continue to be located near sources of raw materials.

2. All other industries are and will continue to be located near the consumption centres, *viz.* the peri-urban areas of metropolitan cities. These include all consumer goods and consumer durables (including motor vehicles as mentioned earlier). The Information Technology industries and factories manufacturing pharmaceutical drugs based on original research are also located in these areas. Even some of the refineries are located near these cities because they are the best locations for distribution of petroleum products. There is not likely to be any significant change in this locational pattern during the next two decades.
3. The principal attractions of the cities is: (a) their large markets and well established networks for distribution of products in their hinterlands; (b) the unions of employees of loss making public enterprises will be progressively reconciled to accepting voluntary retirement packages. The younger workers will with some self-acquired training seek employment in rapid growth industries and modern services.

NOTES

1. Akshay Joshi, quoting report on the sector by NASCOM—Mekinsy study of the IT sector—*Times of India*. May 24th 2000.
2. During 2002-04 the process of disinvestments not only of loss making enterprises but also even of profit making public sector units was expedited. However, after establishment of Congress led-left supported Government in 2004 the process of disinvestments has virtually stopped. (Addition by K. Nath)

REFERENCES

Tata Consultancy Services, *Statistical Outline of India*, 1998-99. Mumbai, 1999. p. 280 Figures based on Annual Survey of Industries.

Tata Consultancy Services, *Statistical Outline of India*, 2001-2002, p. 102.

15

Entrepreneurship in India: Distribution by Regions, Castes and Levels of Economic Development—A Survey[1]

INTRODUCTION

At the turn of the century, economist Joseph Schumpeter emphasized the importance of entrepreneurship as a factor in economic growth. The object of this chapter is to promote thinking and research into the economic, social or political conditions that have led to growth of entrepreneurship among certain regional, religious and caste groups but not among others.

The principal method of raising questions about factors contributing to entrepreneurship (or lack of it) or its demise is to make references to entrepreneurial groups in the principal cities and regions of India.

What changes in the economic and social conditions contribute to the emergence of entrepreneurship among communities? A brief survey of Indian entrepreneurship in terms of regional, caste and religious differentiation points to the need for further research into factors prompting entrepreneurial qualities among communities.

Considering Mumbai and Pune where Maharashtrian entrepreneurship has flowered, only after independence, the question arises: Why is it so?

Calcutta has a tradition of establishment of industries, older than in Mumbai, but after independence the Scots' position has been taken by the Marwaris and not the Bengalis.

The Chettiars owned a large proportion of the rich rice producing lands of Mynmar and managed the exports of rice and timber. They were active in Southern Tamil Nadu. Chennai and Bangalore have become very large industrial cities during the last four decades. Industrial entrepreneurship is also not lacking in Andhra Pradesh and Karnataka.

Gujaratis, Marwaries, Parsees and Sindhis residents in western India are important in trade and industries. In late 19th Century large number of Gujaratis migrated to east African countries. Even the Punjabis have a long tradition of migrating out.

Muslim entrepreneurship has been conspicuous by its absence in India in the post-independence period partly because of migration to Pakistan of entrepreneurial groups like Bohras and Khojas who pioneered establishment of industries there.

The survey explains that there has been little development of modern industries in large parts of some large and populous states of India. Moreover, the states in which entrepreneurs are concentrated are more economically and socially developed than those where there is relative absence of entrepreneurs. The question raised here is what changes in economic or social conditions will contribute to this development?

REGIONS

Consider Mumbai and Calcutta, India's largest cities and the principal centers of large industries. The establishment of cotton textile mills in Mumbai dates back to the 1870s, immediately following the civil war in the U.S. The mills were established by two indigenous groups—the Gujaratis and the Parsees. Labour, unskilled and skilled, was furnished by the Maharashtrians who formed the large majority of the population of the city. However, none of the mills was owned by a Maharashtrian. The industrial structure of Mumbai has greatly diversified with the decline of the cotton textile industry in the post-independence years. Instead of being textile industry cities, Mumbai, its sister city New Mumbai and industrial satellite city Thane, are home to industrial enterprises manufacturing a large variety of goods—machine tools, clothing, fine chemicals and pharmaceuticals, from office to hospital furniture and consumer durable such as automobiles, refrigerators and air-conditioners. The owners and managers of these units include besides Gujaratis and Parsees, other groups such as Maharashtrians, Punjabis, Sindhis and Marwaries.

Maharashtrian entrepreneurship has flowered not in Mumbai but in Pune and in the sugar mill towns such as Dahanu. The sugar mills, owned by cooperatives of sugar cane growers are an outgrowth of production of high yield sugar cane with high sucrose content in the irrigated areas. The house of Kirloskars, the largest Maharashtrian owned industrial house, manufactures a large variety of industrial goods such as pumps for irrigation wells, a large variety of machine tools, and has now diversified into manufacture of passenger cars. It is the most respected manufacturer of compressors for refrigerators and air-conditioners.

The medium and small-scale industrial units established in the sugar mill towns are all ancillaries to the sugar mills. The question arises: Why has Maharashtrian entrepreneurship developed in the post-independence years in and outside Mumbai, when it failed to appear in Mumbai for more than a century.

Calcutta has a tradition of establishment of industries as old or older than in Mumbai. The jute industry, perhaps the oldest and largest in terms of generation of employment and export earnings in pre-independence years, was (and continues to be) located in a large number of small towns situated up to 60 kilometres north of Calcutta along the river Hooghly. Calcutta and its sister city Howrah were (and are) home also to a large steel fabricating industry manufacturing bridges, coaches, wagons and other equipment for the railways, mining equipment and machine tools besides repair of ships. The jute and steel fabrication industries as well as the tea gardens of Darjeeling and Assam were owned before independence by Scots. Tea is one of the largest exports of India and Calcutta is the principal packaging and export centre.

After independence, the Scots' place has been taken not by the Bengalis but mainly by the Marwaris, residents originally of western Rajasthan, who began to go to Calcutta to become traders more than a century ago. The able and affluent Bengali young men were and continue to be content with becoming executives (box wallahs) in large Scottish owned companies and lawyers, physicians, scientists and other professionals. But with the exception of the Indian Iron and Steel Company (now called Steel Corporation of Bengal), established by Biren Mukherjee, and some companies manufacturing pharmaceuticals and toiletries no large industrial enterprise was established by a Bengali. Why is this so when Bengal must have had a millennia old tradition of trading with Mynmar? The word Bengal is derived from the Sanskrit word, *Vangalaya* (literally home of tin). However, tin must have been imported from the mines in Tennaserum in southern Mynmar because none is found in Bengal itself. Buddhist monks from Bihar and Bengal were prominent among those who converted the people of Mynmar, Thailand and other countries of south-east Asia to Buddhism. The Sinhalese people of Sri Lanka trace their conversion to Buddhism by the son and daughter of emperor Ashoka in the 3rd Century B.C. They claim also that many people migrated from Bengal to Sri Lanka. What happened to the trading class which was prominent in the trade with Mynmar and other south-east Asian countries? When did it die out and why?

A large proportion of the people who converted the people of south-east Asia to Hinduism and/or Buddhism went also from Tamil Nadu and Andhra Pradesh. There was active trade between Malaya, Indonesia and Indo-China and south India. Which were the classes who managed this trade. The traditional trading group in Tamil Nadu and the old Mysore state are Chettiars in Tamil Nadu and Shetties in Mysore. The word Shetty is derived from the Sanskrit word Shresthi (literally a superior person), which becomes Seth in north India.

The Chettiars owned a large proportion of the rich rice producing lands of Mynmar and managed the exports of rice and timber. However, after repatriation from Mynmar during the second world war, they would seem to have receded into the background. This is not true, however. The Chettiars are active in southern Tamil Nadu, where one company has a controlling interest in manufacture of scooters, a petroleum refinery and a petrochemical plant.

Chennai and Bangalore have become very large industrial cities during the last four decades. But no large industrial house in Chennai is of Chettiar origin nor is any large industrial house in Bangalore of Shetty origin. The best known industrial house in Tamil Nadu, the TVS group of engineering industries is of brahmin origin. While the best known industrial entrepreneurs in Karnataka, the Mallyas, trace their origin to manufacture of sugar and liquor after establishment of sugar mills in central Mysore following irrigation from a canal on the river Cauvery.

Industrial entrepreneurship is not lacking in Andhra Pradesh and Karnataka. The textile mills located in and around Coimbatore, established following growth of irrigated cotton production after construction of a dam on river Pykara are owned mainly by the Naidus and Reddys whose home is in Andhra Pradesh. They own also rice and sugar mills located in a number of towns in coastal Andhra Pradesh where dependable water supply is available from canals on the Godavari and Krishna rivers. They own a large number of industries manufacturing machinery for rice and sugar mills in these towns and for cotton mills in Coimbatore. A large number of large, medium and small-scale industrial units located in Hyderabad are also owned by Andhra entrepreneurs. With the establishment of a state-of-the-art information technology city, 60 kilometres from Hyderabad, Andhra entrepreneurs are likely to become prominent in these industries also.

Bangalore, capital of Karnataka is today by far the largest centre of the information technology industries. It would be interesting to know the caste composition of the Indian owners and managers of these enterprises. A large number must be brahmins. There is reason to believe this because a large proportion of migrants to the Silicon Valley in California in the USA which is the centre of IT industries in the US are brahmins. To what caste do the others belong? Are the others Shetties or do they belong to a number of different castes.

Traditionally priests and non-cultivating landowners, the brahmins took to English education early to become lawyers, physicians, scientists and teachers besides civil servants and white collar workers all over India. Tens of thousands of them are working as white collar workers in Mumbai, Calcutta, Delhi and other cities. At the time of independence some of the highest officials in the Government of India were Tamil brahmins. However, after being debarred from government service in their home state, while some have become industrial entrepreneurs, many have migrated to other states. They may develop a large class of industrial entrepreneurs, based on their dominance in the information technology industries which are the fastest growing industries and are likely to retain this position during the next decade or more. Furthermore, Chennai itself is a rapidly growing IT industries centre.

The most affluent groups in Kerala are the Syrian Christians and Hindu Nairs. But while Syrian Christians are prominent in trade (import and export) and processing of cashewnuts and manufacture of coir goods, the Nairs have been conspicuous by their absence in these activities. What are the differences in historical tradition and values which have led one high caste, relatively affluent group to enter trade and industry but deterred the other?

Ten per cent of the population consists of Moslems who claim to be descendents of Arab traders who married women of Kerala. Why have they failed to produce a class of traders and industrial entrepreneurs when they claim to be descendants of traders?

More than a million people of Kerala have been going to the oil rich countries of the Persian/Arabian Gulf since the 1950s. They have worked mainly as clerks and shop assistants there. Thousands of nurses have also gone to work in these countries and in various Indian cities. Both groups have invested their savings in repairing or enlarging their houses or building new ones or buying additional farmland. Housing is a primary need and it can be understood that a poor migrant would invest his or her savings in improving the family house or building a new one after coming home. But why have those Keralites, who have held well paid positions in the Gulf countries, not come home to start small or medium sized industrial units manufacturing or assembling from imported components consumer durables such as refrigerators, air-conditioners, television receivers and electrically operated kitchen gadgets which they use?

COMMUNITIES

Gujaratis, Marwaris, Parsees and Sindhis, resident in western India, are important in trade and industry in India. The Gujaratis and Sindhis have a tradition extending over millennia of trade with West Asia, principally Iraq and Iran. The tradition of trade may have been a factor in these groups developing an entrepreneurial class.

The Gujaratis migrated in large numbers to the east African countries of Kenya, Uganda and Tanzania to become traders in the late 19th century, and early 20th century, and also to South African countries including Zambia and South Africa. The largest trading and industrial group in Gujarat is Jains, Hindus and Moslem Khojas and Bohras. After the formation of Pakistan a large number of Khojas and Bohras migrated to Pakistan and became the principal entrepreneur in Karachi, its main industrial city and former capital. They are the most affluent group in Pakistan.

Some of the Hindu Gujaratis became prosperous enough to own sugarcane plantations in Uganda. However, after east African countries adopted policies aimed at expelling them, large numbers went to Britain, the U.S. and Canada while others came back to their home state to establish industrial units manufacturing a wide-variety of goods – textiles, and other consumer goods, pharmaceutical drugs and a wide variety of machine tools. After the discovery of petroleum off the coast of Gujarat, the Gujaratis have developed a large and rapidly growing petrochemical industry. Coastal Gujarat is now an industrial workshop so much so that it has a serious problem of pollution of air and water.

The Parsees are a small group which came to India from Iran in the 8th century to escape persecution by the newly converted Moslems. They were given shelter and freedom to practice their ancient Zoroastrian faith by the Hindu and Moslem rulers of Gujarat. For centuries they remained hard working and prosperous small farmers. In the 19th century, they took early to English education and European lifestyle to become pre-eminent lawyers, physicians, scientists and other professionals. They were prominent in the establishment of the cotton textile mills in Mumbai from the 1870s. They have produced two men of extraordinary vision in the last 100 years. The first was Jamshed N. Tata who established India's first iron and steel mill at Jamshedpur in Bihar and constructed hydroelectric power projects to power industries and light up homes in Mumbai. His successors have, besides steadily expanding capacity in the steel works and power projects, pioneered growth of civil aviation, manufacture of commercial motor vehicles and heavy chemicals and are now active in IT industries. The other, Adi Godrej pioneered manufacture of safety goods from locks to burglar proof safes and cupboards, office and hospital furniture, consumer durable such as refrigerators and soap and toiletries. The products of these two groups command a large market because of their insistence on maintaining the highest standards of quality.

Jains in Gujarat, Marwar, Haryana and some cities in Punjab and Uttar Pradesh have a tradition of trade going back to the founding of the religion about 2,500 years ago. Their religion with its emphasis on not killing any living being (human, animal or insect) debarred them from agriculture because a farmer kills millions of insects in various agricultural operations. They could not become Hindus priests because their religion was different from Hinduism. Trade was virtually the only occupation open to them. A large proportion of the Gujarati and Marwari traders in Gujarat, Maharashtra, Rajasthan, Haryana and western Uttar Pradesh are Jains.

The large majority of the Hindus, Gujaratis and Marwaris belong to the traditional trading castes the *banias*. However, among the Gujaratis, Patels who were hard working and prosperous farmers resident mainly in central districts of coastal Gujarat, became traders after migration to east African countries. After repatriation from these countries, they have migrated in large numbers to the U.S. where, besides working in trade and industry, they own a large number of cheap motels. Others are industrial entrepreneurs in their home state. The Patels take pride in saying "There is not a country in the world, where there is not a Patel".

The Sindhis have a millennia old tradition of trade with Iraq and Iran. After the establishment of British rule in India and other colonies, they began to go to cities in India and the colonies to establish mainly textile stores and supermarkets. There is probably no former British colony which does not have Sindhi traders. Some Sindhis have also established stores in regions ruled by other colonial powers.

After the formation of Pakistan, most Hindu Sindhis migrated from Sindh to settle mainly in Gujarat and Maharashtra. Large proportions of them are concentrated in Mumbai, Pune and other cities of both states. Smaller numbers have gone to Hyderabad, Rajasthan and Delhi.

They have maintained their traditional occupation of running textile stores. They are also prominent in building apartment houses in Mumbai, Pune and other cities. They have turned increasingly to manufacturing consumer durables such as refrigerators and air conditioners and electrically operated kitchen appliances. A large number of those in Delhi and other cities are in government service.

Before the division of British India into the Indian union and Pakistan, about 5 million Hindus and Sikhs were settled in villages and towns of areas which now form Pakistan. Almost half of the Sikhs were hard working and prosperous farmers; others were traders and moneylenders. Almost all the Hindus were traders and moneylenders.

After the formation of Pakistan, both communities settled in East (Indian) Punjab, Haryana, Delhi and a few cities in Rajasthan and western U.P. Large numbers of Hindu and Sikh migrants who settled in Delhi are in government service; so are those in the cities of Punjab, Haryana, Rajasthan and western U.P. Others have maintained their traditional occupation of retail trade. The Sikh farmers from Pakistan have become the most progressive and prosperous farmers in Indian

Punjab, Haryana and a few districts of western Uttar Pradesh. Both Hindus and Sikhs have turned increasingly to manufacturing industries. Delhi and its satellite cities in U.P. and Haryana are full of hundreds of small and medium sized and a few large units established by Hindu and Sikh migrants from Pakistan. Their participation in manufacturing and service industries is expected to increase progressively.

The Punjabis are prominent also in management of hotels and other tourism related activities. They are prominent also in production of films and television serials. Large proportions of the mining and forest contractors in Bihar and Madhya Pradesh are also Punjabis.

Among the Sikhs it is necessary to separate Ramgarhias and others. The former, resident originally in East Punjab, particularly in Ludhiana and neighboring districts, were traditionally artisans—carpenters, smiths and masons. Large numbers migrated to Malaysia and Thailand during the late 19th and early 20th centuries. They have come back to establish small, medium and a few large industrial units in their home city of Ludhiana and neighbouring towns.

The largest business established by a Sikh is in production of pharmaceutical drugs. Large numbers of Punjabi Hindus and Sikhs have migrated to the U.K., the U.S. and Canada after India became independent. Most of the Sikhs who migrated from East Punjab to the U.K. in the 1950s and 1960s worked as labourers in manufacturing industries. Their children have been educated and have become professionals and shopkeepers. A small number of Sikh farmers had migrated to California and British Columbia in Canada in the early years of this century to become hard working and prosperous farmers. Punjabi Hindu migrants to the U.K., the US and Canada from the 1950s onwards have been professionals particularly teachers, research workers and physicians. They have not and are not expected to establish any industrial units there.

The Punjabis have a long tradition of migration. Large numbers went to Mynmar in the late 19th and early 20th centuries primarily to establish shops in small towns of Mynmar. After repatriation from Mynmar, they have re-established themselves in their original occupation in small towns of Punjab and western U.P.

Moslem entrepreneurship has been conspicuous by its absence in India in the post-independence period, partly because the principal Moslem trading group—the Gujarati Khojas and Bohras migrated to Pakistan to pioneer establishment of industries there. In India, Moslem entrepreneurship has begun to appear slowly in small industries and handicrafts in which the workers are Moslems but the traders (and exporters) were mainly Hindus. The decorative brassware industry of Moradabad and the pottery and glassware industries of Khurja and Ferozabad in UP are examples. Another is weaving of silk saris in Aurangabad, a suburb of Varanasi. In all these industries while most of the workers are Moslems, the traders and exporters are Hindus. This position is bound to change and Moslem entrepreneurship will slowly develop in these industries and in industries like manufacture of shoes and leather goods in which most of the traders and workers are Moslems.

There has been little development of modern industries in large parts of U.P., Bihar, Madhya Pradesh and Orissa. Furthermore, most of the managers and skilled workers in the industrial units that have been established in these states by the government or by private companies, are from other states. The reasons for the absence of indigenous entrepreneurs in these states and of skilled workers in industrial units established in them have to be investigated.

ENTREPRENEURSHIP AND ECONOMIC DEVELOPMENT

The states in which entrepreneurs are concentrated have noticeably higher levels of economic and social development than those in which there is a relative absence of entrepreneurs. It will be noticed from Tables 15.1 to 15.4 that Gujarat, Maharashtra in the west, Tamil Nadu, Andhra Pradesh, Karnataka in the south and Punjab, Haryana and Delhi and a part of western U.P. where there are large numbers of entrepreneurs are more developed than central and eastern U.P., Rajasthan, Madhya Pradesh, Bihar, Orissa and West Bengal except the Kolkata Metropolitan District. Even in the large industrial enterprises established by the Government of India—four steel mills, a heavy industry manufacturing unit, plants for generation and transmission of electricity and other industries in Bihar and Madhya Pradesh, skilled workers and sub-contractors are from other states—Punjab or the southern states manufacturing associated products such as cement. The owners of the cement plants or chemical fertilisers plants are not from Bihar, Orissa or Madhya Pradesh. They are Gujaratis, Parsees and Marwaris. The conspicuous absence of entrepreneurship in these large and populous states needs to be explained by further research. Rajasthan has an ample supply of entrepreneurship in its western region. Industrial development in it is hampered however by paucity of natural resources. About half of the state is a semi-desert and the natural resources in the other half can only support industrial units like cement mills.

Except Agarwals and Jains in western U.P. there are no indigenous entrepreneurs in U.P., Bihar, Madhya Pradesh and Orissa. The reasons for this have to be explored. One of them could be the absence of a trading tradition or of migration to foreign countries. However, there must have been trade within these large and populous states. What were the trading groups which managed the trade, and when and why have they disappeared?

Per capita income in all three states of the western region and three states of the north-western region is higher than the national average. Per capita income in Punjab, Maharashtra and Gujarat are higher than the all-India average by nearly 80 per cent, 70 per cent and 30 per cent respectively. In all the four states of the southern region it is close to the national average. At the other extreme are Bihar, Orissa, and Uttar Pradesh, with per capita incomes 33 per cent of the national average in Bihar and just over 60 per cent in the other two states, of the national average. Even in West Bengal with the highly industrialised Kolkata Metropolitan District and the Durgapur-Assansol industrial complex, it is just above 90 per cent of the national average (Table 15.1).

The percentages of urban/rural population given in Table 15.2 follow a similar pattern.

They are close to or higher than the national average in all the four states of the southern region, two of the three states in the northwestern region and Gujarat in the western region. In Haryana and Maharashtra they are close to the national average.

At the other extreme, the figures for Bihar and Orissa are half of the national average. In the other states of the north central and eastern regions, the national average is exceeded only in West Bengal. In Uttar Pradesh it is about 70 per cent of the national average while in Rajasthan and Madhya Pradesh the figures are just above 80 per cent of the national average.

The average male and female literacy rates are above the national average in three of the four states of the southern region (Table 15.3).

Table 15.1: Per Capita Net State Domestic Product at Factory Cost (Current Prices in 1996-97)

State and Region	*Rupees ('000)*
I. Southern Region	
Andhra Pradesh	100
Karnataka	103
Kerala	94
Tamil Nadu	112
II. Western Region	
Goa	197
Gujarat	139
Maharashtra	173
III. North-western Region	
Punjab	182
Haryana	162
Delhi	198
IV. North Central and Eastern Region	
Bihar	38
Orissa	64
Uttar Pradesh	67
West Bengal	94
V. Hilly, Forested and Desert Areas	
Madhya Pradesh	74
Rajasthan	92
VI. Not Classified	
Assam	66
Himachal Pradesh	99
Jammu & Kashmir	74
All-India	**109**

Sources: E.P.W. Research Foundation: *National Accounts Statistics of India 1950-51, 1996-97*, Mumbai, 1998, p. 83.

Table 15.2: Urban Population/Total Population in 1991

State and Region	*Population (Million)*	*Urban Population (Million)*	*Urban/Total Population (Per cent)*
I. Southern Region			
Andhra Pradesh	66.3	17.9	27.0
Karnataka	44.8	13.9	32.2
Kerala	29.0	7.7	26.5
Tamil Nadu	55.6	19.1	33.7
II. Western Region			
Goa	1.17	NA	
Gujarat	41.2	14.2	34.5
Maharashtra	78.7	30.5	26.4
III. North-western Region			
Punjab	20.2	6.0	29.7
Haryana	16.3	4.1	25.2
Delhi	9.4	8.4	89.4
IV. North Central and Eastern Region			
Bihar	86.3	11.4	13.2
Orissa	31.5	4.2	13.3
Uttar Pradesh	138.8	27.6	19.9
West Bengal	68.0	18.7	27.5
V. Hilly, Forested and Desert Areas			
Madhya Pradesh	66.1	15.3	23.1
Rajasthan	43.9	10.1	23.1
VI. Not Classified			
Assam	22.3	2.5	11.2
Himachal Pradesh	5.1	0.4	8.9
Jammu & Kashmir	7.7	1.8	23.4
All-India	**843.9**	**217.6**	**25.8**

Sources: Tata Services, Statistical Outline of India 1998-99, Mumbai, 1998, p. 51.

Table 15.3: Average and Female Literacy Rates in 1991

(*Percentage*)

	State and Region	*Average Literacy Rate*	*Female Literacy Rate*
I.	**Southern Region**		
	Andhra Pradesh	45.1	33.7
	Karnataka	56.0	43.3
	Kerala	90.6	87.0
	Tamil Nadu	63.7	52.3
II.	**Western Region**		
	Goa	77.0	68.2
	Gujarat	60.9	48.5
	Maharashtra	63.0	50.5
III.	**North-western Region**		
	Punjab	57.1	49.7
	Haryana	55.3	40.9
	Delhi	76.1	68.0
IV.	**North Central and Eastern Region**		
	Bihar	38.5	23.1
	Orissa	48.6	34.4
	Uttar Pradesh	41.7	26.0
	West Bengal	57.7	47.2
V.	**Hilly, Forested and Desert Areas**		
	Madhya Pradesh	43.4	28.9
	Rajasthan	38.8	20.8
VI.	**Not Classified**		
	Assam	53.4	43.7
	Himachal Pradesh	63.5	52.5
	Jammu & Kashmir	n.a	n.a
All-India		**52.1**	**39.4**

Source: Tata Services, *Ibid.*, p. 40.

They are higher than the national average in all the three states of the western region. The rates are lower than the national average in all the states of north central and eastern region except West Bengal and the two states of hilly, forested and desert region. The figure for

Rajasthan is just above half the national average and for Bihar it is less than 60 per cent.

Growth rates of population during 1981-91 (Table 15.4) are less than the national averages in three of the four states of the southern region, Andhra Pradesh is the exception.

Table 15.4: Population and Growth Rates

State and Region	*Population (millions) In 1991*	*Growth Rate (Per cent per decade)*	
		1971-81	*1981-91*
I. Southern Region			
Andhra Pradesh	66.3	23.1	23.8
Karnataka	44.8	26.8	20.7
Kerala	29.0	19.2	14.0
Tamil Nadu	55.9	17.5	15.4
II. Western Region			
Goa	1.17	26.7	16.0
Gujarat	41.2	27.7	21.2
Maharashtra	78.1	24.5	25.4
III. North-western Region			
Punjab	20.2	23.9	20.3
Haryana	16.3	28.8	27.7
Delhi	9.4	53.0	50.6
IV. North Central and Eastern Region			
Bihar	86.3	24.0	23.5
Orissa	31.5	20.2	20.2
Uttar Pradesh	138.8	25.5	25.5
West Bengal	68.0	23.2	24.6
V. Hilly, Forested and Desert Areas			
Madhya Pradesh	66.1	25.3	26.8
Rajasthan	43.7	33.0	28.0
VI. Not Classified			
Assam	22.3	23.4	23.6
Himachal Pradesh	5.1	23.7	19.4
Jammu & Kashmir	7.7	29.7	29.0
All-India	**84.4**	**24.7**	**23.5**

Source: Tata Services, *Ibid.*, p. 41.

They are lower than the national average also in Gujarat and Punjab. The high rate for Maharashtra could be due partly to immigration in the Mumbai metropolitan region. The lowest rates are in Kerala and Goa which have also the highest rates of female literacy. The rates in the north central and eastern regions and hilly and forested regions are close to the national average.

This survey of entrepreneurship in different states of India refers to the most prominent entrepreneurial groups. Most of industrial entrepreneurs have a tradition of trading within India and with foreign countries, both western and eastern neighbours of India. Others have a tradition also of migration. Some groups such as the Maharashtrians and certain groups in Karnataka have become industrial entrepreneurs where opportunities were offered for it, with growth of industries in their home state. Some of the Tamil brahmins have participated increasingly in manufacturing and service industries after being debarred from their traditional occupation of government service in their home state of Tamil Nadu.

The survey explains that there has been little development of modern industries in large parts of some large and populous states such as U.P., Bihar, Madhya Pradesh and Orissa. Furthermore, most of the managers and skilled workers, in the industrial units that have been established in these states by the Government of India or by private companies like the Tata Iron & Steel works in Jamshedpur in Bihar, all the skilled workers are from other states. The conspicuous absence of indigenous entrepreneurs in these states has to be explained.

There is no doubt that entrepreneurship will appear among groups and regions in which it is virtually absent at present. What changes in economic or social conditions will contribute to this development? Its appearance is essential for rapid economic development and social change in India. Further research into the factors which will induce the growth would contribute greatly to our understanding of the factors that promote or inhibit growth of entrepreneurship in India.

NOTE

1. *Economic and Political Weekly*, Vol. XXXV, No. 48, November 25, 2000.

Index